Teaching Comprehension
in Grades 1–2

Dynamic Strategies and
Creative Lessons for Early Literacy Success

by
Anthony D. Fredericks
....
Illustrated by
Dave Garbot

Harcourt Achieve
Rigby • Saxon • Steck-Vaughn

Dedication

To Laurie Cornell—for the wonder, excitement, and spirit that fills every corner of her classroom, just as they fill the hearts and minds of her students!

Rigby • Saxon • Steck-Vaughn

ISBN: 0-7398-9950-3

©2006 Harcourt Achieve Inc.

Printed in the United States of America.

1 2 3 4 5 6 7 8 9 862 09 08 07 06 05

Acknowledgments

This book, as should be the case with every teacher resource book, is the result of the combined thoughts, efforts, and investments of many people. Numerous individuals, in conversations, classroom observations, and long-distance communications, were instrumental is getting these ideas into print. I cannot rightly claim sole credit for this effort—it is the product of many minds and many creative friends.

I am particularly indebted to my former student teacher (and now exceptional classroom teacher) Alyssa Skura. Every chapter and every piece of literature within this book is stamped with her creative zeal and impassioned desire to bring out the best in youngsters. She is truly the "best of the best," and it is her students who will reap the rewards of her commitment and energy for many years to come. She stands as a model of desire, passion, and energy for all classroom teachers as much as she does for this writer.

This book could not have been conceived without the thoughts and ruminations of my friend Jane Peipmeier. Jane is one of those dynamic first-grade teachers whose work stands at the forefront of what can be and what should be in primary education. Her classroom is a literacy environment that celebrates learning just as much as it celebrates the purposeful growth and development of each and every youngster. I consider it a professional honor to be able to visit and observe her engaging wisdom in promoting both cognitive and affective growth throughout the elementary curriculum.

To my editor, Anne Souby, I extend my praise and a long-standing round of applause. She is that rare editor who truly cares about her authors—she communicates, stimulates, and supports the creative process from beginning to end. It has been an honor to have worked with her on this project.

I would like to extend my sincerest thanks to the scores of teachers throughout the country who invited me into their classrooms to peer over the shoulders of their students, observe from the back of their classrooms, and interview them with a constant barrage of questions. From east to west and north to south they tested, evaluated, and successfully implemented "Comprehension Circles" into their literacy programs with triumph and enthusiasm. I am indebted to all for your contributions and participation.

But, it is to you the reader that I owe my greatest thanks. I celebrate your quest for professional growth and your desire to stimulate the intellectual growth of students. You are about to embark on a magical adventure full of joy, wonder and endless discoveries. I thank you for your passion and investment in all the possibilities!

Preface

Ever since I first began teaching more than three decades ago, I have been fascinated by the literacy growth and development of beginning readers. As I watched my students learn to master sounds, words, and stories, I was intrigued with the mental processes that were taking place inside their heads. I soon learned one of the age-old maxims of reading instruction: we can never see inside the head of a youngster as she/he is reading, so we may never fully understand the mental processes taking place in that "textual interaction." As I observed my own children throughout their involvement in books and literature, I was equally fascinated by their literary engagements and interpretations.

"How do children comprehend and how can I facilitate that process?" was a question I found myself asking over and over again. I sought out experts in print and in person. I conversed with colleagues and teachers both near and far. I attended conferences and conventions. I examined, experimented, and tested theories and strategies of every size, shape, and dimension (also known as "the good, the bad, and the ugly"!). And, after more than thirty years (O.K., I'm a slow learner), I came to an inescapable conclusion—comprehension is an active engagement with text; **it is an act of thinking.**

At this point, let's stop and look at another definition of comprehension: "Comprehension is the ability to construct meaning by interacting with text" (Cooper, 2003). As teachers, we naturally and easily associate the word *comprehension* with the word *reading*. In fact, in all our college courses and in every teacher manual the term *reading comprehension* was used with natural frequency. In essence, whenever we heard the word *comprehension*, we always heard the word *reading* tagged to it. But I'd like to look at comprehension in just a little bit different light.

If you look at Cooper's definition above, you'll note that one of the key phrases is "interacting with text." That is to say that students can have a relationship with different types of texts—oral texts as well as written texts. Take that one step further and you can begin to see that if we can help beginning readers successfully interact with oral text, then they will be on the road to successfully interacting with written text as they develop those all-important connections between oral language and written language. In short, the strategies of reading comprehension can be universally applied to many different types of learning situations. We can help students construct meaning not only in reading, but across the curriculum in an ever-increasing spiral of learning situations.

Now let's go back to an earlier point—that is, comprehension is a process of thinking about text. Many elementary teachers subscribe to the notion that reading involves an active and energetic relationship between the reader and the text. The reader-text relationship is reciprocal and involves the characteristics of the reader as well as the nature of the materials. This philosophy of reading, often referred to as a *transactional approach to reading*, is based on the seminal work of Louise Rosenblatt (1978) and has particular applications for first and second grade teachers. Here are two principles of that philosophy (adapted from Rosenblatt, 1978) that serve as the foundation upon which this book is based and which have been successfully used by thousands of primary teachers around the country:

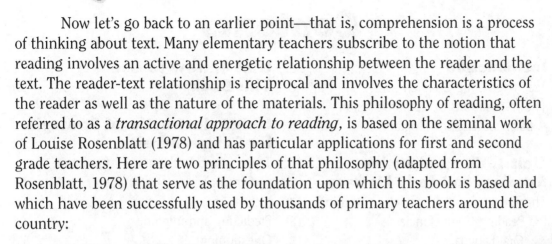

- Reading is a lived-through experience or event. Children "evoke" the text, bringing a network of past experiences with the world, with language, and with other texts.

- The meaning is neither in the child nor in the text, but in the reciprocal transaction between the two.

I hope you will agree with me that reading is indeed a process of thinking. If we can guide our students in the practices and procedures of thinking about text, then we can also assist them in learning about the practices and procedures of comprehending text — whether that text is presented to them in an oral format or in a written format. In other words, if we are committed to helping youngsters achieve a measure of success in all their reading experiences, we should be equally committed to helping students learn and use strategies that will assist them in a wide variety of language experiences.

This raises an interesting question, perhaps one that was in the back of your mind as you picked up this book:

How can I become a better teacher of comprehension and how can my students comprehend better?

I believe the answer will always be an exciting challenge for us. But, I hope that you will discover, as have elementary teachers throughout the country, that a systematic and sustained focus on comprehension development (in all matters literary) offers unlimited learning possibilities and a plethora of literacy adventures for all your students. Indeed, many magical discoveries await!

Let's begin the journey!

—Tony Fredericks

Contents

Introduction

The first-grade classroom was a beehive of activity. Students were working on assignments, various individuals were congregated around selected literacy centers, children were listening to audiotapes, others were curled up in a corner silently reading, and the middle-aged teacher was working with a small group of youngsters in a guided reading activity. Many things were taking place, but while the conversation was animated, the organization and management kept everyone focused and on task.

I was lurking along the periphery, clipboard in hand and pen at the ready. I carefully observed all the literacy activities taking place and would occasionally jot some notes or transcribe part of a conversation. One youngster watched me with rapt attention. Finally, his curiosity could stand it no more and he approached me.

"Who are you and what are you doing here?" he asked.

"Mrs. Perillo invited me to come into your class today to see what everyone is doing," I replied.

A quizzical look crossed his face as he carefully considered my answer.

"Oh, then you must be her grandfather!" he volunteered.

It was then that I noticed the poster for the forthcoming Grandparent's Day at the school. I tried to save face.

"No," I responded. "I'm visiting here because I'm writing a book."

Without missing a beat, he responded, "I'm a writer, too! I learned this year. I didn't have to wait until I was old like you."

Further conversation, I knew, would be fruitless. I humbly slunk into a corner and began to observe another group of somewhat less inquisitive students.

Teaching Young Children

Children come to school eager to learn. They want to learn about the world. They want to learn about snakes and sharks and elephants and dolphins and all sorts of

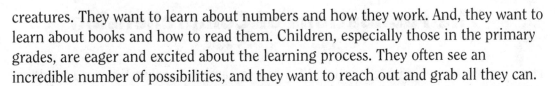

creatures. They want to learn about numbers and how they work. And, they want to learn about books and how to read them. Children, especially those in the primary grades, are eager and excited about the learning process. They often see an incredible number of possibilities, and they want to reach out and grab all they can.

First- and second-grade teachers are the same way. They are ready for these eager-to-learn students. They want to provide them with a classroom overflowing with incredible learning opportunities and possibilities. They want shelves overflowing with books, bins spilling over with letters and numbers, and walls overcrowded with words and letters and signs and names and anything else that conveys the magic of reading. These are exciting times, and they are times embraced by children and teachers alike.

I recently came across a document that had been in my files for some time. It was a policy document (not something we typically choose for bedtime reading) drafted nearly two decades ago by the National Association for the Education of Young Children in conjunction with the Early Childhood and Literacy Development Committee of the International Reading Association. The document, entitled *Literacy Development and Early Childhood,* presented a series of issues, premises, concerns, and recommendations regarding the literacy growth of youngsters.

Several of the recommendations in that report are shared within the context of this book. I believe some of those recommendations (summarized below) are worthy of a second look:

1. Build instruction on what the child already knows about oral language, reading, and writing.

2. Ensure feelings of success for all children.

3. Provide reading experiences as an integrated part of the communication process.

4. Encourage risk-taking in first attempts at reading and writing.

5. Use reading materials that are familiar or predictable.

6. Present a model for children to emulate.

7. Take time to read to children from a wide variety of sources.

8. Foster children's affective and cognitive development.

9. Encourage children to be active participants in the learning process.

I think those recommendations make as much sense today as when they were written many years ago. In many ways those recommendations are a celebration of *what can be* as much as they are a validation for *what should be.* They serve notice that teachers and children enter into a unique partnership each and every school year. Filled with energy and suffused by possibilities, they work together to create a community of learners that knows no limits and has no boundaries.

The Foundations of Comprehension

Have you ever eaten with chopsticks? Do you remember the first time you tried to do it? You may have fumbled the sticks, dropped food on the table, or become very frustrated at your efforts. Learning how to use chopsticks takes lots of practice and, perhaps, someone to assist you in mastering a proper technique. That individual may have invited you to observe someone else (in a restaurant, for example) using a set of chopsticks. She/he may have helped you hold the chopsticks. She/he could have demonstrated how to get the food from the plate to your mouth. At times, that person may have held the chopsticks with you to assist in the learning process. Your instructor may have allowed you to make a few mistakes during the practice cycle. She/he may have encouraged you to keep the cycle going.

In many ways, learning how to use chopsticks is similar to learning language. Few of us are perfect language users the first time we try to say a sentence or read a story. We need to be surrounded by lots of oral language (for example) in order to understand the dynamics of speaking. We need to be surrounded by lots of books in order to understand the dynamics of reading. Children need to have valid opportunities to see language in action and to practice language in order to become competent language users.

When you think about the "chopsticks" example above, several elements seem to predominate. Interestingly, these elements, or conditions, are also part of effective classroom instruction that supports comprehension instruction. (Yes, I'm tempted to call this the "Chopsticks Philosophy of Comprehension Instruction," but I won't.) Indeed, there is a growing legion of classroom teachers and university researchers who recognize the importance and significance of these conditions for comprehension instruction (Cooper and Kiger, 2003; Fredericks et al., 1997; Strickland, 1995). A literacy program that is focused on comprehension development is one in which the following conditions are integrated:

1. Reading aloud to children

2. Active student involvement

3. Support and encouragement

4. Holistic learning

5. Approximations

6. Student responsibility

7. Teacher response

8. Teacher modeling

Condition 1: Teachers read aloud to students.

At the heart of any classroom are the daily opportunities for teachers to read aloud to their students. Reading aloud introduces children to quality literature in a pleasurable and comfortable format. Reading aloud also models for students the strategies, practices, and processes mature readers (teachers) use as well as the pleasure obtained from a variety of genres. In the "chopsticks" example above, the observation of another diner in the restaurant and the enjoyment she/he had while eating moo gai pan (for example) are comparable to a pre-school teacher reading *Brown Bear, Brown Bear, What Do You See?* to a group of eager youngsters.

Condition 2: Students are actively involved in their own learning.

Good classroom instruction helps students assume a sense of self-responsibility for their own learning. A challenge for many teachers is in providing the framework in which students can begin to "take charge" for some of the learning in a classroom. When an "invitational learning environment" is created, then students are eager and willing to participate. There is interaction between teachers and students and between students and students. Student decisions and input are actively solicited and acted upon.

Condition 3: Students are given support and encouragement.

Children need to know that they have the support and encouragement of others. At the same time, teachers must convey the attitude that students can succeed, learning will occur, and progress will be made. The emphasis is on what children can do, rather than on the errors or mistakes that are always a natural byproduct of the learning process. In short, there are positive expectations woven throughout any academic endeavor.

Condition 4: Learning is holistic.

Children do not learn to read (or learn to comprehend) independently from the other language arts. What is clear from observing scores of teachers around the country and conversing with dozens of others, as well as from a cursory review of research, is the fact that language learning is multidisciplinary. That is, instruction in reading should also be supported by other language skills such as listening and speaking. Indeed, the integration of the language arts in every lesson is holistic, complete, and meaningful. In short, comprehension is NOT just an element of the reading process—it is enhanced and facilitated in concert with other language arts, too.

Condition 5: Learning is a series of approximations.

How did you learn how to talk? I doubt that you were able to recite the Gettysburg Address during the first year of your life. Undoubtedly, you began to babble and chatter some type of incomprehensible language (incomprehensible to everyone except your parents) beginning with one syllable "words" (e.g., "Da da," "Ma ma"). Later, you learned to put two or more words together to form some sort of makeshift sentence (e.g., "Me go."; "Dog woof."). Still later, you learned to put more words together into comprehensible units and began communicating with others outside your immediate family. In short, you learned to talk through a series of approximations. In other words, part of the individual language learning of all of us came about through a series of approximations. The implications are that all approximations of language use need to be supported and rewarded by teachers—for it is through that process that success is built and language becomes a valuable tool for additional learning.

Condition 6: Students are given choices.

It is my fervent belief (as well as that of many other teachers) that students need to develop a sense of self-responsibility in all their academic endeavors. Self-selection is an important aspect in the literacy education of any child. In fact, when children are provided with opportunities to make their own choices and to follow through on those choices (sometimes referred to as "risk-taking"), then they are making an *investment of self*—an intellectual contribution that forms the foundation for individual motivation and personally meaningful discoveries.

Condition 7: Teachers provide supportive feedback.

Children need to receive feedback about their learning—particularly about their language learning. Response implies that children are provided with verbal and nonverbal information about their progress and that that data is critical to students' continuing advancement in learning about and using language.

Condition 8: The teacher is a model.

One of the most powerful tools teachers have at their disposal is that of modeling. That is, teachers should demonstrate to their students the processes and practices that they use as language learners or accomplished readers. In so doing, teachers show children what a successful reader does. Another way to think about this is a maxim that is pounded into the heads of many nonfiction children's authors (myself included) at conferences and in professional journals—"Show, don't tell!" In other words, providing regular and sustained opportunities for students to look inside the head of a successful reader (you, for example) while she/he reads can have a positive impact on any youngster's reading development.

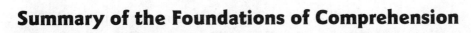

Summary of the Foundations of Comprehension

Condition	Value to Students
Reading Aloud	• Exposes children to a wide range of literature • Assists children in matching oral and written language • Helps develop knowledge of text structure • Develops a sense of story • Demonstrates fluent reading • Enhances vocabulary development (oral and written)
Active Student Involvement	• Promotes active (vs. passive) learning • Encourages students to develop a sense of self-responsibility • Fosters an invitational learning environment • Excites students to become eager and willing to participate • Enhances a dynamic relationship between teacher and students
Support and Encouragement	• Fosters "empowerment" • Values student input • Sets forth expectation of progress • Expands learning opportunities • Promotes and enhances confidence, attitudes, and self-concept
Holistic Learning	• Offers a social context and support structure for learning • Assures that students do not view reading as an isolated subject • Promotes and enhances all language arts • Ensures that reading becomes a learning tool in all subject areas • Integrates the curriculum
Approximations	• Allows learning to happen in "little steps" • Rewards tiny "successes" • Recognizes that mastery of a task may be long-term • Enhances confidence • Provides time to learn
Student Responsibility	• Provides students with realistic opportunities to use reading strategies independently • Allows students to make choices and follow through on those choices • Encourages risk-taking • Stimulates motivation • Allows students to "try" newly learned strategies in a supportive learning environment
Teacher Response	• Supports learning as a continuing process • Promotes self-confidence • Encourages further involvement • Encourages further learning • Recognizes achievement
Teacher Modeling	• Models enjoyment of learning or reading • Allows students to "see" inside the head of an accomplished reader • Allows teachers to "practice what they preach" • Allows students to value the teacher as a co-learner • Demonstrates interaction between reader and text • Enhances the development of metacognitive abilities

Just for fun (as well as for an interesting point of comparison), let's return to our earlier "chopsticks" example. Using the same conditions that we outlined above as essential in comprehensive comprehension instruction, let's see how they might also apply to "chopsticks instruction."

Corollary Application of Conditions

Comprehension Condition	Corollary to "Chopsticks"
Reading Aloud	You watched another diner as she/he ate with chopsticks.
Active Student Involvement	You used a set of your own chopsticks for practice.
Support and Encouragement	Your "teacher" believed that you, too, could become an accomplished chopsticks user.
Holistic Learning	You realized that the use of chopsticks was part of a series of steps that would eventually nourish you.
Approximations	You learned (and re-learned) little steps. You also made a few mistakes along the way.
Student Responsibility	You took responsibility for learning a new skill. No one told you that you had to do it.
Teacher Response	You received some feedback on your progress.
Teacher Modeling	You watched an "expert" as she/he used chopsticks.

Suffice it to say, the dynamics of comprehension instruction, like the learning of any new task (e.g., using chopsticks), is dependent on a select array of valuable and necessary conditions. You will, of course, note that nowhere in this list of conditions has the assumption been made that children are able to read independently. Rather, it is important to point out that the conditions of effective comprehension instruction are not necessarily reading-related; instead they are related to the environment in which children participate in thinking about text—whether that text be oral text (as in the initial stages of literacy development) or written text (as in the later stages of literacy development). In short, comprehension development can be, and should be, a precursor to more formal encounters with printed materials.

A Balanced Literacy Program

In my work with youngsters and in my conversations with teachers around the country, I have discovered that there are two factors that make comprehension development. The first is the idea that reading (and any attendant comprehension instruction) is not only a part of every school day, but is also an element of the primary curriculum from "Day One." Children need to be exposed to language and the ways they can interact with that language from their first days in school. This not only helps them build a familiarity with language, books, and reading, but also helps ensure that they know that literacy development is an important element of everyday instruction.

The second factor, related to the first, is that comprehension instruction can and should be part of a balanced literacy program. As emphasized throughout this book, it is vitally important for youngsters to understand that comprehension is also a way of thinking about text. Helping children develop their thinking abilities is a natural outgrowth and extension of any and all literacy development.

A balanced literacy program is one in which students are provided with direct instruction, a support structure, and opportunities to utilize reading comprehension strategies in meaningful text. In short, they are encouraged, supported, and sustained in many literacy activities. Margaret Mooney (1990) defines this process as reading *to*, reading *with,* and reading *by* students.

Reading To: Children are provided with regular opportunities to listen to a reading expert (the classroom teacher) read from a variety of texts and books. Typically referred to as "read-aloud" time, this is the time when children hear language in use by practiced and accomplished models. This is also an opportunity when teachers can model appropriate reading behaviors through "think-alouds"— times in which they talk out loud about the thought processes they are using as they read a piece of text. These models of thinking can be promoted as appropriate strategies for beginning literacy users to emulate.

Reading With: Children are gathered into groups (e.g., whole class, large, or small) for direct instruction. This is sometimes referred to as "shared reading" time. It is also the time when reading strategies are introduced to youngsters and children are guided in applying those strategies to appropriate reading materials. This is typically when Comprehension Circles take place.

Reading By: Children have opportunities to utilize their reading strategies in independent activities. Students can select their own reading materials, work at literacy centers, and engage in activities such as Drop Everything And Read (D.E.A.R.) or Sustained Silent Reading (S.S.R.).

The following chart illustrates the components of a balanced literacy program for youngsters in first and second grade:

Gradual Release of Responsibility ⟶

Sustained Silent Reading

Focused Reading

Comprehension Circles

Shared Reading

Teacher "Think-Alouds"

Reading Aloud to Children

Teacher Directed ⟶ Student Directed

Student Dependent ⟶ Student Independent

Reading TO ⟶ **Reading WITH** ⟶ **Reading BY**

Here's the bottom line: From "Day One" it is important that youngsters perceive themselves to be readers in order to be successful in reading. When students are *actively engaged* in the dynamics of literacy development from the moment they first walk into the classroom, they will begin to feel that reading is an important element in their learning cycle. They will also begin to believe that they can be successful in all their encounters with books and the magic to be found within them.

Unit 1

Comprehension, Reading, and Early Literacy

The Transactional Approach to Reading

Many teachers subscribe to the notion that reading involves an active and energetic relationship between the reader and the text. That is, the reader-text relationship is reciprocal and involves the characteristics of the reader as well as the nature of the materials. This philosophy of reading, often referred to as a **transactional approach to reading**, is based on the seminal work of Louise Rosenblatt (1978) and has particular applications for teachers building effective student-based reading programs. As you might expect, it serves as a foundation for the construction, implementation, and effectiveness of balanced reading programs. Here are some principles of reading instruction (adapted from Rosenblatt, 1978) particularly useful for primary-level teachers seeking to implement effective comprehension practices:

1. Reading is a lived-through experience or event. The reader "evokes" the text, bringing a network of past experiences with the world, with language, and with other texts.

2. The meaning is neither in the reader nor in the text, but in the reciprocal transaction between the two.

3. There is no single correct reading of a literary text.

4. In any specific reading activity, given agreed-upon purposes and criteria, some readings or interpretations are more defensible than others.

> "*T*he reader-text relationship is reciprocal and involves the characteristics of the reader as well as the nature of the materials."

We all have our own unique backgrounds of experience that we bring to any reading material. As a result, we will all have our own unique and personal interpretation of that material—an interpretation that may or may not be similar to the interpretations of others reading the same text. Thus, reading a piece of literature opens up interpretive possibilities for youngsters and provides opportunities for extending that literature in personal and subjective ways.

Unit 1

The Transactional Approach to Reading

The transactional approach to reading instruction is significant because it places emphasis on three critical and interrelated stages in the reading process. Together, these stages are essential in the comprehension and appreciation of all types of reading materials:

Before Reading: Processes designed to link students' background knowledge and experiences to the text

During Reading: Processes designed to help students read constructively and interact with text

After Reading: Processes designed to deepen and extend students' responses to text

The emphasis (at all stages and all levels) is on the development of appropriate reading strategies. Strategies are those mental processes that readers use (independently) to obtain meaning from text. Mature readers use a wide variety of strategies to comprehend written material. Beginning readers must be taught necessary strategies in order to ascend through the various stages of reading development. Indeed, the *heart and soul* of every reading program is to assist youngsters in comprehending what they read.

Pre-Reading Competencies

Students need a solid background of pre-reading skills as they begin their journey "down the literacy road." Reading is a developmental process, and certain attributes or skills must be in place as children begin their journey. These include (but are not limited to): maturation, ability to converse, ability to work with others, ability to share, ability to listen, and attentiveness. We also know that students' future success in reading is built upon the foundation of certain pre-reading competencies. These include **oral language ability, concepts of print,** and **phonemic awareness.**

Oral Language

Many children, throughout the early years of their lives (e.g., birth to age five), have been surrounded with language (being read to, listening to adults, watching TV, etc.). Those language experiences provide youngsters with the foundational support upon which the other language arts (reading, writing, listening) rest. Indeed, even before children learn to read and write, they learn to talk and communicate with those around them. In fact, oral language begins to develop in most children from the day they are born.

So too do children learn that speaking is a way of satisfying their immediate needs (hunger, thirst, etc.), as well as their secondary needs (entertainment, clothing, etc.). Most children discover that speaking is not only a method of communicating with others but is also a way in which they can express their emotions and desires. Indeed, there is a convincing body of research that suggests that sustained oral languaging opportunities, both in and out of the classroom, form the foundation upon which successful learning rests (Fredericks et al., 1997).

Although young children certainly wouldn't use the terminology in the chart, they quickly learn some basic attributes of language even before they enter a formal educational setting (e.g., school). The chart on the right shows some basic concepts that youngsters between the ages of birth and five years old typically learn.

Language Concept	Definition
Phonology	An understanding that language is made of sounds
Morphology	An understanding of how words are formed (letters in patterns)
Semantics	An understanding that language is used to convey meaning
Vocabulary	An understanding that words have different meanings
Pragmatics	An understanding that language can be used to learn things

Facility with oral language is an important precursor to reading instruction and comprehension development. Indeed, there is a convincing body of research that concludes that students who have less well-developed oral abilities will also experience limited success in the other language arts (Fredericks et al., 1997). Teachers who plan oral language activities for both fluent and non-fluent children will be helping youngsters in later comprehension instruction. Here's why:

1. Oral language development forms the foundation upon which successful reading and writing experiences rest.

2. When youngsters are encouraged to use and practice their oral language skills, their vocabulary development improves concomitantly.

3. Systematic instruction in developing oral language abilities enhances personal feelings of self-worth and facilitates individual self-concepts.

4. Regular opportunities to participate in oral language activities demonstrate the "active" nature of language as a tool to communicate and a tool to comprehend.

5. Through speaking, children are engaged in positive languaging opportunities that enhance, stimulate, and encourage the development of and "comfortableness" with all the language arts (adapted from Fredericks et al., 1997).

It's important to note that facility in speaking also translates into facility in reading, writing, and listening skills. To this end, it becomes important for teachers to provide sufficient language development opportunities throughout the entire elementary curriculum. Here are some suggestions:

- Planned opportunities for students to engage in the exchange of information need to be woven throughout the school day.

- Lots of read aloud experiences—books shared by the teacher and other adults— provide good models of oral language use.

- Informal drama activities and productions provide engaging opportunities for children to put language "into action."

- Provide classroom discussions or informal storytelling through the use of concrete objects such as a baseball, a bird feather, a rock, a specific photograph.

- Out-of-classroom common experiences—field trips, movies, stories—that children have experienced together offer many opportunities for discussion and appreciation.

- Provide opportunities for students to work in pairs, triads, small groups, and other cooperative learning ventures.

- "Show and Tell"

What is most critical to know is that oral language development does not stop once students enter a formal educational setting (a classroom, for example). Rather, students should be adding to, enhancing, and polishing their oral language abilities throughout their educational careers. In doing so, they are also enhancing the necessary requisites for good comprehension development.

Concepts of Print

Simply put, this concept of reading refers to how a book "works." That is, children must have knowledge of the organizational structure of a book, its components,

and the way in which it is designed. Young readers need to understand the separate parts of a book (front, middle, back), the progression of a story in the book (from front to back), directionality cues (top to bottom, left to right), the arrangement of letters into words, the meaning of punctuation, and other details about printed materials.

The significance of this skill is that it provides youngsters with an awareness of how every piece of written material "operates." For teachers, it is a way of knowing what children know about reading before they can actually read. Much of children's concepts about print come from home experience (e.g., parents who have read to their children on a regular basis). Children who have adequate concepts about print are ready to move into the preliminary stages of reading instruction. These concepts are illustrated in the chart at the right.

Phonemic Awareness

Phonemic awareness instruction provides children with opportunities to experience spoken language before they start to learn written language. The ability to hear and manipulate sounds is referred to as *phonemic awareness*. Implicit in this definition is the fact that children need to hear the sounds of language (for example, "Hickory, Dickory, *Dock*; The mouse ran up the *clock*"). Hearing the sounds of words is completely independent of recognizing the meaning of those words (a skill that is developed later in the reading process). It is also important for children to identify the sequence of sounds within an oral unit (what we call a word). For example, "What is the last sound you hear in the word *book*? Third, phonemic awareness is the ability of children to understand the relationship that phonemes play in word formation. For example, "Let's take the sound /s/ and add it to the beginning of the sound /at/. What word do we have?"

The importance of phonemic awareness lies in the fact that it lets children know that language can be manipulated. By combining sounds, subtracting sounds, and rearranging sounds, we can create elements known as words. These words help us communicate with each other. For young children, the path to that communication begins with the ability to hear the sounds in words, determine the various positions of those sounds within one or more words, and understand the role of those sounds within a single word. Phonemic awareness is a sequenced series of oral language skills that precede a child's transition into written language.

It is important to understand that phonemic awareness does not just "happen." Phonemic awareness is a sequential and developmental process. Certain abilities precede others and must be mastered before other skills can be learned. A

Concepts of Print

- Books have a front and a back.
- Reading begins at the front of a book.
- Letters in words are read from left to right.
- Words can be long or short.
- Words on a page are read from left to right.
- Words on a page are read from top to bottom.
- There are spaces between individual words on a page.
- Words appear in groups or clusters known as sentences.

strong foundation in phonemic awareness abilities is a precursor to the foundation of reading skills that takes place later in the reading process. Following is a sequential ordering of phonemic awareness abilities children need to acquire. Notice the connections with **oral language** abilities.

Sequence of Phonemic Awareness Skills

1. Awareness of spoken words (we can communicate orally via logical units of speech).
2. Many words have similar or matching sounds (words can rhyme with each other).
3. Many words begin with the same sound (alliteration). For example, "Tommy's toy turtle is on the table."
4. Words have syllables (words can be divided into distinct parts).
5. Words have onsets (the sounds of a word that come before the first vowel).
6. Words have rimes (the first vowel in a word and all the sounds that follow).

7. The sounds in a word appear in specific locations (each sound has a specific position, e.g., beginning, middle, end).
8. Words have individual sounds (consonants and vowels have one or more different sounds).
9. The sounds of a word can be separated (a word can be divided into its component phonemes). For example, "Can you tell me the three sounds in the word *mouse*? [/m/ /ow/ /s/]
10. The sounds of a word can be manipulated (beginning, middle, and ending sounds in a word can be replaced with other beginning, middle, and ending sounds; also, beginning, middle, and ending sounds can be eliminated from a word).

Assessing Phonemic Awareness

The following assessment instrument is designed to help you determine the appropriate stage of phonemic awareness development for individual students in your classroom. It is not designed as a group or class test, but rather an instrument that will assist you in targeting instruction for individual students.

1. The Assessment is to be administered in an oral format—one child at a time. The actual administration will take approximately ten minutes per child, and an entire class can be assessed in less than a week (depending on your schedule of regular activities).

2. It may not be appropriate or necessary to assess every child in the class. Some children will have sufficient phonetic skills that will preclude them from this assessment process.

3. It is not necessary to "go through" the entire test with every child. Some children will indicate early stages of phonemic awareness development (e.g., rhyming), but will become frustrated when attempting later stages (e.g., sound positions). Teacher judgment in stopping the testing process at an appropriate point is always preferable to "forcing" a child through a complete assessment procedure.

Comprehension,
Reading, and
Early Literacy

Phonemic Awareness Assessment

Student Name: _____

Date: _____

Test Administrator: _____

Stage One—Rhyming and Alliteration

Rhyming Identification

Read each pair of words orally. Circle each pair the child correctly identifies.
"I will read two words to you. Tell me if the two words rhyme. Here are two words
that rhyme: **ball — fall**. Here are two words that don't rhyme: **ball — bat**."

bed — red	crack — pink	pill — grill	tuck — tack
boat — float	nose — close	mail — rake	bank — rice

Rhyming Utility

Read each word orally. Write the word the child supplies on the appropriate space.
"I will read a word to you. Tell me another word that rhymes with the first word.
Here's an example: **meet — feet**."

nail _____	sick _____	bug _____
bake _____	map _____	cot _____

Alliteration Identification

Read each set of words orally. Circle each set the child correctly identifies.
"I will read three words to you. Tell me if the three words all begin with the same
sound. Here's an example of three words that all begin with the same sound: **nose,
nail, nice**."

set, sail, soar	rub, frog, rack	pen, pat, poke
bun, best, ton	hole, hair, help	gate, goat, goose

Alliteration Utility

Read each pair of words orally. Write the word the child supplies on the
appropriate space.
"I will read two words to you. Tell me one more word that has the same beginning
sound as the first two words. Here's an example: **bank, boy, boat**."

meet, mail, _____	coat, cap, _____
fog, fast, _____	date, deer, _____
nice, nail, _____	tape, tail, _____

Possible Score: 26 / Student's Score: _____

Teaching Comprehension in Grades 1–2

Unit

1

Pre-Reading
Competencies

Stage Two—Word Parts

Onsets

Say each sound orally. Write the word the child says next to the sound.
"I will make the sound of a letter. Tell me a word that begins with that sound.
Here's an example: /**d**/ — **dive**."

/s/ _____   /t/ _____
/b/ _____   /m/ _____
/j/ _____   /k/ _____

Rimes

Say each sound orally. Write the word the child says next to the sound.
"I will make a sound. Tell me a word that ends with that sound. Here's an example:
/**ad**/ — **dad**."

/ed/ _____   /op/ _____
/ing/ _____   /ake/ _____
/ell/ _____   /id/ _____

Syllabication

Say each two-syllable word slowly. Circle each word the child correctly blends.
"I'll say a word very slowly. I'll say it in two parts. Put the two parts together and
tell me what the word is. Here's an example: **birth...day — birthday**."

base...ball   fun...ny   pop...corn
mop...ping   sun...set   can...dy

Phoneme Blending

For each word, say the individual phonemes slowly. Circle each word in which the
child correctly blends the phonemes.
"I will say some sounds very slowly. Put the sounds together and tell me the word
you hear. Here's an example: /**b**/ /**ō**/ /**t**/ — **boat**."

/i/ /t/   /p/ /e/ /n/   /f/ /r/ /o/ /g/
/s/ /ō/   /j/ /um/ /p/   /s/ /t/ /o/ /p/

Possible Score: 24 / Student's Score: _____

Stage Three—Sound Positions

Beginning Sounds

Read each word orally to the child. Circle the words the child correctly identifies.
"Tell me the sound you hear at the beginning of each word I say to you. Here's an example: **five** — **/f/**."

say	pail	dice
jump	old	chain

Middle Sounds

Read each word orally to the child. Circle the words the child correctly identifies.
"Tell me the sound you hear in the middle of each word I say to you. Here's an example: **chain** — **/ā/**."

green	big	yes
ride	mouse	rack

Ending Sounds

Read each word orally to the child. Circle the words the child correctly identifies.
"Tell me the sound you hear at the end of each word I say to you. Here's an example: **pain** — **/n/**."

top	ride	flat
duck	skill	plum

Possible Score: 18 / Student's Score: _____

Stage Four—Sound Separation

Phoneme Counting

Say each word for the child. Circle the words the child correctly identifies.
"I will say a word. For each word, tell me how many sounds you hear. Here's an example: **dig** — **there are three sounds, /d/ /i/ /g/**."

hen (3)	cow (2)	but (3)
horse (3)	this (3)	me (2)

Phoneme Segementation

Say each word for the child. Circle the words the child correctly identifies.
"I will say a word. Then I would like you to say the word back to me very slowly so I can hear each sound in the word. Here's an example: **bell** — **/b/ /e/ /l/**."

brown	eat	help
truck	pig	gum

Possible Score: 12 / Student's Score: _____

Stage Five—Sound Manipulation

Sound Deletion

Say each sentence for the child. Circle the sentence the child correctly responds to. "I will say a word. Then, I will ask you to say the say word, but to leave off a sound that I tell you. Here's an example: Say *jet* without the /j/ — /et/."

Say *bird* without the /b/.
Say *sad* without the /s/.
Say *work* without the /w/.

Say *must* without the /t/.
Say *sleep* without the /p/.
Say *flag* without the /g/.

Say *ball* without the /a/.
Say *run* without the /u/.
Say *well* without the /e/.

Sound Substitution

Say each sentence for the child. Circle the sentence the child correctly responds to. "I will say a word. Then, I will ask you to change something about the word and say it back to me. Here's an example: Take away the first sound in *sell* and replace it with a /f/ — fell."

Take away the first sound in *hit* and replace it with a /b/.
Take away the first sound in *dog* and replace it with a /f/.
Take away the first sound in *best* and replace it with a /n/.

Take away the last sound in *bug* and replace it with a /t/.
Take away the last sound in *skin* and replace it with a /p/.
Take away the last sound in *rock* and replace it with a /b/.

Take away the middle sound in *cat* and replace it with a /u/.
Take away the middle sound in *bell* and replace it with a /i/.
Take away the middle sound in *tub* and replace it with a /a/.

Possible Score: 18 / Student's Score: _____

Phonemic Awareness Assessment Scoring Rubric

	Child is very competent.	Child is moderately competent.	Child is minimally competent.	Child is not competent.
Rhyming and Alliteration	24–26 points	20–23 points	15–19 points	0–14 points
Word Parts	22–24 points	18–21 points	13–17 points	0–12 points
Sound Positions	16–18 points	12–15 points	8–11 points	0–7 points
Sound Separation	10–12 points	7–9 points	5–6 points	0–4 points
Sound Manipulation	16–18 points	12–15 points	8–11 points	0–7 points

Directions: Add up the total number of points for each of the five sections of the Assessment. Using the rubric above put a check mark in one of the four boxes following the title of each section to indicate the child's score for that section. The column with the most number of checkmarks is indicative of the student's overall level of competency in phonemic awareness (**Very Competent, Moderately Competent, Minimally Competent, Not Competent**).

Instruction in phonemic awareness provides young children with multiple opportunities to "experience" oral language. As a result, children begin to understand, use, and apply oral language in a host of situations. They develop proficiencies in the appreciation, utility, and manipulation of language that help solidify an understanding of how language "works." This understanding is the foundation upon which written language abilities are based. It is also the foundation for phonics instruction and later, for reading instruction.

The relationship between phonemic awareness and reading instruction is considerable. Without proficiency in phonemic awareness, children may not have the necessary foundation for later reading competency. What becomes abundantly clear from an enormous body of reading research is that children who have difficulty in learning to read or who have failed to learn to read are often those who also lack phonemic awareness abilities. Equally clear is the fact that phonemic awareness is a precursor for later reading success and forms the foundation upon which young children can begin to develop (and appreciate) early literacy skills.

Unit

1

Pre-Reading
Competencies

Summary of Pre-Reading Competencies

The chart below lists the pre-reading competencies essential for later reading
success. They also form the foundation upon which successful comprehension
development is based.

Oral Language	Concepts of Print	Phonemic Awareness
• Language is composed of sounds. • Words are formed by arranging letters in patterns. • Language is used to convey meaning. • Different words have different meanings. • Language can be used to learn about the world. • Oral language forms the foundation for vocabulary development.	• Books have a front and a back. • Reading begins at the front of a book. • Letters in words are read from left to right. • Words can be long or short. • Words on a page are read from left to right. • Words on a page are read from top to bottom. • There are spaces between individual words on a page. • Words appear in groups or clusters known as sentences.	• There are word patterns that are similar (rhyming) and there are similar sounds at the beginning of words (alliteration). • Words can be divided into more than one sound, and the sounds in a word occur in a particular sequence (beginning sound + ending sound). • Each sound within a word has a specific and logical position within that word (beginning, middle, end). • Sounds in a word (phonemes) can be separated. • The sounds in a word can be manipulated, rearranged, resequenced, and reconfigured.

When to Start Comprehension Instruction

● ● ● ● ● ● ● ● ● ● ● ● ● ● ● ●

For comprehension instruction to be effective, it must be predicated on several
factors that will ensure its success, especially for youngsters in first and second
grade. The following concepts must be in place before
comprehension instruction can begin. Students must:

- Know that people communicate with words.
- Be able to express themselves through oral language.
- Know how to listen to others.
- Have a listening vocabulary of approximately 1,000 words.
- Know that words appear in groups or clusters known as sentences.
- Know that people read books silently and out loud.
- Know that reading makes sense.
- Understand the left-to-right progression of reading.
- Know that there is a match between oral language and written language.
- Be able to obtain some information from illustrations.

Teaching Comprehension

Looking at Comprehension

The central goal of reading instruction is comprehension. Comprehension is based on one's ability to make sense of printed materials. It goes beyond one's ability to remember details or recall factual information from text. What does it mean for a student to comprehend? Several researchers (Wiggens and McTighe, 1998; Wiske, 1998) suggest that students comprehend when they are able to:

- *connect* new knowledge to their prior knowledge, including prior knowledge about other topics and other ideas;

- *interpret* what they learn;

- *apply* their knowledge to new situations; and

- *explain* and predict events and actions.

In examining these studies, one should note that phonics instruction does not necessarily precede comprehension instruction. In other words, the strategies of comprehension can be taught and learned prior to (and along with) other regular forms of reading instruction.

> "*You* can guide pre-reading students to interpret, apply, explain, and make new connections."

For example, if students understand the "flow" of ideas from page to page in the first half of the book *Brown Bear, Brown Bear, What Do You See?* by Bill Martin, Jr., they will be able to make predictions about the text as you read aloud successive pages in the book. In short, they can learn the very important comprehension strategy of prediction as an element of read alouds even before it becomes part of their reading repertoire with written text. What is important here is the fact that you can guide students to interpret, apply, explain, and make new connections—in short, you can teach for comprehension.

This vision of reading education is one in which all children have the opportunity to engage in reading as a process of inquiry. It implies that children can explore, examine, and "play with" ideas in print even before they learn how to decode that print. Helping youngsters deal with the strategies of comprehension *before* or *as* they learn decoding skills can assist them tremendously as they are learning to become accomplished readers. It is essential to create a community of

learning that is supportive, encouraging, and committed to exploring the dynamics of comprehension across the curriculum and across the various learning styles in any classroom.

Guiding Principles and Practices of Learning

Here's a statement every teacher knows intuitively: Learning is a complex and multidimensional process. (By the same token, ALL primary teachers will equally agree with the corollary to that statement: **Teaching** is a complex and multidimensional process!) Suffice it to say that we have reams of research about how learners learn and especially about how learners learn to read. While it is certainly beyond the scope and intent of this book to address all of that pertinent research, I think you might find the chart below to be a "quick and easy" synthesis of that data. This summary focuses on five critical principles about children's learning and cognitive development (adapted from Carin and Bass, 2001).

Guiding Principles and Practices

Constructing Knowledge and Understanding	• The ultimate goal of reading instruction is comprehension. Instruction that supports comprehension development must be constructed. • In the process of understanding text, students connect new knowledge to prior knowledge. • Constructed knowledge is refined and elaborated in successive encounters with text.
Alternative Conceptions	• Children often have alternative ideas about text that may interfere with learning. • Moving toward reading comprehension requires student awareness and effort. It also demands the assistance and support of a teacher.
Cognitive Development	• In the course of cognitive development, knowledge becomes more flexible. Students learn to use knowledge in an ever-increasing variety of learning tasks.
Scaffolding	• Teachers need to effectively model and scaffold knowledge construction. Teachers are an important resource for youngsters in the learning cycle.
Learning Communities	• Learning occurs best when students are active participants in a community of learners. Learning is a social activity.

What Readers Do

One of the seminal research documents in the field of reading education investigated what proficient readers do to comprehend text (Pearson, Dole, Duffy, and Roehler, 1992). Also included in this document was research-based data that indicated what unsuccessful readers do and, most importantly, what teachers can do to move students to higher levels of comprehension. This research also identified comprehension strategies that youngsters **of all ages** (emphasis added) use to construct meaning. One of the report's conclusions was that teachers need to teach these strategies explicitly and for long periods of time (Miller, 2002).

The chart below presents a synthesis of the necessary strategies for comprehension to occur. Quite obviously, these strategies address competencies that <u>readers</u> need to master. But, as you review this list, think about how these strategies might also apply to students in your classroom. I hope you agree with me that these strategies have specific application for all students in the primary grades.

Comprehension Concepts and Strategies

Concept/Strategy	Description	Source
Schema (Making Connections)	• Readers activate prior knowledge before, during, and after reading. • Readers connect the known with the unknown.	Anderson and Pearson, 1984. Fredericks et al., 1997.
Mental Imagery	• Readers use concrete or past experiences to create "mind pictures" or visual images. • Mental imagery takes place before, during, and after reading.	Fredericks, 1986. Pressley, 1976.
Predicting and Inferring	• Readers make "educated guesses" to form conclusions, make critical judgments, and create unique interpretations. • Readers predict future events in text.	Hansen, 1981.
Questioning	• Readers ask questions of themselves, the authors, and the texts they read. • Teachers model appropriate question-asking strategies.	Fredericks, 2003. Raphael, 1984.

Unit 2

What Readers Do

Concept/Strategy	Description	Source
Important Information	• Readers determine the most important ideas and themes in a text. • Readers group or classify ideas into recognizable categories.	Palinscar and Brown, 1984.
Synthesizing (Retelling)	• Readers synthesize and summarize (in their own words) what they read. • Readers rethink what they encounter in text.	Brown, Day, and Jones, 1983.

Modeling Comprehension

Do you remember how you learned to ride a bicycle? Undoubtedly, you watched someone (an older sibling or other child) as she/he rode around the neighborhood. Perhaps a parent assisted you by demonstrating how to hold the handlebars, how to position your feet on the pedals, how to make the necessary circular motions with the pedals, and the all-important need to maintain your balance. If you were like me, you probably fell down a lot, skinned your knees, bumped your head, fell off, or careened into a lamppost or the family car. Looking back at those experiences, you can probably smile now with some fond memories, although at the time it was a pretty scary experience.

In many ways learning to read is similar to learning how to ride a bicycle. There is something you want to master (perhaps because everyone else is doing it), and you need a guide or instructor to help you learn necessary skills or competencies. That guide often demonstrates how he/she performs a selected skill and then gives you an opportunity to do the same. After one skill is mastered, others are taught in a certain sequence. When you were learning bicycle skills, you probably had someone who modeled important abilities—you got to see what an accomplished bicycle rider could do. So can it be with reading instruction.

Modeling is the process of showing or demonstrating for someone how to use or do something she or he does not know how to do; most human behaviors are acquired in this way (Bandura, 1986). When a child watches someone writing a letter, modeling is taking place. When an individual observes a game of chess, modeling is taking place. And when a beginning reader listens to an adult (teacher or parent) talking about the thoughts in his/her head as he/she reads, modeling is taking place. We all need experts in our journey into and through many learning tasks—whether that journey involves riding a bicycle or learning to think like a reader.

Types of Modeling

Roehler and Duffy (1991) identify two types of modeling that teachers traditionally practice. The first is **implicit modeling**, which takes place when the processes or ideas being modeled occur as part of an experience. They are not directly identified or stated. Examples of implicit modeling include reading aloud to children and having youngsters watch you as you engage in some independent reading with a self-selected book. **Explicit modeling** involves directly talking with and showing youngsters what is being modeled. Two types of explicit modeling involve *talk-alouds* and *think-alouds*.

Talk-Aloud: The teacher presents students with a series of steps or procedures for completing a task and asks questions to guide them through the procedure. Each step in a procedure is presented to students and the teacher talks the students through those steps.

Think-Aloud: In this modeling technique, the teacher actually talks about the thinking processes he/she uses. Children have an opportunity to actually "look inside" an expert's head (the teacher) to "see" what goes on as he/she reads. This is modeling at its best simply because youngsters have a "front-row seat" for the reading process. They hear what an accomplished reader does. Most important, they learn that there is a measure of responsibility on the part of a reader to make a connection between what the reader knows and what the reader is encountering in text. When pre-readers watch what accomplished readers do and when those accomplished readers guide children to engage in the same thought processes, then students are well on the way to comprehension success.

Here's an example of a think-aloud (focusing on the comprehension strategy of *Predicting and Inferring*) using the book *Good Night, Gorilla* by Peggy Rathman:

"Boys and girls, when I look at the picture on the front of this book, I can see a gorilla holding some keys. He has his fingers up to his lips, so I guess he wants us all to be quiet. I see a watchman walking in the opposite direction. I'm thinking that he doesn't know that the gorilla has his keys. He seems to be looking for something else. I'm guessing that maybe the gorilla is going to do something sneaky and that he doesn't want the watchman to know what he's doing. Maybe he is going to let all the other animals in the zoo out of their cages. Hmmm, I think I'm going to have to read the story to find out what happens."

Modeling is one of the most powerful teaching tools we can share with youngsters. As stated earlier, it is how we learn many tasks throughout our lifetime. As such, it can be used in a wide variety of classroom activities and experiences, particularly those involving reading. But, for modeling to achieve its greatest potency, it must be done within the context of a specific text (Roehler and Duffy, 1991). For example, when we learned how to ride a bicycle, we actually watched someone else ride a bicycle and then emulated some of the actions or motions of that expert. We didn't just hear about how people ride bicycles; rather, we saw someone in action with a real bicycle. By the same token, modeling the thinking behaviors that take place in our heads as we read a book with children is very powerful. As such, how we think as we read should not be presented to children as an isolated skill but should be demonstrated with authentic text (e.g., books, songs, fingerplays, etc.).

Scaffolding

Have you ever watched a new building—particularly a tall building—being erected in a downtown area? Typically, there will be lots of machines, lots of people, and lots of activity. In many cases there will be a framework or metal structure on the outside of the building. This frame allows workers to attend to outside tasks on the building (painting, masonry, etc.) in addition to providing them with egress into the upper floors of the building without going through the interior. This structure is known as a scaffold. It is both a form and a construction aid.

Scaffolding (use of instructional scaffolds) is important in education, too—particularly reading education. By definition, scaffolding is when a teacher provides instructional assistance to enable students to learn at higher and higher levels (just like a building scaffold assists construction people to work on a structure at higher and higher levels). Several researchers (Grigorenko, 1998; Roehler and Cantlon, 1997) have outlined the following practices as essential in any learning task:

- set challenging and interesting learning tasks with an appropriate degree of novelty;

- simplify the task so that the learner can manage its components and achieve intermediate steps;

- facilitate student talk in small group and large group settings;

- ask meaningful questions at just the right time;

- lead students to clarify, elaborate, or justify their responses;

- supply necessary information or direct learners to appropriate sources;

- provide models of thinking processes;

- provide external support to aid students in making connections.

Modeling is an effective aid in helping children acquire necessary comprehension abilities. But, it is equally important that those same children begin to take on the reading/thinking behaviors of the "expert" through more and more encounters with textual materials. Often referred to as a "gradual release of responsibility," this process implies that youngsters must have authentic opportunities to practice those behaviors. These opportunities are accomplished by scaffolding the instruction—"passing the instructional baton," so to speak.

This instructional scaffold provides direction and support for any learner. Eventually these scaffolds will be removed as students become more proficient and comfortable in the acquisition of reading strategies. Obviously, the ultimate goal is to have students develop their own self-regulated strategies in a wide variety of textual materials.

Guidelines for Effective Modeling

Strategies are taught in context.	Students are provided with opportunities to engage in meaningful interactions with real text.
Modeling is continuous.	Students observe modeling in a wide variety of daily activities (sing-alongs, show and tell, etc.) and in a wide variety of curricular areas.
Implicit modeling is a daily experience.	Students have multiple opportunities to observe the teacher reading independently, writing independently, and reading aloud.
Explicit modeling is a daily experience.	Students have multiple opportunities to "see" inside the head of an accomplished reader through talk-alouds and think-alouds.
Modeling is done one strategy at a time.	Students should have concentrated experiences with a single reading strategy. Although reading involves the use of multiple strategies at the same time, youngsters require repeated experiences with each strategy to attain competency.
Cooperation is emphasized.	Youngsters and the teacher work collaboratively to support each other in a variety of interactive tasks and activities.
Instruction is scaffolded.	Responsibility for learning is gradually released to students. After modeling a strategy several times for children, invite them to 1) model it for each other, and 2) use it on their own.
Invite parents' participation.	Parents can serve as implicit modelers of reading behaviors—reading to their children, writing letters and notes, setting aside a family reading hour, etc. Encourage their active participation.
Invite student response.	Invite students to discuss and talk about the strategies you demonstrate. Encourage them to share ways in which your models can be used in various educational (or recreational) tasks.

Unit 3
Comprehension Lessons

Comprehension strategies can be taught to beginning readers as well as accomplished readers. Children can be presented with, and given practice in, the types of thinking that accomplished readers do. As youngsters begin to realize that reading and thinking go hand-in-hand, they also begin to understand that reading is much more than simply decoding printed symbols in a book—it involves a dynamic interaction between the reader and the text.

Lesson Planning

Comprehension Circles are instructional plans that stimulate and emphasize comprehension development in a wide range of texts. They differ from "regular" reading instruction in that they do not depend on the reading ability of any single individual or the class as a whole. In short, the ability to decode text is not a prerequisite for the success of comprehension development, nor is it a prerequisite for the success of Comprehension Circles.

The success of comprehension instruction is highly dependent upon the opportunities provided to students for actively engaging in the dynamics of text. What follows is a structure that has been used successfully in hundreds of classrooms across the country. While this format provides you with a working outline for the necessary elements of a Comprehension Circle, it is important to note that there is a great deal of flexibility inherent within this design. You are encouraged to modify or alter this plan in line with the structure of your own instructional program. For example, the time limits are suggestions only and can be easily changed in accordance with your daily schedule of activities.

This sequence of processes and procedures is designed to help students become comfortable in using the strategies of

Comprehension Circles

The term "Comprehension Circle" was chosen intentionally. It underscores the concept of comprehension as a continuous process—a process that is ever evolving and always moving forward (there is no finite end). Also embodied in this term is the idea that learning is a collaborative event between and among teachers and children. We all come together in a focused group (e.g., a circle) for a common purpose and a common experience.

competent readers. It is a model that can be easily changed as the competencies of class members change.

The following five elements are important components in a Comprehension Circle:

1. **Engagement (Schema)** is the initial element in any lesson—the stage at which the strategy of schema is emphasized. It is here that you would 1) activate the background knowledge of youngsters, or 2) provide necessary background knowledge for those lacking sufficient backgrounds of experience.

2. **Modeling** includes those activities that allow you to demonstrate, either implicitly or explicitly, the thinking you use while reading. This modeling will be focused on a specific comprehension strategy used in Stage 4.

3. **Read Aloud** is the stage at which a book is shared orally with youngsters. Sometimes it may be necessary (depending on the comprehension strategy to be demonstrated) to do a read aloud before the Modeling stage. Another option may include stopping periodically during the read aloud to do a think-aloud focused on a selected strategy.

4. **Guided Instruction** is the stage at which a specific comprehension strategy is emphasized. At this stage you invite youngsters to use one of the four strategies (Mental Imagery, Predicting and Inferring, Questioning, or Identifying Important Information) you demonstrated in Stage 2 in selected portions (or the entire book) shared during read aloud time. In some cases, you may wish to use a comparable book (e.g., same theme, same author, same genre) for children to practice.

5. **Synthesize and Summarize** is the final strategy for a Comprehension Circle. This is the time to "debrief" with students—talking about what they learned, how successful they were in using a particular strategy, and reflecting on how they might use that strategy in future books.

The chart on pages 38–39 offers several suggestions for these five elements. This does not mean that you need to do *all* activities for every Comprehension Circle. For example, you may know from your own prior experience that your students have extensive experience with farm animals (particularly if you live or teach in a farming community). Thus, activating students' schema may just entail a simple statement ("Let's think about some farm animals.") rather than extensive explanations or supplementary illustrations. The ultimate key to successful Comprehension Circles is flexibility.

Unit 3

Lesson Planning

Suggested Comprehension Circle Strategies and Activities

Component	Strategies and Activities	Suggested Time Frame
Engagement (Schema)	• Gather students together as a whole class or a smaller group. • Present the theme or topic of a forthcoming book. • Talk about the topic. • Ask questions about the theme or topic. • Invite students to share **relevant** experiences (keep the conversation <u>focused</u>). • Talk about any misperceptions or misconceptions. • Provide illustrations or photos that illuminate the theme or concept. • Share (as necessary) other AV resources that stimulate schema development. • Show the book cover and encourage discussion about its topic or theme. • Draw "straight-line" connections between what youngsters know and the book's main idea. • Link the book to a similar story/book.	2–3 minutes
Modeling	• Introduce the book. • Vocalize your purpose for reading. • Read and discuss the title. • Talk about the illustrations. • Do a "mental walk" through the book. • Demonstrate a talk-aloud (focused on a specific strategy). • Demonstrate a think-aloud (focused on a specific strategy). • Provide multiple opportunities for students to "see" inside your head.	3–4 minutes
Read Aloud	• Read the selected book out loud to children. • Use expression and intonation as appropriate. • Consider using a big book. • Occasionally "track" the print with your finger or a pointer. • Occasionally use a Shared Book experience with children. • Consider periodic stops (as necessary) to model your thinking. • Demonstrate your enthusiasm for the book while reading.	4–5 minutes

Component	Strategies and Activities	Suggested Time Frame
Guided Instruction	• Teacher and students return to text. • Conduct class/group reading conference. • Identify one specific comprehension strategy. • Clarify reading strategy in "kid terms." • Demonstrate the strategy within the context of the book. • Re-model (as necessary) your use of the strategy in that book. • Invite youngsters to "try out" the strategy (by using their own talk-about or think-about conversations). • Encourage retellings. • Discuss transfer of strategy. • Pose open-ended questions. • Reread a portion of the book (as necessary) and talk about how the strategy can be used there. • Provide positive feedback.	4–5 minutes
Synthesize and Summarize	• Invite children to talk about what they learned. • Encourage active discussion among all class/group members. • Use open-ended questions. • Students may need thinking time before responding. • Help youngsters focus on 1 or 2 significant points. • Invite students to reflect on the modeling you did throughout the lesson. • Recap (in kid terms) the strategy used.	2–3 minutes

Note: A Comprehension Circle (as described above) takes approximately 15–20 minutes. This time suggestion, however, is very flexible and is ultimately dependent upon the attention span of the youngsters with whom you work. For most first- and second-grade students, this time frame is more than sufficient. Nevertheless, as students gain more and more confidence with Comprehension Circles, you are certainly encouraged to expand these time frames on an "as needed" basis. The most important determinant of the length of any Comprehension Circle experience is the active engagement of youngsters in all five stages.

On pages 40–42 you will find a *Comprehension Circle Lesson Planner*. It has been designed to offer you a workable and flexible document that will help you design appropriate lessons for your students. Please feel free to modify and adapt this plan in accordance with the dynamics of your own philosophy and classroom organization.

Teaching Comprehension in Grades 1–2

Unit 3

Lesson Planning

Comprehension Circle Lesson Planner

I. Engagement (Schema)

Purpose/Objective(s) of lesson:

Questions to ask:

Illustrations to show:

Concrete objects to use:

Other:

2. Modeling

Introduction of the book:

Talk-Aloud (describe scenario):

Think-Aloud (describe scenario):

Comprehension Circle Lesson Planner

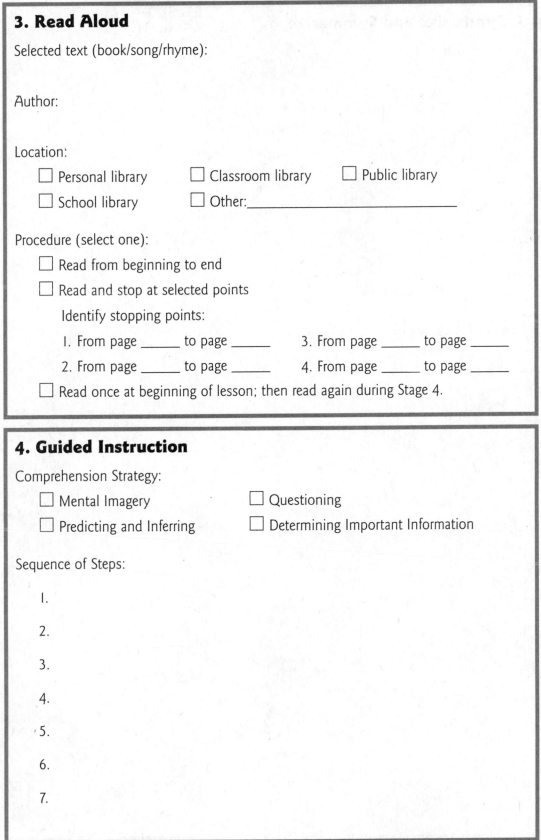

3. Read Aloud

Selected text (book/song/rhyme):

Author:

Location:

☐ Personal library   ☐ Classroom library   ☐ Public library

☐ School library   ☐ Other:_____

Procedure (select one):

☐ Read from beginning to end

☐ Read and stop at selected points

    Identify stopping points:

    1. From page _____ to page _____   3. From page _____ to page _____

    2. From page _____ to page _____   4. From page _____ to page _____

☐ Read once at beginning of lesson; then read again during Stage 4.

4. Guided Instruction

Comprehension Strategy:

☐ Mental Imagery   ☐ Questioning

☐ Predicting and Inferring   ☐ Determining Important Information

Sequence of Steps:

1.

2.

3.

4.

5.

6.

7.

Unit

3

Lesson Planning

Comprehension Circle Lesson Planner

5. Synthesize and Summarize

Important points

    1.

    2.

    3.

Open-Ended Questions:

Additional Modeling:

Designing and Teaching a Comprehension Circle Lesson

Comprehension Circles can be used with a wide variety of materials. While the intent is to eventually assist children in understanding written materials, the practices and procedures of Comprehension Circles are universal. Thus, whenever the word *text* is used, it can refer to books, songs, rhymes, or any other type of printed material that conveys a message. Later sections of the resource guide demonstrate how comprehension strategies can be used with materials other than books.

1. Select a group of students (whole class, large group, or small group) for a Comprehension Circle activity.

2. Select an appropriate text and record it on the Planner. You may wish to choose the material or invite students to select the text or book the day before the actual lesson. Use a text that will help demonstrate the use and utility of a selected comprehension strategy.

3. Determine the purpose or objectives of your lesson.

4. Identify an appropriate comprehension strategy (in concert with the theme or plot of a selected text) and record it.

5. Think about the background knowledge youngsters may have relevant to the text. Record your impressions.

6. Plan appropriate activities that will solicit students' background knowledge. Or, if appropriate, consider activities that will provide the necessary schema for the text.

7. Ask questions that will assist students in activating the necessary background knowledge related to the text (e.g., "How is the cover of this book similar to the ant colony we saw on the playground last month?").

8. Consider and plan for the modeling you will use. Since your modeling will undoubtedly be explicit, consider how you will use talk-alouds and think-alouds.

9. Introduce the text to students and orient them to its major features. Consider one or more of the following:

    a. Talk about the general plot of the story.

    b. Link the book to a previous story, book, or experience.

    c. Do a "walk-through" of the illustrations or photos.

d. Talk about the author or illustrator.

e. Ask students to make a prediction about the cover or title.

f. Stimulate a purpose for reading (e.g., "Let's read this book to see what happens to the puppy on the cover.").

10. Model how you use the appropriate comprehension strategy.

11. Read the text (or sing the song) to students.

12. Insert "stopping points" where appropriate.

13. Use a pre-determined sequence of steps to share the selected strategy with youngsters.

14. Discuss the use of the strategy within the context of the text.

15. Teach the strategy in the context of the text.

16. Encourage youngsters to actively participate with you. Intervene and guide as necessary. Interventions are short and are guided by prompts that help students focus on the strategy.

17. Engage youngsters in synthesizing and summarizing textual information.

18. Keep the summarization direct and to the point.

19. Encourage discussion and collaboration among all children. This is a cooperative venture, not a competitive one.

20. Provide multiple exposures to the comprehension strategy by using additional texts.

Please keep in mind that this sequence of planning and teaching activities is one way of designing your own lessons. Obviously, you will not want to include everything suggested above for your lessons, nor should you. This design provides you with a number of options, which are dependent upon the nature of the text, the attention span and maturity levels of the children, and the resources you have available. You can modify and adapt these suggestions in keeping with your unique classroom situation and the evolving development of your students. As you become more comfortable in designing your own Comprehension Circle lessons, you will adjust this outline to your own teaching style and philosophy.

Note:

"Engagement (Schema)" and "Synthesize and Summarize" are comprehension strategies that are part of every Comprehension Circle lesson.

A Sample Comprehension Circle Lesson

Heather Simmons is a first-grade teacher in western Colorado. A primary teacher for eight years, she thoroughly loves working with beginning readers. "This is an exciting age," she says. "Youngsters are filled with energy, wonder, and an insatiable desire to learn—especially to learn about reading. I can't think of anything I'd rather be doing than sharing a good book with my students or working with a child on understanding a new piece of literature. This is an exciting age and an exciting time to be a teacher!"

Heather, like her students, is a passionate learner. She is always willing to seek out new possibilities and new learning opportunities for her class. For the past three years, she has immersed her students in Comprehension Circles. "This is exciting," she emphasizes. "I can see all kinds of intellectual growth in these kids. They are really into reading in a big way, and I couldn't be happier!" One look in Heather's classroom and it quickly becomes apparent that she embraces and celebrates reading as much as any teacher. Books are spilling down from shelves and bookcases, words are liberally sprinkled across the walls and doors, and a wonderland of posters, banners, and other displays herald a new author or some old familiar books in intriguing and interesting ways. Literacy is at the forefront of Heather's classroom, and the celebration is contagious!

As she shares Comprehension Circles with the children in her room, Heather has discovered some marvelous thinking taking place. She notes that youngsters are "doing a lot of thinking outside the box" and that they are more engaged in the books and literature she shares with them every day. Most important, she notes, is the fact that language development and comprehension development go hand-in-hand. "My students know that they are learning and using the same thinking processes that can be part of everything we do in first grade!"

Heather has selected the book *In the Tall, Tall Grass* by Denise Fleming (New York: Henry Holt and Co., 1991). She wants to help her students use the strategy of mental imagery to help them create "mind pictures" as they read. Following are some of the planning, thinking, and teaching interactions that took place during a 20-minute Comprehension Circle experience with youngsters.

I. Engagement

Heather: O.K., guys. Today I want to share with you a brand new book. The title of the book (points) is *In the Tall, Tall Grass*. The author of the book (points) is Denise Fleming. Mrs. Fleming has written lots of books for boys and girls. Many of them are about animals and the places where animals live.

Let's think about the title of this book. What kinds of animals do you think might live "in the tall, tall grass"?

José: I think there are lots of bugs.

Martin: Caterpillars, yeah, caterpillars!

April: Worms?

Peter: Creepy crawly things.

Josephina: Deer, just like the one in my backyard last week!

Heather: Those are all good ideas, and I'm going to write them here on the board. Now, in a few minutes we're going to listen to this book, but before we do, I want to tell you about some of the things I do in my head when I see a new book.

Robert: Are we going to see inside your brain?

Heather: Yes, I'm going to let you see some of the things I think about, especially some of the pictures I make in my head when I look at a book.

Layton: Cool! We get to see Miss S's brain!

2. Modeling

Heather: Let's look at the cover of this book. Here (points) you can see a boy peeking through the grass. Down here (points) you can see a caterpillar crawling through the grass. Look all over the cover and you can see lots and lots of green grass all around.

Franklyn: It's like he's in a jungle, right?

Heather: That's right, Franklyn. But you know what? Even though I can see all these things on the cover, I can still make some more pictures in my head— pictures about other things that could live in the tall, tall grass. Here are some of the things I can see in my head:

When I look at the cover of *In the Tall, Tall Grass*, I see the boy. I see the grass all around. And I see the little caterpillar crawling through the grass. Because of the title of the book and because of this picture on the cover, I can guess that this story will take place outdoors. It might even take place in a large field or meadow. So, now I'm painting a picture in my head of a field with lots and lots of grass all over the place.

Carlo: My uncle lives in Michigan, and he has lots of fields on his farm.

Heather: Let's keep focused, O.K.? So I now have this picture in my head of a big open field. I can see the sun overhead and it's a warm day. There are a couple

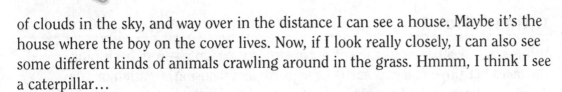

of clouds in the sky, and way over in the distance I can see a house. Maybe it's the house where the boy on the cover lives. Now, if I look really closely, I can also see some different kinds of animals crawling around in the grass. Hmmm, I think I see a caterpillar…

April: Jus' like the one on the cover?

Heather: Yes. I can also see some other animals in the picture that's in my head. I can see a green snake slithering through the grass. I can see a tiny mouse scurrying through the grass. I can see a worm crawling along. And way over there I think I can see some ladybugs crawling up a blade of grass. It seems like there's lots of things happening in the picture that's in my head!

   Well, now I'm going to read a couple of pages at the beginning of the book. I want to see if I should add anything to the picture that's in my head. I'm going to listen carefully to the words and look closely at the illustrations Denise Fleming put in the book.

(Heather reads the first few pages [the book is un-numbered] through to "…hummingbirds sip.")

   Hmm, it looks like I might have to change some of the things that are in the picture in my mind. I know from reading these first few pages that the story takes place outside in a field. I also know that there are some different kinds of animals in the story—animals that may not be the same as the ones in my head.

Josephina: Are there any deer?

Heather: No, but now I can put the caterpillars on these pages (points) into the picture in my mind. And I can put the hummingbirds on these pages (points) into the picture in my head. So, now I know that there might be some animals that live in the grass and there might be some animals that can fly over the grass. So maybe I should add some more birds to the picture in my head. What other kinds of animals could I add to my picture?

Brian: You could add bumblebees.

Michael: You could add turkeys.

LaToya: You could add big giant eagles.

Josephina: You could add deer!

Heather: Well, I'll tell you what we can do. I'll read the whole story to you from the beginning. After I finish, I'll go back and read it again and give you a chance to make some pictures in your own heads. O.K., let's go!

Unit

3

A Sample
Comprehension
Circle Lesson

3. Read Aloud

At this stage Heather reads the entire book to her students—from beginning to end. She takes her time, savoring each of the words and focusing attention on the rhyming pattern of the book. This slow reading also allows her students to begin the process of mental imaging when she does the follow-up read aloud in the next stage.

4. Guided Instruction

Heather: O.K. Now we have heard the entire book. I'm going to go back and read the story again. But this time I want you to make your own pictures in your own heads. Remember there is no right or wrong way to make a mind picture. Your mind picture may be different from someone else's or it may be the same. That's O.K. What's important is that you make up your own picture in your own mind.

Enrique: You mean like the picture you made in your head?

Heather: The picture you make doesn't have to be the same as my picture. Just make it your own picture.

O.K., now I'm going to read the story again, but I'll read it very slowly and stop after each set of pages. That will give you a chance to add some things to the picture that's in your head.

First of all, I want each of you to paint a picture in your head of a field. Now put some animals in that field. They can be some animals you have heard about, or they might be some animals you would like to discover in a field.

Josephina: Can I put in some deer?

Heather: It's your picture; you can put any animals you want in your own mind picture. O.K., now take a few moments to begin painting your mind pictures.

(Heather allows the children 1–2 minutes to initiate their mental images.)

Now, I'll read the story again—very slowly—and you can add some things to the picture you now have in your head as you listen to the story.

(Heather reads the entire book to her students, pausing after each two-page spread to allow sufficient time for students to add to or modify their mental images.)

5. Synthesize and Summarize

Heather takes time to allow selected students to share their mental images. (It's not necessary for everyone to contribute.) She then discusses some of the mind pictures and some of the modifications children made in their images as the story was read.

Heather: Well, it seems that we were able to do lots of things with this story, right?

Franklyn: Yeah, we had some really neat pictures in our brains.

Jenny: Some pictures were just like the book. And some pictures were different.

Heather: What do you think we learned today?

Enrique: We learned how to make some pictures in our head.

Robert: We learned about things that live in the grass.

Crystal: We learned that the pictures in our head might be just like the pictures in the book.

Franklyn: Or they might be different.

Heather: I think we also learned that when we make pictures in our head, we can enjoy a story a lot more. And, guess what, we can make our own mind pictures about any book we share in class.

Josephina: You mean even books about deer?

Heather: (sighing) Yes, Josephina, even books about deer!

You will note in the transcription above that there is a great deal of flexibility inherent in any Comprehension Circle. Heather's students have been previously introduced to the mental imagery strategy, and Heather is now providing them with a text that will allow them to use this strategy in a meaningful way. The success of this lesson was largely due to a certain degree of independence Heather had given her students, as well as the opportunity to use a strategy in a planned and systematic way. The Comprehension Circle lesson plan described in this chapter is an outline, not a formula. It is respectful of the developing nature of children and the specific dynamics of your individual classroom.

It's also important to realize that comprehension development takes time. It is not something that "happens" the first or second or third time we present it to youngsters. Children need many opportunities to engage in the strategies and processes of comprehension. Comprehension development is not a "once and done" procedure. It is sustained, developmental, and long-term. The lessons, activities, and ideas in this book will help you integrate comprehension development into all aspects of your classroom literacy program throughout the entire school year.

Unit 4

How to Use This Book

The success of your comprehension program will revolve around regular, systematic, and sustained strategies naturally incorporated into your entire classroom program. As mentioned earlier, comprehension instruction should be one element in your overall literacy program. The strategies, activities, and lesson plans in this book are designed to offer you a plethora of possibilities and opportunities for engaging students in the dynamics of thinking and understanding. Here are some ideas to consider:

- Comprehension Circles should be a regular and daily occurrence. Plan sufficient time each day for students to participate in appropriate engagement activities.

- Remember that comprehension is one element—albeit an important one—in the overall reading program. Plan sufficient time for the other components, too—shared reading, reading aloud, individualized reading, paired reading, and sustained silent reading.

- Be aware that students' instructional needs change throughout the year. Provide strategies appropriate to each individual's level of development.

- Comprehension Circles can be used with all types of literature and within all types of reading programs. One of their great advantages is that they are easily adaptable to any type of reading curriculum or school/district philosophy.

- Feel free to experiment with Comprehension Circles. Any piece of literature can be coupled with this basic concept to enhance the teaching of both thinking and reading.

- Keep in mind that the basic comprehension strategies throughout this book can be viewed as generic in nature. They have been designed as applicable to a wide range of literature and a wide range of teaching/learning situations.

- Remember that students' needs, attitudes, and abilities change and evolve throughout the year. Those changes will have an impact on the success of Comprehension Circles. Sensitivity to those ongoing changes will help ensure the success of the overall reading program.

- The key to success with Comprehension Circles is flexibility— flexibility in designing your lessons, flexibility in selecting appropriate literature, flexibility in grouping students, flexibility in choosing reading strategies, and flexibility in the integration of comprehension into your overall instructional plans.

> *"The key to success with Comprehension Circles is flexibility."*

All of the activities, strategies, and lesson plans in this book have been classroom-tested and "kid-approved." All are designed to offer you and your students some wonderful adventures and exciting discoveries. Make these ideas a regular part of your overall instructional program, modify them according to the specific needs of students in your classroom, and add to them via the ideas and suggestions that naturally occur in any dynamic curriculum.

Unit 5
Instructional Strategies for Comprehension

One of the primary objectives of reading instruction is assisting children in understanding and integrating the behaviors of accomplished readers. This is done through explanations or demonstrations of those behaviors by the teacher, gradually releasing responsibility for those behaviors to a group of students, and supporting and encouraging students as they begin to use those behaviors. In short, teachers assist beginning readers in becoming independent thinkers who are able to use a variety of strategies to comprehend various texts.

It is important to remember that reading is a constructive process—that is, readers build meaning and understanding by interacting with text (Pearson et al., 1990). This implies that there is an interaction between the reader's prior knowledge and the "knowledge" in text. This interaction is achieved through the use of strategies that assist readers in solving problems at all stages of the reading process. Mastery of specific strategies is essential in helping youngsters become successful readers.

I suspect that there are two questions that may be at the forefront of your thinking now:

- Is it possible to teach comprehension strategies to youngsters in the beginning stages of reading development?

- What are the critical or essential strategies that students need to become accomplished readers?

> *"**M**astery of specific strategies is essential in helping youngsters become successful readers."*

The answer to the first question is an unqualified "Yes!" If we remember that reading is a thinking process, then we should also know that whatever skills or talents we can provide children that will enhance their thinking and processing of text—both oral and written text—will be useful throughout their growth in all stages of reading development.

In response to the second question, many research studies (Harvey and Goudvis, 2000; Pearson et al., 1992; Pressley, 2000; Cooper and Kiger, 2003) identify six critical reading strategies necessary for developing readers. These include:

1. Tapping into background knowledge (schema)

2. Mental imagery (visualizing)

3. Predicting and inferring

4. Questioning

5. Identifying important information

6. Synthesizing and summarizing

The first strategy (tapping into background knowledge) and the last strategy (synthesizing and summarizing) should be part of every literacy encounter (at the beginning and at the end). One of the other four strategies (mental imagery, predicting and inferring, questioning, identifying important information) is selected for a literacy lesson depending on the needs of youngsters and the nature of the text used. This multiplicity of comprehension strategies in any single lesson helps underscore the need for accomplished "comprehenders" to use several strategies in combination.

Tapping into Background Knowledge (Schema)

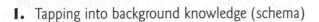

Background knowledge is what we already know about a topic or concepts. We use (or tap into) our background knowledge to make sense of new ideas or new information. Thus, it stands to reason that the more background knowledge we have about a forthcoming topic, the better we will be able to understand (and remember) the topic.

For students, the essential concept to keep in mind is that what they already know affects what they will learn from text. That is, their prior knowledge interacts with text to create meaning. Or to put it another way, more background knowledge equals more understanding. Background knowledge is often called schemata, which are the mental frameworks we have for organizing and understanding information. Our ability to tap into our schemata (known as schema theory) determines how we process new data.

Unit 5

Tapping into Background Knowledge (Schema)

Youngsters are continually and constantly exposed to all types of new information. In the younger years, this is done through exposure to lots of concrete experiences—playing in a sandbox, moving across the floor on a wheeled vehicle, touching and handling objects. It is clear that the more concrete experiences a youngster has throughout her/his developmental years, the more background knowledge she/he will accumulate. Helping children tap into their background knowledge prior to any literacy activities is a major determinant of their success in those activities. For example, a child who has experienced a giraffe at a zoo will have a much better foundation for understanding giraffes encountered in stories and in print. In short, the depth and breadth of our background knowledge help us make sense of the world.

An emphasis on background knowledge or schema is particularly important when working with pre-readers. This is because young learners will bring a diversity of background knowledge to any classroom discussion. As a result, there are two questions you need to ask yourself:

1. How can I help youngsters activate their background knowledge (turn it on)?

2. How can I "fill in the gaps" or develop the necessary background knowledge about a topic before discussion so that children will have an adequate foundation for comprehension?

In working with a diversity of youngsters in your classroom, you may not be able to assess every youngster's background knowledge (or lack of background knowledge) about a topic. However, you can get a "status of the class" by utilizing one of the following techniques for assessing prior knowledge (Holmes and Roser, 1987):

1. **Free recall:** "Tell me what you know about _____."

2. **Word Association:** "When you hear the words *ball, bat,* and *base,* what do you think of?"

3. **Recognition:** Share the following key terms, phrases, or sentences and ask youngsters to tell which ones they think may be related to the book they are about to read, *Is This a House for Hermit Crab?* (McDonald, 1990): *hermit crab, shore, sand, sea, wave.*

4. **Structured Question:** In preparation for reading the book *A Chair for My Mother* (Williams, 1982), ask children a set of prepared questions that will help you assess prior knowledge: "What does a waitress do in a restaurant?" "Why do people put money in big jars?" "What sometimes happens during a house fire?"

5. **Unstructured Discussion:** "We are going to read a story about horses. What do you know about them?"

There are several strategies primary teachers can use with young students to 1) assess the prior knowledge of youngsters, and 2) assist youngsters in developing the necessary prior knowledge for an understanding of a text. These are summarized in the chart below (adapted from Cooper and Kiger, 2003):

Strategies to Develop Prior Knowledge

Strategy	Benefit(s)	Comments
1. Prediction	One of the most effective in assisting children to "build bridges" between prior knowledge and text	Provide students with an opportunity to look at the cover illustration of a book or share the title with them. Ask them to make "educated guesses" about what they will hear.
2. Discussion	Supports children's oral language development and provides a model for student-to-student discussions	To achieve the greatest benefits, discussions must be focused on the topic, theme, or concept rather than free-for-all conversations. Move beyond simple "yes" or "no" questions and invite children to generate their own queries.
3. Brainstorming	Easy, comfortable method for accessing prior knowledge Allows for later "corrections" if there are misconceptions Also an aid to later writing activities	This strategy works best when children have some knowledge of a forthcoming topic. Transcribing their ideas is also important so they can "see" how ideas are connected. Again, it is important to keep the conversation focused on a specific topic.
4. Picture Walk/ Text Walk	This procedure is one of the most successful because it effectively activates prior knowledge by placing the specific concepts of a text into listeners' minds.	Before a read aloud, show students the book/text and take them page by page through the book, highlighting illustrations and some key words. Invite youngsters to make some preliminary predictions as you "journey" through the text.

Strategy	Benefit(s)	Comments
5. Prequestioning	This strategy models what all good readers do when they encounter a new piece of text. It assists youngsters in establishing their own purposes for reading.	Before sharing a book with students, ask them a focused question about the main idea or story line. The question should also be based on their prior knowledge. For example, "Here is a book called *The Snowy Day* (Keats, 1962). I wonder what kinds of things kids do when it snows."
6. Read Aloud	Read alouds are most helpful in assisting youngsters to build adequate backgrounds of information and to "restructure" any misconceptions they may have about a specific topic. They have limited assessment value.	The basic elements of read alouds are discussed in another section of this book. However, it is often beneficial to tell youngsters what a book is about and *why* you are reading it prior to any read aloud session. This helps listeners tap into their own background knowledge before hearing a story.
7. Role Playing	Role playing is particularly helpful for youngsters who need concrete experiences. It is also helpful for second language learners. It is very effective in assessing background knowledge as well as misconceptions or misperceptions about a topic or concept.	Invite students to take parts and act out a situation related to the main idea or basic concepts of a book. This pre-reading activity needs to be carefully planned to be successful. Puppets can also be used as an alternative strategy.
8. Concrete Materials; Realia; Hands-on Experiences	For many children, particularly young learners, the use of concrete objects, or realia, is necessary to provide adequate background knowledge and to develop appropriate schemas.	Provide youngsters with one or more concrete items prior to reading a text. Objects may be demonstrated for children or may be handled, as appropriate. Illustrations, CD-ROM's, field trips, videos, and other items are all appropriate.

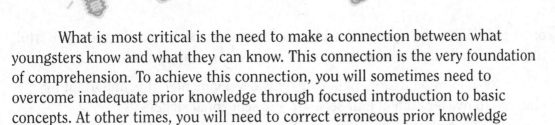

What is most critical is the need to make a connection between what youngsters know and what they can know. This connection is the very foundation of comprehension. To achieve this connection, you will sometimes need to overcome inadequate prior knowledge through focused introduction to basic concepts. At other times, you will need to correct erroneous prior knowledge before students participate in an oral language experience. It is important to keep in mind that *students who experience difficulties in constructing meaning (comprehension) often have limited or erroneous prior knowledge* (Lipson, 1984) [emphasis added].

The strategies above are valuable in activating and developing necessary backgrounds of information. What is most important is that 1) you vary the strategies used throughout the year, and 2) you include the assessment or activation of prior knowledge as a prelude to all literacy encounters. When used in conjunction with students' needs and textual considerations (e.g., narrative, expository), these strategies can provide you with powerful tools that will help guide students on the road to comprehension success.

> ### Some Suggested Literature for Teaching "Tapping into Background Knowledge (Schema)"
>
> *Ira Sleeps Over* by Bernard Waber
>
> *On the Day You Were Born* by Debra Frasier
>
> *The Relatives Came* by Cynthia Rylant
>
> *The Snowy Day* by Ezra Jack Keats
>
> *The Teacher from the Black Lagoon* by Mike Thaler
>
> *Pumpkin Eye* by Denise Fleming
>
> *Guess How Much I Love You?* by Sam McBratney
>
> *Noisy Nora* by Rosemary Wells
>
> *There's a Nightmare in My Closet* by Mercer Mayer
>
> *No, David!* by David Shannon
>
> *Goodnight Moon* by Margaret Wise Brown
>
> *Miss Bindergarten Celebrates the 100th Day* by Joseph Slate
>
> *Miss Nelson Is Missing!* by Harry Allard

Mental Imagery

Mental imagery is the creation of pictures in a reader's mind prior to, during, or after reading. Once images are created (and colored by the reader's experiences), they become a permanent part of long-term memory. Thus, creating images during any literacy activity will result in learning and comprehension.

However, it is important to know that imagery is a sequentially learned skill. For students who do not have this skill, simply telling them to create pictures in their minds is not sufficient. This may be due in large measure to the increasing amount of visual information (TV, movies, etc.) to which youngsters are subjected during the course of a day. Many of those images have been artificially created by

Unit 5

Mental Imagery

other people in order to convey a message (e.g., advertising). Yet the most powerful, meaningful, and lasting images are those we create in our own minds.

Keep in mind that mental imagery is developmental. It is important for children to master each of four separate and sequential stages:

Stage 1. Provide children with opportunities to create images of concrete and tangible objects.

Place a toy car in front of students.

"Look directly at this object until you are familiar with it. Study it very carefully. Now close your eyes. Imagine that you still see the car in front of you. Look at the picture in your mind. Notice the size of the car. Notice the color of the car. Look at the doors, the windows, the tires. Is there anything special about your car? Open your eyes. Compare the picture of the car in your mind with this car. Is there anything you did not see in your mind picture? What is the same?"

Stage 2. Encourage youngsters to visualize and recall familiar objects, scenes, or past experiences outside the classroom.

"Close your eyes. Picture yourself in your room at home. Look at the walls. Look at the furniture. Look at any toys on the floor. Look at the floor—what is it made of? What color are the walls? Look at your bed. What is on your bed? Look at the closet. Where is the closet? Are there any other doors in your room? Are there windows in the room? Now open your eyes. Take a piece of paper and some crayons and draw a picture of the picture you saw in your mind. Try to include as many details as you can. Afterwards, we will talk about your picture."

Stage 3. Provide youngsters with opportunities to listen to high imagery stories that utilize common experiences or knowledge.

Begin reading a story that has good description and action. Stop periodically and allow youngsters opportunities to create mental images of the scenes just read in the story. Encourage children to share their "mind pictures" orally. At the end of the reading, invite youngsters to illustrate one or more of their visual images.

Stage 4. At this stage, students should begin to create their own mental images as they listen to stories. Continuing read aloud sessions and storytelling experiences enhances the development of mental imaging abilities. The development of mental imaging abilities facilitates listening comprehension and a greater appreciation (and personal involvement) in the stories shared. This cyclical process continues, expanding students' horizons and influencing the development of all the language arts.

Assisting children in creating mental images while listening is a valuable instructional strategy and an important part of the entire language arts curriculum. However, as Fredericks (1986) points out, effective mental imaging activities should be structured around several guidelines:

- Children need to understand that their images are personal and are affected by their own backgrounds and experiences.

- There is no right or wrong image for any single child. Teachers should not attempt to change students' images, but rather assist them in clarifying details or strengthening "mind pictures."

- Creating "mind pictures" is something all readers do before reading and while reading.

- Students should be provided with sufficient opportunities to create their mental images prior to any follow-up discussion. Some children will need more time to create or "illustrate" their images.

- Provide adequate time for children to discuss the images they have created. The object is not to have everyone arrive at a "correct" image, rather to encourage sharing of ideas and perceptions in a supportive environment.

- You can stimulate image creation through a series of open-ended statements or questions. Queries such as the following can assist children in the development and elaboration of their mental images:
    "Tell me more about your image."
    "Please describe your mind picture in more detail."
    "What other items do you see in your mind?"
    "Tell us more. What does it look like?"
    "Are there other details that could be part of your 'picture'?"

Assisting children in creating mental images facilitates listening and reading comprehension and also offers numerous speaking opportunities. An additional benefit is that youngsters begin to use thinking skills in concert with listening skills. In turn, they learn to focus on the processes of comprehension moreso than just the products.

Introductory Activities

Following are examples of selected **Mental Imagery** activities that can be used with students. Note that the intent is to provide children with an authentic opportunity to listen, formulate mental images, and use those images as a prelude to a book or some other piece of written text. You will also note the opportunities here for students to extend this listening sequence into a host of

Unit 5

Mental Imagery

other language arts activities such as journal writing, story creation, storytelling, related children's literature, oral presentations, and the like.

Activity 1

Sit on the floor and relax.
Close your eyes and imagine yourself as a beautiful flower.
Feel the warmth of the sun on your petals.
Feel your petals beginning to open.
Feel them opening wide to take in the sun's rays.
Listen to a nearby honeybee as it searches for nectar.
Feel the bee inside your petals as it looks for nectar.
Feel the bee as pollen from your flower clings to its legs.
Feel the grains of pollen sprinkle down inside your flower.
Watch as some of the grains fall onto a long slender stalk (the pistil).
Observe as the grains work their way down the stalks.
Look as the grains reach the bottom and join with a tiny egg.
Watch them begin to grow into new seeds.
See yourself returning to the classroom.
When I count to five, slowly open your eyes.
Take a few minutes to share your mind picture with a classmate.

Activity 2

Sit on the floor.
Close your eyes and paint a picture in your head of a lake.
Put lots of fish in your lake.
See the water everywhere.
It is blue, clear, and cold.
Imagine yourself to be a fish.
You are swimming in the lake.
See yourself swimming through the clear blue water.
Imagine yourself swimming from one side of the lake to the other.
See yourself swimming back and forth.
Look around you and see some other fish.
You are all swimming together.
The water is cold and clear.
Now, slowly open your eyes.
Let's take a few minutes to talk about the pictures in our heads.

Activity 3

Sit on the storytelling rug.
I want you to close your eyes and imagine that you are in a forest.
You are walking through a big forest.
There are lots of trees all around you.
There are some branches on the ground.
Look carefully, and you will see a deer behind a nearby tree.
The deer is looking right at you.
The deer is standing still, not moving.
Carefully watch the deer.
Soon, the deer begins to walk away; it is not afraid.
Look over to your right and see a log on the ground.
There is an animal on top of the log.
It is a squirrel.
Look at the squirrel.
He scampers over the log and across the ground.
Continue walking through the forest.
Look at all the trees.
Now, slowly open your eyes.
We want to talk about some of the things you saw in your head.

Sample Lesson Plan

The following lesson is an example of a Comprehension Circle focusing on the
strategy of **Mental Imagery**. The text is *The Salamander Room* by Anne Mazer
(New York: Knopf, 1991). As with all Comprehension Circles, there are many ways
of sharing a specific comprehension strategy. The chart on the next page shows
one approach.

Unit

5

Mental
Imagery

The Salamander Room

Component	Strategies and Activities	Instruction
Engagement (Schema)	• Gather students together as a whole class or a smaller group. • Present the theme or topic of a forthcoming book. • Talk about the topic. • Ask questions about the theme or topic. • Invite students to share relevant experiences (keep the conversation focused). • Talk about any misperceptions or misconceptions. • Provide illustrations or photos that illuminate the theme or concept. • Share (as necessary) other AV resources that stimulate schema development. • Show the book cover and encourage discussion about its topic or theme. • Draw "straight-line" connections between what youngsters know and the book's main idea. • Link the book to a similar story/book.	Introduce the book *The Salamander Room* to students by sharing the cover illustration, the author, and the illustrator. Ask one or two students to share any experiences they may have had with salamanders. Show illustrations of salamanders from various books (National Audubon Society's Field Guides are excellent.). Talk about some physical features of salamanders. Point out those features on the cover illustration.
Modeling	• Introduce the book. • Vocalize your purpose for reading. • Read and discuss the title. • Talk about illustrations. • Do a "mental walk" through the book. • Demonstrate a talk-aloud (focused on a specific strategy). • Demonstrate a think-aloud (focused on a specific strategy). • Provide multiple opportunities for students to "see" inside your head.	Share the following think-aloud with youngsters: *When I read the title of this book and see the picture on the cover, I have a painting in my head of a small room. The room is in someone's house. In the room I can see a couple of tiny salamanders. Each of the salamanders is orange. Each one has a long tail. Now I see more salamanders. Some are scurrying across the floor. Some salamanders are sleeping in the corner. Some are eating from a plate. The picture I see in my head is a whole room full of salamanders. Some are orange, some are red, some are green, and some are blue. There is*

Component	Strategies and Activities	Instruction
Modeling (*continued*)		*nothing else in the room except lots and lots of salamanders.*
Read Aloud	• Read the selected book out loud to children. • Use expression and intonation as appropriate. • Consider using a big book. • Occasionally "track" the print with your finger or a pointer. • Occasionally use a Shared Book experience with children. • Consider periodic stops (as necessary) to model your thinking. • Demonstrate your enthusiasm for the book while reading.	Read the book aloud to students, stopping at the end of the second page of text (Pages are unnumbered.)—after "...him good-night stories." Model the changes you need to make in your original mental image (above) and talk about them. Tell children that they will create their own "mind pictures" as you read the rest of the story aloud (do not show the illustrations to the students as you read).
Guided Instruction	• Teacher and students return to text. • Conduct class/group reading conference. • Identify one specific comprehension strategy. • Clarify reading strategy in "kid terms." • Demonstrate the strategy within the context of the book. • Re-model (as necessary) your use of the strategy in that book. • Invite youngsters to "try out" the strategy (by using their own talk-about or think-about conversations). • Encourage retellings. • Discuss transfer of strategy. • Pose open-ended questions. • Reread a portion of the book (as necessary) and talk about how the strategy can be used there. • Provide positive feedback.	Invite youngsters to create a mental image of Brian's bedroom based on what they have heard so far in the story. Take some time to talk about selected images. Read the story to the bottom of the page ending with "...juiciest insects are there." Briefly talk about selected images that children have created. Invite them to focus on specific details. Finish the remainder of the book.

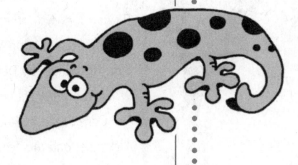

Mental
Imagery

Component	Strategies and Activities	Instruction
Synthesize and Summarize	• Invite children to talk about what they learned. • Encourage active discussion among all class/group members. • Students may need thinking time before responding. • Help youngsters focus on 1or 2 significant points. • Invite students to reflect on the modeling you did throughout the lesson. • Recap (in kid terms) the strategy used.	Invite other students to discuss their mental images. Talk briefly about some of the changes or modifications that needed to be made in those images as the story continued through to the end. Read the book a second time, this time sharing the illustrations as you read. Invite youngsters to observe the illustrations and how they are similar to or different from the images in their heads. When the second read aloud is finished, talk about any differences between the pictures in their heads and those in the book. Talk about how their images helped them enjoy the story.

Some Suggested Literature for Teaching "Mental Imagery"

The Napping House by Audrey Wood

Barn Dance by Bill Martin, Jr.

Night in the Country by Cynthia Rylant

The Paper Crane by Molly Bang

In the Tall, Tall Grass by Denise Fleming

Harold and the Purple Crayon by Crockett Johnson

The Salamander Room by Anne Mazer

Tar Beach by Faith Ringgold

A Chair for My Mother by Vera B. Williams

Owl Babies by Martin Waddell

Barnyard Banter by Denise Fleming

Where the Wild Things Are by Maurice Sendak

The Carrot Seed by Ruth Krauss

Alexander and the Terrible, Horrible, No Good, Very Bad Day by Judith Viorst

Predicting and Inferring

Predicting is the process of extrapolating information based on a minimum of data or information already known. It is also a process of making "educated guesses" about future events, whether those events may happen one minute from now or several years from now. Predicting is highly dependent upon the depth and breadth of one's background knowledge. The more concrete experiences one has had, the better able she/he is able to make predictions. Making predictions is one of the most powerful pre-reading and reading abilities children can learn. That's simply because predicting is a "mental investment" in a future event—one about which the learner now wants to discover more.

Readers often need to make conjectures and suppositions on the basis of a minimum of data. Inferring is of two types: deductive (going from the general to the specific) and inductive (going from the specific to the general). Making inferences, just as in making predictions, requires that youngsters have a sufficient background of personal experiences as well as opportunities and encouragement to draw tentative conclusions or explanations. Also, just as with predictions, inferences are "educated guesses." The primary difference between the two is that predicting is an educated guess about a future event while inferencing is an educated guess about something that is happening here and now. Here are some examples:

> "*Making predictions is one of the most powerful pre-reading and reading abilities children can learn.*"

"What will the weather be tomorrow?" (Prediction)

"Look at the picture on the cover of this book.
Where do you think this story takes place?" (Prediction)

"Why is everybody so happy today?" (Inference)

"How do you think the main character feels about his lost dog?" (Inference)

For predicting and inferring to be successful, there must be a certain level of background knowledge. Both of these strategies are "educated guesses"—the "educated" part is a measure of the depth and breadth of prior knowledge. Without adequate background knowledge, predictions and inferences are quite difficult to make (for youngsters as well as for adults). It is important, therefore, that you are aware of or provide for the necessary prior knowledge that will form the foundation for future predictions and inferences.

Children also need to know that predictions and inferences are temporary. They are based on the best available knowledge at the time. As more knowledge is obtained, predictions and inferences are modified or altered. In this way, competent readers monitor and adjust their reading as they "blend" their prior knowledge with new knowledge encountered in the text. This adjustment is an

Unit 5

Predicting and Inferring

active response— one that engages an individual in the dynamics of comprehension. It can best be taught through lots of modeling and lots of "think-alouds" by the teacher as she/he reads.

Introductory Activities

Following are some **Predicting and Inferring** activities that can be introduced to students. These will provide youngsters with opportunities to experience this comprehension strategy prior to sharing it in Comprehension Circle lessons with books and other texts.

1. At the end of each day, invite children to make a prediction about the weather for the following day. Engage students in a discussion about the weather for the current day. You may wish to discuss the temperature, cloud conditions, humidity (in very general terms), wind, or any other observations children may have. Ask youngsters to think about the outside conditions for the day and invite them to make an "educated guess" or prediction about tomorrow's weather. Make sure children know that there are no right or wrong responses, rather that they are making their best guesses based on the current day's weather. You may wish to construct a chart divided into two columns: "Today's Weather" and "Prediction for Tomorrow's Weather." Plan time during your morning activities to talk about the previous day's prediction and how accurate it was.

2. Take several photographs of various scenes and activities throughout your school. These could include cafeteria workers preparing lunch, custodians working on a furnace, superintendent at her/his desk, or secretary sorting mail. Each day show one of the photos to youngsters and invite them to speculate on what may be happening in each picture. Ask the class to create their own original story about the individual and what she/he is doing. Transcribe the stories and post them along with the photos on a special bulletin board. For variety, invite students to select several pictures from a variety of old magazines. Cut these out and post them. Ask students to create their own oral stories about each of the magazine pictures.

3. Occasionally read a story to your students, but leave off the ending. Engage the children in an active discussion about a possible ending. Take time to discuss important details and how they might assist everyone in determining an appropriate ending for the story. As students make predictions, write them on the board. Complete the rest of the story and then discuss their initial predictions and how well they matched with the "real" ending.

Sample Lesson Plan

The following lesson is an example of a Comprehension Circle focusing on the strategy of **Predicting and Inferring**. The text is *The Very Hungry Caterpillar* by Eric Carle (New York: Philomel, 1983). As with all Comprehension Circles, there are many ways of sharing a specific comprehension strategy. Here is one approach:

The Very Hungry Caterpillar

Component	Strategies and Activities	Instruction
Engagement (Schema)	• Gather students together as a whole class or a smaller group. • Present the theme or topic of a forthcoming book. • Talk about the topic. • Ask questions about the theme or topic. • Invite students to share **relevant** experiences (keep the conversation <u>focused</u>). • Talk about any misperceptions or misconceptions. • Provide illustrations or photos that illuminate the theme or concept. • Share (as necessary) other AV resources that stimulate schema development. • Show the book cover and encourage discussion about its topic or theme. • Draw "straight-line" connections between what youngsters know and the book's main idea. • Link the book to a similar story/book.	Start by discussing the topic of "caterpillars" with students. Show some illustrations or pictures of caterpillars from various books. If possible, bring a live caterpillar into the classroom and allow children to observe it for a while. Take some time and encourage youngsters to describe the caterpillar. Write some of their observations on the board or post them on a bulletin board. If practical, set up a temporary terrarium for the caterpillar for a few days. Take time each day to share additional observations about the "visitor."
Modeling	• Introduce the book. • Vocalize your purpose for reading. • Read and discuss the title. • Talk about illustrations. • Do a "mental walk" through the book. • Demonstrate a talk-aloud (focused on a specific strategy). • Demonstrate a think-aloud (focused on a specific strategy). • Provide multiple opportunities for students to "see" inside your head.	Read the title of the book to students. Show the cover illustration. Tell students, *"As I look at the cover of this book, I can see a caterpillar. It makes me think about the caterpillar I saw on my driveway last weekend. It, too, was green and hairy. Then, I think about the title of the book. Now, I want to make a guess about this book. I predict that this book is about a caterpillar that is very*

Component	Strategies and A...	
Modeling *(continued)*		
Read Aloud	• Read the selected ... to children. • Use expression a... as appropriate. • Consider using a... • Occasionally "tra... with your finger ... • Occasionally use a Shared Book experience with children. • Consider periodic stops (as necessary) to model your thinking. • Demonstrate your enthusiasm for the book while reading.	*was a story about a caterpillar and that the caterpillar might eat lots of food? It looks like my predictions were all right. Now, I'm going to look at the next couple of pages.* (Pages are cut in a staggered fashion so that the next five can all be seen at once.) *I see an apple, a pear, a plum, a strawberry, and an orange. So, I'm going to make a prediction that the caterpillar is going to eat all of those fruits. Let's read and find out.* (Read through to the end of the "oranges" page.) *I think my predictions are O.K. so far. So, are you all ready now to make your own predictions?"*
Guided Instruction	• Teacher and students return to text. • Conduct class/group reading conference. • Identify one specific comprehension strategy. • Clarify reading strategy in "kid terms." • Demonstrate the strategy within the context of the book. • Re-model (as necessary) your use of the strategy in the book.	(Turn to the next two pages.) *"Let's look at these two pages. Maybe we can all make a prediction about some of the things the little caterpillar will eat next.* (Encourage youngsters to look at the illustrations and make predictions about what the caterpillar will eat next. Read through the line ending with "...slice of watermelon.") *Now, let's make an inference.*

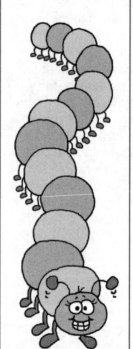

Component	Strategies and Activities	Instruction
Guided Instruction *(continued)*	• Invite youngsters to "try out" the strategy (by using their own talk-about or think-about conversations). • Encourage retellings. • Discuss transfer of strategy. • Pose open-ended questions. • Reread a portion of the book (as necessary) and talk about how the strategy can be used there. • Provide positive feedback.	*How do you think the caterpillar felt after eating all that food?"* (Invite youngsters to make their guesses and then read the last sentence on that page. Talk about the "connections" youngsters made between the clues in the story and the predictions and inferences they made. Finish reading the rest of the book.)
Synthesize and Summarize	• Invite children to talk about what they learned. • Encourage active discussion among all class/group members. • Students may need thinking time before responding. • Help youngsters focus on 1 or 2 significant points. • Invite students to reflect on the modeling you did throughout the lesson. • Recap (in kid terms) the strategy used.	Invite children to discuss some of the important events of the story. Selected students can share their own retelling of the story or their favorite part of the story. Consider posing one or more of the following open-ended questions: *"What did you like best about this story?" "What did you like about the ending?"* or *"Tell me three things you learned from this story."*

Some Suggested Literature for Teaching "Predicting and Inferring"

Oliver Button Is a Sissy by Tomie dePaola

Goodnight, Gorilla by Peggy Rathmann

Q Is for Duck: An Alphabet Guessing Game by Mary Elting and Michael Fulsom

Fly Away Home by Eve Bunting

The Very Lonely Firefly by Eric Carle

Bringing the Rain to Kapiti Plain by Verna Aardema

Is This a House for Hermit Crab? by Megan McDonald

The Very Hungry Caterpillar by Eric Carle

Good-Night, Owl! by Pat Hutchins

Jack and the Beanstalk by Steven Kellogg

The Little Old Lady Who Was Not Afraid of Anything by Linda Williams

Lyle, Lyle, Crocodile by Bernard Waber

Is Your Mama a Llama? by Deborah Guarino

There Was an Old Lady Who Swallowed a Fly by Simms Taback

We're Going on a Bear Hunt by Michael Rosen

Three Billy Goats Gruff by Glen Rounds

Rosie's Walk by Pat Hutchins

Questioning

Self-questioning is an important reading comprehension strategy for all students. Although considerable attention has been given to the development of teacher questions over the years, it is equally important that students be offered viable and authentic opportunities to generate their own questions about the text as they read. In fact, the opportunity for students to ask questions of themselves (metacognition) can be one of the most significant processes we can teach.

Although questions are widely used and serve many functions, teachers frequently overrely on factual questions. There is a convincing body of research (Fredericks and Cheesebrough, 1993; Fredericks et al., 1997) which suggests that as much as 80% of all the questions asked of students during the course of a day are of the literal or recall variety. This seems to suggest that little creative or divergent thinking (hallmarks of comprehension) may be taking place.

One of the most significant and important statements I've encountered in more than three decades of teaching is the following:

> **Students tend to read and think based on the types of questions they anticipate receiving from a teacher.**

This means that if students are constantly bombarded with questions that require only low levels of cognitive involvement (literal or recall questions, for example), they will tend to think accordingly. Conversely, children who are given questions based on higher levels of cognition will tend to think more creatively and divergently. In other words, if we want our students to engage in higher levels of problem solving and creative thought, we need to ask questions that promote a multiplicity of responses.

"If we want our students to engage in higher levels of problem solving and creative thought, we need to ask questions that promote a multiplicity of responses."

As you might expect, the kinds of questions we ask youngsters serve as models for the kinds of questions they can begin asking themselves (metacognition). In fact, helping students begin asking their own self-initiated questions can be a powerful element in any instructional activity. In order to do that, students need models to emulate. The goal of asking students appropriate metacognitive questions is to gradually release responsibility of question-asking and place it squarely in the hands of students.

The following chart will assist you in asking appropriate metacognitive questions as you share stories with youngsters.

Teacher-posed questions are listed down the left side of the chart. The objective is to gradually reduce the number of teacher questions and increase the number of student-posed questions—questions that children begin asking themselves as they listen to stories.

Sample Metacognitive Questions

Teacher-Posed	Student-Posed
1. Is this story similar to anything you may have heard before?	1. Why would this be important for me to know?
2. What were you thinking when you listened to this part of the story?	2. Is this character similar to any other(s) I know?
3. What have we learned so far?	3. Does this information give me any clues about what may happen later in the story?
4. What is the major point of this section?	4. How does this information differ from other things I know?
5. Did you change your mind about anything after hearing this part of the story?	5. Why is this difficult for me to understand?
6. Do you have any questions about this book?	6. Do I need additional information to help me understand this topic?
7. What did you do when you didn't understand something in the story?	7. Can I summarize this part of the story?
8. What new information are you learning?	8. What do I know so far?
	9. What did the author do to make me think this way?
	10. Am I satisfied with this story?

Providing students with opportunities to initiate their own questions throughout a storytelling session can be a valuable goal of literacy development. The chart on page 72 provides you with a list of questions that accomplished and mature readers tend to ask themselves. Here is a modeling procedure you may wish to follow:

1. Select a piece of children's literature.

2. Ask yourself (out loud) some of the *Before Reading* questions and provide answers for yourself and youngsters (again, out loud).

3. Read the book aloud to a group of students.

4. Periodically through the reading continue to ask yourself additional questions (this time from the *During Reading* list).

5. Complete the oral reading and ask yourself a sampling of questions from the *After Reading* section.

6. Model these metacognitive questions for children during each read aloud session.

7. Using think-alouds, invite students to assist you in answering your own questions.

Unit

5

Questioning

Note: It is not r ... all the questions in any one section. S ... e, During, After) during each read ... oose for successive readings with oth ...

... es

Before Readi ...

Is this similar to a ...

Why am I reading ...

Why would this i ...

Do I have any questions about this story before I read it? If so, what are they?

During Reading

Am I understanding what I'm reading?

What can I do if I don't understand this information?

Why am I learning this?

Are these characters or events similar to others I have read about?

How does this information differ from other things that I know?

Why is this difficult or easy for me to understand?

Is this interesting or enjoyable? Why or why not?

Do I have any questions about this text that have not been answered so far?

What new information am I learning?

What information do I still need to learn?

After Reading

Can I share a brief summary of the story?

What did I learn in this story?

Where can I go to learn some additional information on this topic?

Did I confirm (or do I need to modify) my initial purpose for reading this text?

Is there anything else interesting I'd like to find out about this topic?

Do I have some unanswered questions from this text?

When youngsters are offered genuine, stimulating invitations to participate actively in question asking, they assume a higher level of independence and motivation throughout any literacy task and throughout any piece of text. This can be achieved when teachers establish themselves as good models of question asking.

Introductory Activities

1. Display photographs of people in your local community (plumber, postal worker, banker, nurse, high-school coach). Show a photo to children and ask them to come up with some questions they would like to ask that person (about what they are doing, how old they are, where they live, etc.). Encourage youngsters to develop a list of about 4–6 questions. Then, tell them that you will take on the role of the person in the picture and answer their questions (this can be either serious or silly). Talk with youngsters about the importance of asking questions—especially asking questions about the pictures or illustrations in books.

2. If appropriate, you may want to play a variation of the game show Jeopardy® with your students. Initially, you can demonstrate this by providing an "answer" for students (e.g., "clouds") and then providing an appropriate question for that "answer" ("What is in the sky?"). Illustrate this with several more examples and then invite students to suggest some "answers" for which you will then provide the questions. As children become more practiced, invite them to offer questions for some "answers" that you provide. This can be a fun and engaging activity to use as part of your daily morning meeting time.

3. At the beginning of the week, show the children the covers of several selected books that you plan to read to them in the coming days. Invite youngsters to discuss and select one question they would like to find the answer to when that book is read. Write the selected question for each book on a separate index card and place each card inside its respective book. Later, when each book is selected for presentation to the class, remove the index card and briefly discuss the question printed on the card. Remind children that this was a question they posed earlier in the week and that they want to listen carefully to the story to see if they can figure out the answer. Plan time after a reading to talk about the question and any possible answer(s)/response(s).

Sample Lesson Plan

The following lesson is an example of a Comprehension Circle focusing on the strategy of **Questioning**. The text is *Leo the Late Bloomer* by Robert Kraus (New York: HarperCollins, 1971). As with all Comprehension Circles, there are many ways of sharing a specific comprehension strategy. Here is one approach:

Teaching Comprehension in Grades 1–2

Unit 5

Questioning

Leo the [...]

Component	Strategies and [...]	
Engagement (Schema)	• Gather students [...] whole class or a [...] • Present the them[...] forthcoming boo[...] • Talk about the t[...] • Ask questions a[...] or topic. • Invite students t[...] **relevant** experi[...] conversation <u>focused</u>). • Talk about any misperceptions or misconceptions. • Provide illustrations or photos that illuminate the theme or concept. • Share (as necessary) other AV resources that stimulate schema development. • Show the book cover and encourage discussion about its topic or theme. • Draw "straight-line" connections between what youngsters know and the book's main idea. • Link the book to a similar story/book.	[...]time needed to learn some of those skills. Emphasize the fact that every person takes a different amount of time to learn something new. That's great! Use an example from your own life with a sibling (when you each learned how to ride a bicycle, for example). Emphasize the concept that everybody is different and everybody learns at different times and at different rates. Keep the conversation positive and upbeat.
Modeling	• Introduce the book. • Vocalize your purpose for reading. • Read and discuss the title. • Talk about illustrations. • Do a "mental walk" through the book. • Demonstrate a talk-aloud (focused on a specific strategy). • Demonstrate a think-aloud (focused on a specific strategy). • Provide multiple opportunities for students to "see" inside your head.	Read the title to youngsters. Say something like, *"When I read this title, I have a question in my mind. That question is, 'Why is Leo late?' I wonder if he is always late or just late some of the time. I guess I'm going to have to read the book to find out."* (Read through the page ending with "...never said a word." Pages are unnumbered.) *"Hmmm, I still don't know why Leo is late. I know that there are some things that he can't do. But, I still wonder why he is late."*
Read Aloud	• Read the selected book out loud to children. • Use expression and intonation as appropriate. • Consider using a big book.	Before reading the next page, beginning with "What's the matter... ," say to children, *"I'm still wondering why Leo is always late. Will I find out on*

Component	Strategies and Activities	Instruction
Read Aloud *(continued)*	• Occasionally "track" the print with your finger or a pointer. • Occasionally use a Shared Book experience with children. • Consider periodic stops (as necessary) to model your thinking. • Demonstrate your enthusiasm for the book while reading.	*this page?" (Read the page. Say to the youngsters,) "Ahhh, it looks like Leo is late because he takes his time to learn things. It looks like I found some answers to my questions."*
Guided Instruction	• Teacher and students return to text. • Conduct class/group reading conference. • Identify one specific comprehension strategy. • Clarify reading strategy in "kid terms." • Demonstrate the strategy within the context of the book. • Re-model (as necessary) your use of the strategy in that book. • Invite youngsters to "try out" the strategy (by using their own talk-about or think-about conversations). • Encourage retellings. • Discuss transfer of strategy. • Pose open-ended questions. • Reread a portion of the book (as necessary) and talk about how the strategy can be used there. • Provide positive feedback.	Say to youngsters, *"Do you have any questions that you would like answered in the rest of the story?"* Record three or four very focused questions as suggested by children. Review each question orally. Tell students that you will continue reading the story but that everyone needs to listen carefully for any answers to the questions on the board. Tell students that they can signal you when they think they hear a possible answer. You can place a check mark next to a posted question when an appropriate answer has been discovered. Read through to the end of the book.
Synthesize and Summarize	• Invite children to talk about what they learned. • Encourage active discussion among all class/group members. • Students may need thinking time before responding. • Help youngsters focus on 1 or 2 significant points. • Invite students to reflect on the modeling you did throughout the lesson. • Recap (in kid terms) the strategy used.	Invite youngsters to do a retelling of the story. Ask youngsters to talk about the things that Leo couldn't do in the beginning of the story. Then, ask children to talk about the things that Leo could do at the end of the story. Afterwards, invite them to talk about some of the questions that were asked (by you and by themselves) and how the answers to those questions were found. Plan time to talk about any unanswered questions and how to find answers.

Some Suggested Literature for Teaching "Questioning"

Monarch Butterfly by Gail Gibbons

Miss Bindergarten Gets Ready for Kindergarten by Joseph Slate

Baby Whale's Journey by Jonathan London

Barn Dance by Bill Martin, Jr.

The Three Bears by Paul Galdone

Harry the Dirty Dog by Gene Zion

Leo the Late Bloomer by Robert Kraus

Jump, Frog, Jump by Robert Kalan

Two Bad Ants by Chris Van Allsburg

When I Was Young in the Mountains by Cynthia Rylant

The Mitten by Jan Brett

Ten, Nine, Eight by Molly Bang

A Kiss for Little Bear by Else H. Minarik

Happy Birthday, Moon by Frank Asch

The Napping House by Audrey Wood

Identifying Important Information

One of the significant strategies all readers use is to identify important information in text. This strategy is not one learned quickly or easily. It is part of a developmental process that is highly dependent upon the amount and quality of reading material to which a child is exposed. In other words, children's schema for important ideas is developed through sustained and constant exposure to books and read aloud sessions. More experience with good literature equates to more familiarity with the components of a good story.

As you might expect, important ideas vary from book to book and from genre to genre. The chart on the next page shows some of the important features teachers can share with youngsters:

Expository	Narrative Text
• Main idea	• Story line
• Details	• Beginning, middle, end
• Topic sentence	• Story grammar
• Photographs	• Main character(s)
• Captions	• Setting
• Headings	• Problem/solution
• Diagrams	• Conclusion
• Bold print	
• Table of Contents	

While the strategies discussed earlier in this chapter will have their greatest application in narrative text, they are also important for expository text. On the other hand, Identifying Important Information, while appropriate for narrative text, will have its greatest application with nonfiction materials.

Many youngsters have a tendency to focus on a few isolated facts as they listen to a story or read a book. It is a constant challenge for teachers to assist youngsters in connecting factual information to form complete concepts. To do that effectively means helping them (over extended periods of time) to select the most important elements of a nonfiction book. This can be facilitated and enhanced through systematic and sustained teacher modeling of the previous four comprehension strategies in selected nonfiction literature. For example:

1. **Engagement (Schema):** *"When I look at the title of this book—**In the Small, Small Pond** (Denise Fleming; New York: Holt, 1993)—I remember the time when my family and I went to a lake in New York. We saw lots of fish, ducks, and dragonflies there. It was a very busy place."*

2. **Mental Imagery:** *"When I see the book **Zebras** (Anthony D. Fredericks; Minneapolis, MN: Lerner Books, 2001), I get a picture in my head of a large open plain in Africa. I can see tall trees way off in the distance. I see some giraffes standing next to a pool of water. There is a lion hiding in the bushes nearby. The sun is overhead and is shining brightly. It is a very hot day. And coming into the picture now is a herd of zebras. There are about 20 zebras. There are mothers, fathers, and three or four babies. They are moving very slowly to the pool of water. They are thirsty, but they are also careful. There are many things in this picture in my head."*

3. Predicting and Inferring: *"When I see the cover of the book **Into the Sea** (Brenda Guiberson; New York: Holt, 1996), I want to make a prediction. I predict that this is a story about a little turtle. I predict that this story is about a turtle who swims through the ocean looking for food. Maybe there is some danger, like a shark. I also predict that the turtle will grow up to be a large turtle."*

4. Questioning: *"When I see the cover of the book **Penguins** (Gail Gibbons; New York: Holiday House, 1998), I have some questions in my head. Some questions I would like to know are "Where do penguins live?" "How big do penguins get to be?" "What kinds of food do they eat?" When I ask questions like those, it helps me look for the answers as I listen to a book or as I read a book on my own."*

One of the most significant things we can do to assist children in identifying important information is to help them establish a purpose for reading prior to listening to a book or story. This can be as simple as asking, "Why do we want to read this book?" or "What do we want to learn?" As with other similar questions, it is important to keep the responses short and focused. This can be accomplished by:

- Modeling through *think-alouds* how you identify 2–3 items you want to discover before reading a book.

- Modeling through *mental imagery* 2–3 significant facts that are part of your initial response to a book or story.

- Modeling through *questioning* 2–3 specific questions you ask prior to reading a book or story.

The critical factor is the need for children to have a very specific purpose or reason for reading expository text. Guide them in establishing group or individual purposes prior to a wide variety of classroom activities including (but not limited to) recess, nap time, snack time, center time, etc. In each case, transcribe their ideas and help them focus on the connection between the pre-activity purpose and the important details of the activity.

Another technique that helps youngsters identify important information is to plan time each day to work with illustrations and photographs. Invite youngsters to look at a selected illustration and determine 2–3 significant details. Ask them to defend their choices. Here is one suggested procedure:

1. Show an illustration or photograph that has some action (people swimming, horses jumping, birds flying over trees). There should be no text on the illustration/photograph.

2. Invent a caption or title for the illustration/photograph and share it with students.

3. Tell youngsters that when you think about the title/caption, it helps you look for 2–3 important details in the picture. At this point it's important to provide a strict limit (2–3) on the number of important details.

4. Inform children that your purpose for "reading" the illustration is to identify the 2–3 most important parts of the picture.

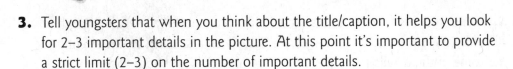

5. Identify a single significant detail related to your title/caption. Explain to youngsters your rationale for selecting that detail.

6. Repeat with 1–2 more important details.

This activity is short and can be made part of your regular daily schedule. As students become more familiar with this process, you can invite them to select a photograph/illustration from a file box and post one on a wall of the classroom at the start of each day. As a feature of your opening activities for that day, spend time developing a title for each picture and related details. This information can be written on strips of oaktag and posted alongside each picture. Review these postings periodically.

Introductory Activities

1. Invite each youngster to lie down on a large sheet of newsprint. Use a marker to trace around each youngster's body. With the assistance of an aide or volunteer, cut out each student's body outline. Invite each child to tell you five important facts about herself/himself. These could include the following: name, age, hair color, hair type (curly, straight), eye color, etc. Use a marker to print the "details" about each child on her/his respective "body map." Post these along one wall of your classroom. Plan some time to discuss the facts of each person. For example, select one or two individuals each day and talk about their "details." Let children know that the details about each person are similar to the details we hear in books and stories.

2. Show a large picture or photograph to the class for one minute. Invite youngsters to look at the picture very carefully and to note as many details as possible. Remove the picture from their sight and engage the class in a discussion of the details they remember. You may wish to jot those details on the board. Allow the children to see the picture again. Take time to talk about the details they saw the first time and those they can see the second time. An adaptation of this activity would be to supply the class with a prepared question, the answer to which is a detail from a picture. Show the picture for one minute and ask youngsters to locate the detail that is the answer. You may wish to successively reduce the viewing time from one minute to 30 seconds to 20 seconds, etc.

3. Invite students to listen to a selected radio program for a specified length of time (two minutes, for example). As they listen, ask them to pay attention to some of the details (names of songs, commercials, public service announcements, etc.). At the end of the time period, take time to discuss some of the things they heard. What details were common? What details were uncommon? Take some time to talk about why it is easier to remember some details and not others. A variation of this activity would be to select a particular time of the day (between 10:35 and 10:40, for example). Invite youngsters to listen for as many classroom sounds that occur in that time span as possible. Afterwards, take time to discuss and share their responses.

Sample Lesson Plan

The following lesson is an example of a Comprehension Circle focusing on the strategy of **Identifying Important Information**. The text is *Under One Rock: Bugs, Slugs and Other Ughs* by Anthony D. Fredericks (Nevada City, CA: Dawn Publications, 2001). As with all Comprehension Circles, there are many ways of sharing a specific comprehension strategy. Here is one approach:

Under One Rock: Bugs, Slugs and Other Ughs

Component	Strategies and Activities	Instruction
Engagement (Schema)	• Gather students together as a whole class or a smaller group. • Present the theme or topic of a forthcoming book. • Talk about the topic. • Ask questions about the theme or topic. • Invite students to share **relevant** experiences (keep the conversation <u>focused</u>). • Talk about any misperceptions or misconceptions. • Provide illustrations or photos that illuminate the theme or concept. • Share (as necessary) other AV resources that stimulate schema development. • Show the book cover and encourage discussion about its topic or theme. • Draw "straight-line" connections between what youngsters know and the book's main idea. • Link the book to a similar story/book.	Before reading the book, invite students to imagine that they are outside on a hike. While hiking, they come across a rock by the side of the path. Invite them to imagine that they lift up the rock. Ask children to suggest some of the animals or creatures they might possibly find under a single rock. Transcribe their suggestions on the board. Invite children to give you a rationale for each particular animal. ("It's small." "It can crawl under a rock." "I saw one once when I went to my grandmother's farm.")

Component	Strategies and Activities	Instruction
Modeling	• Introduce the book. • Vocalize your purpose for reading. • Read and discuss the title. • Talk about illustrations. • Do a "mental walk" through the book. • Demonstrate a talk-aloud (focused on a specific strategy). • Demonstrate a think-aloud (focused on a specific strategy). • Provide multiple opportunities for students to "see" inside your head.	Show the cover of the book to children. Tell them, *"You know, when I see this illustration, I can imagine myself doing the same thing. I can imagine myself peeking under a rock in a field. I can imagine myself lifting that rock and seeing all kinds of animals crawling around. In fact, I predict that if I lifted a rock I would certainly find at least three animals—they would be a spider, a worm, and a bunch of ants. That's because I see a lot of those kinds of animals whenever I go outside my house. So, as I read this story, I want to see if this boy (point) on the cover discovers ants, worms, and spiders."* Record "Ants," "Worms," and "Spiders" on the chalkboard.
Read Aloud	• Read the selected book out loud to children. • Use expression and intonation as appropriate. • Consider using a big book. • Occasionally "track" the print with your finger or a pointer. • Occasionally use a Shared Book experience with children. • Consider periodic stops (as necessary) to model your thinking. • Demonstrate your enthusiasm for the book while reading.	Begin to read the book to students. As each of the predicted creatures (ants, spider, worms) is encountered in the book, stop and talk about your initial predictions and the words on the chalkboard. Place a check mark on the board to indicate that your original prediction(s) were verified with the important details found in the book. After locating the spider (the third animal in the sequence of the story), continue reading to the bottom of the "spider page" ending with "...on a summer's day."
Guided Instruction	• Teacher and students return to text. • Conduct class/group reading conference. • Identify one specific comprehension strategy.	Invite youngsters to make predictions about two more creatures that they think will be found under the rock. Make a class decision on only two creatures. Post these on the

Teaching Comprehension in Grades 1–2

Unit 5

Identifying Important Information

Component	Strateg...	
Guided Instruction *(continued)*	• Clarify ... "kid ter... • Demon... the con... • Re-mod... use of th... • Invite yo... the strat... talk-abou... conversa... • Encourag... • Discuss t... • Pose open-ended questions. • Reread a portion of the book (as necessary) and talk about how the strategy can be used there. • Provide positive feedback.	...n that you ...and that ...ee if their ...n the ...k. Again, ...each
Synthesize and Summarize	• Invite children to talk about what they learned. • Encourage active discussion among all class/group members. • Students may need thinking time before responding. • Help youngsters focus on 1 or 2 significant points. • Invite students to reflect on the modeling you did throughout the lesson. • Recap (in kid terms) the strategy used.	Invite youngsters to relate 3 or 4 of the most important animals in the book. Invite and encourage them to make their suggestions in the form of complete sentences. "*Which animals were the most important?*" is a question you could ask. Afterwards, ask students to come up with a one-sentence summary of the book. In one sentence, what would they tell their parents or friends is the main idea of the story?

Some Suggested Literature for Teaching "Identifying Important Information"

Under One Rock: Bugs, Slugs and Other Ughs by Anthony D. Fredericks

What Do You Do with a Tail Like This? by Steve Jenkins and Robin Page

Around One Cactus: Owls, Bats and Leaping Rats by Anthony D. Fredericks

In the Small, Small Pond by Denise Fleming

Bugs by Nancy Parker and Joan Wright

Great Crystal Bear by Carolyn Lesser

Sky Tree by Thomas Locker

The Great Kapok Tree by Lynn Cherry

Slugs by Anthony D. Fredericks

Look! by April Wilson

Everybody Has a Bellybutton by Laurence Pringle

Listen to the Rain by Bill Martin, Jr., and John Archambault

Into the Sea by Brenda Guiberson

Synthesizing and Summarizing (Retelling)

Synthesizing is the process of combining elements to form a new whole. It is a way for children to engage in creative and original thinking. Combining story elements from two or more sources to form a new idea or interpretation is a valuable and important reading comprehension ability. It is a way for students to combine new information (in the text, for example) with old information (schema theory). Synthesizing is appropriate for both expository and narrative text. In many ways, synthesizing is a personal reaction to key elements in the text.

Summarizing is the process of assembling major ideas in a text into a single statement or idea. It is a way that readers sift through important and unimportant data to arrive at the major point or major thought in a piece of text. While many people summarize at or near the end of a piece of text, it is often a strategy that can be effectively employed throughout the text, particularly in longer books or stories. When we ask students to conceptualize the main idea of a story, we are providing them with a means to create a summary—one couched in their own words, terminology, and interpretation of text.

Synthesizing and summarizing (retelling) should be part of every literacy encounter. Retelling involves children in several critical processes:

- Promotes decision making about important details

- Fosters good listening skills

- Enhances appreciation of story sequence

- Stimulates a personal monitoring of individual levels of comprehension

- Brings important ideas to a level of consciousness or awareness

- Helps youngsters think about what they hear

- Underscores the value of cooperative sharing

Retelling achieves its greatest potency when children have positive models to emulate. Thus, it is important for you to demonstrate appropriate retelling behaviors—significant details, brevity, complete thoughts, and focus. These behaviors can be demonstrated and actively modeled in a wide range of classroom activities: after a recess period, following the viewing of a video, after a storytelling session, after a playtime activity, or immediately following a structured lesson. It is important for youngsters to "see inside your head" as they do during any mental imagery activity. By providing students with insights about the thought processes you use in synthesizing and summarizing a story, you are helping them focus on the important elements of this strategy.

I have found that one of the most effective strategies for engaging children in synthesizing and summarizing text is called "What iffing." In this strategy, you take some of the questions that you would normally ask students at the conclusion of a read aloud (for example) and tag the two words "What if" to the front of each question. With these questions, children have to use the knowledge they gained from the text in order to think divergently—a primary benefit of "what iffing." For example, instead of asking "What kind of day did Alexander (in *Alexander and the Terrible, Horrible, No Good, Very Bad Day*) have?," it would be appropriate to ask, "What if Alexander had a wonderful, fantastic, delightful, and very good day?"

It is important to note that there are no right or wrong answers with "What iffing." Rather, students are given opportunities to "play" with language and the possibilities that might exist within a story or beyond that story. Students' divergent thinking is stimulated and enhanced in a wide variety of reading materials.

As an example, I recently asked a group of kids to generate a list of "What if" questions for the story *The Three Little Pigs*. Here is a partial list of some of their queries:

- What if the story was *The Three Little Wolves*?

- What if all three houses had been made of brick?

- What if the wolf smoked cigarettes?

- What if the story took place in the city?

- What if the wolf was much smaller than the pigs?

You will notice that "What if" questions encourage and stimulate the generation of multiple queries and multiple responses. Its advantage lies in the fact that all students are encouraged to participate and all responses can be entertained and discussed. Just as important, it provides a creative opportunity to summarize text in very inventive ways.

I'm equally fond of an opportunity for retelling that Debbie Miller (2003) describes. When a youngster returns after an absence, she invites one or more children in the class to retell a story for the returning student. For example, "We're glad to have you back, Parker! Yesterday, we read a book called *Tar Beach*. Would you like to have someone retell the story for you?" Or "We read a book about animals in winter while you were out. Would someone like to retell what we learned for Parker?"

Another retelling opportunity I used quite often occurred at the end of the week. I would gather students together on the carpet and we would review the events, happenings, significant details, and special moments of the week. Then, we would complete a "Learn and Share" sheet (on page 86). Students would share information with me and I would transcribe it on a master sheet as follows:

3. What are **three** things we learned this week?

2. What are **two** things you would like to share with someone else?

1. What is **one** thing you would like to learn more about?

As information was volunteered by students, I would write it in the appropriate spaces on the sheet. Then, I would duplicate the sheet and hand a copy to each student on her/his way out the door on Friday afternoon. Students were encouraged to share the sheet with parents or other caregivers. The benefits, as you might imagine, were enormous. Students and parents were often engaged in active conversations about the events of the preceding week. Students had opportunities to summarize and synthesize valuable information. And parents had some very concrete information in response to that age-old question, "What did you learn in school today?"

Some Suggested Literature for Teaching "Synthesizing and Summarizing"

In One Tidepool: Crabs, Snails and Salty Tails by Anthony D. Fredericks

Smoky Night by Eve Bunting

Click, Clack, Moo: Cows That Type by Doreen Cronin

Sheep in a Shop by Nancy Shaw

Sheep in a Jeep by Nancy Shaw

The Day Jimmie's Boa Ate the Wash by Trinka Kakes Noble

Inch by Inch by Leo Lionni

Frog and Toad Together by Arnold Lobel

Frog and Toad Are Friends by Arnold Lobel

"More, More, More," Said the Baby by Vera B. Williams

Mouse Soup by Arnold Lobel

The Very Busy Spider by Eric Carle

Unit 5

Synthesizing and
Summarizing
(Retelling)

Learn and Share

Name: _____   Date: _____

3. Three things I learned this week:

_____

_____

_____

2. Two things I would like to share with someone else:

_____

_____

1. One thing I would like to learn more about:

_____

Six Strategies

• • • • • • • • • • • • •

The six essential comprehension strategies are summarized in the chart below.
Included with each one is a selection of questions or prompts that help developing
readers focus on the elements of each strategy.

Essential Comprehension Strategies

Strategy	Description/Explanation	Questions/Prompts
Background Knowledge (Schema)	Background knowledge forms the foundation and the structure for all reading experiences. What readers know affects what they can learn.	• "What does this remind you of?" • "Is this similar to anything you've read before?" • "I like the way you remembered that other story." • "How are you and this character similar?"
Mental Imagery	Good readers create "mind pictures" as they read. Visualizing the characters, elements, or events of a story is critical to overall comprehension.	• "Close your eyes. What do you see in the picture in your head?" • "Can you create a picture of this in your mind?"
Predicting and Inferring	Good readers are able to combine background knowledge and text knowledge as they read. This combination helps them make "educated guesses" about the content of the text throughout the reading process. These "educated guesses" take place in advance of reading as well as during the reading act.	• "What is happening here?" • "What makes you think that?" • "How did you arrive at that idea?" • "What do you think will happen next?" • "You're making some good guesses about the story."
Questioning	Readers continually ask themselves questions throughout the text. This is done to check or confirm an understanding of the book or story. Metacognitive questions are ways in which readers self-assess their understanding as well as stay engaged in the dynamics of a story.	• "What would be a good question to ask here?" • "Would you please think out loud for us?" • "What question could you answer now?" • "You're using some good thinking skills here."

Component	Strategies and Activities	Instruction
Identifying Important Information	Good readers are able to separate important from unimportant information in the text. They can identify critical details and separate them from extraneous material.	• "What is the most important information here?" • "What is the main information?" • "Why do you think this is important?" • "I like the way you find important information."
Synthesizing and Summarizing	Good readers are able to pull together all that they have read into an inclusive statement. Their comprehension is based on their ability to synthesize and summarize setting, characters, plot, theme and point of view into a single statement.	• "What was this about?" • "Can you combine everything we read into one sentence?" • "What would you tell someone else about this story?" • "It sounds as if you can tell someone at home what this story is all about."

The six comprehension strategies described above are appropriate for all youngsters—those who have not yet learned how to read, beginning readers, and accomplished readers. Indeed, these are strategies that all readers use throughout the reading process. More important, however, is the fact that they are also "thinking" strategies—that is to say, they can be taught and promoted through both verbal and written text. In short, they are not dependent on reading ability; rather, they are dependent upon any kind of interaction with text.

For teachers familiar with the three primary stages of guided reading instruction (Before, During, After), the six comprehension strategies have the greatest instructional value and application at selected stages of reading. These are illustrated in the chart below:

	Before Reading	During Reading	After Reading
Background Knowledge	X	X	
Mental Imagery	X	X	
Predicting and Inferring	X	X	
Questioning	X	X	X
Identifying Important Information		X	X
Synthesizing and Summarizing		X	X

Unit 6

Literature-Based Activities

In this section you will discover a wide range of trade books that can be used to highlight and develop appropriate Comprehension Circle lessons for your students. These books represent only a small fraction of the wonderful literature resources you can share with youngsters.

Included with each book is a variety of activities, procedures, and strategies useful in designing engaging and dynamic lessons. For some books you will discover a complete Comprehension Circle. For other books you will discover a selection of potential activities you can use to design and develop your own lessons. This is not to suggest that you use all these activities for any single lesson. Rather, you will find many possibilities that can assist you in developing several different Comprehension Circle lessons for the same book.

This section offers loads of teaching possibilities and loads of learning possibilities for the trade books you normally share with youngsters. Use these ideas as samples for the incredible array of activities, projects, and ideas that can be part of all your literacy efforts—particularly those directed at comprehension development.

Click, Clack, Moo: Cows That Type
by
Doreen Cronin
(New York: Simon and Schuster, 2000)

Summary In this rollicking tale, Farmer Brown has a problem. His cows are making demands—they want electric blankets. Then the chickens get involved, and before long Farmer Brown has a real uprising on his hands. The duck comes in as a mediator and eventually finds a solution to the problem...sort of. This book, a perfect classroom read aloud, will bring giggles and guffaws from any audience.

Component	Strategies and Activities	Instruction
Engagement (Schema)	• Gather students together as a whole class or a smaller group. • Present the theme or topic of a forthcoming book. • Talk about the topic. • Ask questions about the theme or topic. • Invite students to share **relevant** experiences (keep the conversation <u>focused</u>). • Talk about any misperceptions or misconceptions. • Provide illustrations or photos that illuminate the theme or concept. • Share (as necessary) other AV resources that stimulate schema development. • Show the book cover and encourage discussion about its topic or theme. • Draw "straight-line" connections between what youngsters know and the book's main idea. • Link the book to a similar story/book.	Provide students with photographs of various farm scenes. Plan to offer lots of photos of farm animals. After students have been sufficiently "prepped" with the photos, ask them to generate a list of typical farm animals. Record their suggestions on the chalkboard. Then, ask youngsters to think of a "job" for each animal listed. For example, an appropriate "job" for a cow would be "giving milk." An appropriate "job" for a chicken would be to "lay eggs." Create a master list of farm animals and the various "jobs" they would be expected to do on the farm.
Modeling	• Introduce the book. • Vocalize your purpose for reading.	Say to children, *"When I see the title of this book, I wonder if this book is going to be different*

Component	Strategies and Activities	Instruction
Modeling *(continued)*	• Read and discuss the title. • Talk about illustrations. • Do a "mental walk" through the book. • Demonstrate a talk-aloud (focused on a specific strategy). • Demonstrate a think-aloud (focused on a specific strategy). • Provide multiple opportunities for students to "see" inside your head.	*from other kinds of books about animals. I can see a bunch of cows on the cover of the book. The cows are gathered around a typewriter.* (Make sure youngsters know what a typewriter is. Many children may only be familiar with computer keyboards and may never have seen a real old-fashioned typewriter.) *"A chicken and a duck are looking at the typewriter, too. I know that one of the things that good readers do is to create pictures in their minds before they read. So, I'm going to make a mind picture in my head and let you 'see' inside my brain while I think. O.K., here goes. I am thinking about a farm. I have a picture in my head of a farm with a farmhouse, a barn, fields of corn and beans, a tractor and some other machines, and lots and lots of animals. As I look at my picture, I can see some cows in the barn. The farmer is milking the cows in the barn. I can see some chickens in the chicken house. The chickens are laying eggs. And, I can see some ducks. The ducks are swimming around on a pond. I can see lots and lots of things in the picture in my head—a picture that I'm creating before I read this story."*
Read Aloud	• Read the selected book out loud to children. • Use expression and intonation as appropriate. • Consider using a big book. • Occasionally "track" the print with your finger or a pointer. • Occasionally use a Shared Book experience with children.	Demonstrate your enthusiasm for the book while reading Invite the students to close their eyes and to create a mental image of a farm in their heads. When the students are ready, read the book to them. Stop at the end of the page where the farmer gets another

Unit

6

Click, Clack,
Moo:
Cows That Type

Component	Strategies and Activities	Instruction
Read Aloud (*continued*)	• Consider periodic stops (as necessary) to model your thinking. • Demonstrate your enthusiasm for the book while reading.	note from the cows about the hens being cold and demanding electric blankets.
Guided Instruction	• Teacher and students return to text. • Conduct class/group reading conference. • Identify one specific comprehension strategy. • Clarify reading strategy in "kid terms." • Demonstrate the strategy within the context of the book. • Re-model (as necessary) your use of the strategy in that book. • Invite youngsters to "try out" the strategy (by using their own talk-about or think-about conversations). • Encourage retellings. • Discuss transfer of strategy. • Pose open-ended questions. • Reread a portion of the book (as necessary) and talk about how the strategy can be used there. • Provide positive feedback.	Invite selected youngsters to briefly discuss their mental images at this point in the story. Make sure they understand that their mental images and the illustrations in the book may be different—that's O.K. Engage students in a discussion of how the mental images helped them understand and appreciate the story more. Comment that readers usually create mental images before they read as well as while they read in order to appreciate a story more. After this discussion, invite students to close their eyes once again, re-create their mental images, and listen to the rest of the book. Finish reading the book to them.
Synthesize and Summarize	• Invite children to talk about what they learned. • Encourage active discussion among all class/group members. • Use open-ended questions. • Students may need thinking time before responding. • Help youngsters focus on 1 or 2 significant points. • Invite students to reflect on the modeling you did throughout the lesson. • Recap (in kid terms) the strategy used.	Invite one or two selected youngsters to do a retelling of the story. Ask them to focus on the specific information in the book and how that information may or may not have matched with the mental images in their heads as they listened to the book. Use the **Retelling Form** from the Appendix to assist children in focusing on significant information. Review the steps and procedures used during the read aloud.

How I Became a Pirate
by
Melinda Long
(New York: Harcourt, 2003)

Summary Jeremy Jacob is in for the adventure of his life when a rag-tag group of pirates suddenly appears on the beach. The pirates take Jeremy on board, and he soon learns that the life of a pirate is a little different than he had originally imagined. Oh, sure, they don't have to eat their vegetables or brush their teeth, but there are storms and other calamities to deal with. And, then, they have to bury the treasure in a very secret place. But, all's well that ends well—at least when there's soccer practice! Put a little "pirate" in your voice and watch the smiles every time you read this book. Yo ho, yo ho!

Engagement (Schema)

Obtain some pictures or illustrations of pirates (these can be found in a wide variety of "pirate books" such as Treasure Island and other related literature). Invite youngsters to view the pictures and note some of the features of pirates and pirate ships. Create two lists on the chalkboard—one of the features of pirates and the other of the features of pirate ships. As always, keep the conversation focused and specific.

Mental Imagery

Say to the children, *"Close your eyes and paint a picture in your head. Imagine that you are on the beach. Create a mind picture of you standing on a beach somewhere. You are building a sand castle on the beach. It is just you and the sand castle. The sand castle is getting larger and larger. You are very proud of your sand castle. Then, you look out to sea. You see a ship. You look closely and see that it is a pirate ship. You can see a black flag flying at the top of the ship. You can see lots of pirates on the ship. One pirate has a patch over one eye. Another pirate has a cloth wrapped around his head. Another pirate has a sword hanging from his side. And, there are other pirates working on the ship. The ship is headed towards the beach. It is coming right towards the beach you are standing on. Suddenly, all the pirates are pointing at you. They are saying something. The pirate ship is coming closer and closer to the beach. It stops just offshore, and a small rowboat is put into the water. Some pirates get into the rowboat and row to shore. Now slowly open your eyes, and we'll listen to a story about a young boy and the day he became a pirate."*

Questioning

Model for children some of the questions you might ask yourself as you read this book. Do a think-aloud to share some of the thought processes you use as you read. Possible questions/thoughts include:

- "I wonder if these pirates are dangerous or kind."
- "I wonder if Jeremy is scared."
- "I wonder where they are going."
- "I wonder if Jeremy will ever come back to his beach."
- "I wonder if Jeremy will stay a pirate forever."
- "I wonder how this story will end."

If You Give a Mouse a Cookie
by
Laura Joffe Numeroff
(New York: HarperCollins, 1985)

Summary When a little mouse shows up at the door, he is naturally hungry and wants a cookie. Then, he needs some milk. Then, he needs a straw. Then, he needs…. This is a timeless "circle" story that will keep kids in stitches. Youngsters never cease to enjoy this tale's light sense of humor and colorful array of engaging illustrations. It is one of a series that should be part of every classroom.

Questioning

Model for students some of the questions you would ask yourself as you read this book. Do a think-aloud for students using some of the following examples:

- "Do I have any questions about this story before I read?"
- "What do I like about the cover of this book?"
- "What can I do if I don't understand something?"
- "Am I enjoying the story so far?"
- "Can I retell this story to someone else?"
- "Would I want to read another book like this?"

As you do an initial read aloud, slip some of the questions above into the storytelling. Pause each time and allow students to "see inside your head" as you model each question and as you think about how you might respond to each one. For example, if you asked yourself (in a talk-aloud), *What can I do if I don't understand something?*", you could make up the following response: *"Well, I guess if I didn't understand something, I could continue reading and hope that the author gives me some new information. Or maybe I could ask a friend to help me figure out what is going on in the story."* The scenarios don't have to be long, just illustrative of the thinking you might do as you ask and answer your own thought processes.

Making the World
by
Douglas Wood
(New York: Simon and Schuster, 1998)

Summary With lyrical descriptions and rich watercolor paintings, this book takes readers on a trip around the world to show how everything in nature works together to re-create the world every day. This is one of those magical books that celebrates each individual's role in nature and how every person is a very special part of the web of life. This is a book to be read over and over and one that will be favorite read-aloud for many years.

Engagement (Schema)

Before you read this book to children, show them the book and take them, page by page, through the book, highlighting the illustrations and some key words. Invite youngsters to make some preliminary predictions as you "journey" through the text. Afterwards, talk to children about a time when they made a difference or a time when they contributed something to someone else to help them feel better. You may wish to engage youngsters in a short role-playing scenario that illustrates one of the scenes in the book. Ask one or more students to role-play one of the children described in the book. What might he or she be thinking? What might he or she be doing? Afterwards, discuss how each and every person makes important contributions to nature and the world. You may wish to make a chart of some of the contributions children have made to "helping nature" during the course of the past week. It would be appropriate for you to model some of your behaviors in this regard as well.

Unit

6

Making the World

Questioning

Model for students some of the things you might ask yourself as you read this book. Here are some possibilities:

- "I wonder why the author called this book 'Making the World.'"

- "I wonder how a morning breeze helps to make the world.

- "I wonder how a cloud helps to make the world."

- "I wonder how a child in Japan, or another country, helps to make the world."

- "I wonder what I have done recently to help make the world."

- "I wonder how I can continue to make the world."

Plan time to discuss some of your possible responses to those queries. Invite children to suggest their own responses to your thoughts.

The Napping House
by
Audrey Wood
(San Diego, CA: Harcourt, 1984)

Summary Young listeners will want to hear this story again and again. The tale is simple, but the action is complex. There's a bed, a snoring granny, a dreaming child, a dozing dog, a snoozing cat, and all sorts of creatures that add up to a madcap assembly of action and participation. Watch out for all the fun!

Component	Strategies and Activities	Instruction
Engagement (Schema)	• Gather students together as a whole class or a smaller group. • Present the theme or topic of a forthcoming book. • Talk about the topic. • Ask questions about the theme or topic. • Invite students to share **relevant** experiences (keep the conversation <u>focused</u>). • Talk about any misperceptions or misconceptions. • Provide illustrations or photos that illuminate the theme or concept. • Share (as necessary) other AV resources that stimulate schema development. • Show the book cover and encourage discussion about its topic or theme. • Draw "straight-line" connections between what youngsters know and the book's main idea. • Link the book to a similar story/book.	Show the cover of the book. Invite students to describe what is happening on the cover. Ask students to think of a time when they were taking a nap in their own bed. <u>Ask them to describe that scene</u> (keep the conversation focused). How did they feel? How were they positioned? Do they think they were snoring? You may wish to draw an illustration on the chalkboard that features a child sleeping in a large bed. Include some of the ideas shared by youngsters.
Modeling	• Introduce the book. • Vocalize your purpose for reading. • Read and discuss the title. • Talk about illustrations. • Do a "mental walk" through the book. • Demonstrate a talk-aloud (focused on a specific strategy). • Demonstrate a think-aloud (focused on a specific strategy). • Provide multiple opportunities for students to "see" inside your head.	Share the following think-aloud with youngsters: "*When I read the title of this book and see the picture on the cover, I have a painting in my head of someone's bedroom. The room is in someone's house. In the room I can see a large bed. I can see a woman sleeping in the bed. I can see her snoring in the bed. I can see a child sleeping in that same bed. The child is sound asleep. I can also see a dog sleeping in the bed. The dog, too, is sound asleep. Everybody on the bed is sound asleep. Everybody is snoring. This is a picture I make in my head when I see the title and when I look at the picture on the cover.*"

kid not see pictur

Unit

6

The Napping House

Component	Strategies and Activities	Instruction
Read Aloud	• Read the selected book out loud to children. • Use expression and intonation as appropriate. • Consider using a big book. • Occasionally "track" the print with your finger or a pointer. • Occasionally use a Shared Book experience with children. • Consider periodic stops (as necessary) to model your thinking. • Demonstrate your enthusiasm for the book while reading.	Read the book aloud to students, stopping at the end of the page where the cat is sleeping on the bed. (The pages are unnumbered.) Model the changes you need to make in your original mental image (above) and talk about them. Tell children that they will create their own "mind pictures" as you read the rest of the story aloud (do not show the illustrations to the children as you read).
Guided Instruction	• Teacher and students return to text. • Conduct class/group reading conference. • Identify one specific comprehension strategy. • Clarify reading strategy in "kid terms." • Demonstrate the strategy within the context of the book. • Re-model (as necessary) your use of the strategy in that book. • Invite youngsters to "try out" the strategy (by using their own talk-about or think-about conversations). • Encourage retellings. • Discuss transfer of strategy. • Pose open-ended questions. • Reread a portion of the book (as necessary) and talk about how the strategy can be used there. • Provide positive feedback.	Invite children to create a mental image of the bedroom based on what they have heard so far in the story. Take some time to talk about selected images. Read the story to the end of the page where the flea joins the group. Briefly talk about selected images that youngsters have created. Invite them to focus on specific details. Finish the remainder of the book.
Synthesize and Summarize	• Invite children to talk about what they learned. • Encourage active discussion among all class/group members. • Use open-ended questions. • Students may need thinking time before responding. • Help youngsters focus on 1 or 2 significant points.	Invite other students to discuss their mental images. Talk briefly about some of the changes or modifications that needed to be made in those images as the story continued through to the end. Read the book a second time, this time sharing the illustrations as you read. Invite

Literature-Based Activities

Component	Strategies and Activities	Instruction
Synthesize and Summarize *(continued)*	• Invite students to reflect on the modeling you did throughout the lesson. • Recap (in kid terms) the strategy used.	youngsters to observe the illustrations and how they are similar to or different from the images in their heads. When the second read aloud is finished, talk about any differences between the pictures in their heads and those in the book. Talk about how their images helped them enjoy the story.

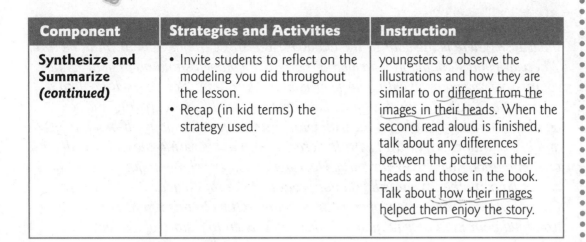

No, David!
by
David Shannon
(New York: Blue Sky Press, 1998)

Summary Just like every other kid, David is always getting in trouble. And, just like every other kid, his mother is always telling him "No." This is a madcap and rollicking series of events that will resonate with every child (and many adults, too). Children will delight in this simple tale that will bring back lots of memories and spark lots of laughter.

Engagement (Schema)

Engage students in a discussion about some of the things they do at home that perhaps their parents don't always approve. What are some of the events they have been part of that met with some type of disfavor on the part of adults in the family? You might want to spark this discussion by sharing some events from your own childhood that were not particularly appreciated by your parents. This brainstorming session should be very focused. Students should not take off on tangents—telling about scrapes their baby brother got into or their cousin Alyssa's adventure with the black crayon or the neighbor down the street who rode her bicycle across the old man's lawn. Help children concentrate on specific events in their own lives.

Mental Imagery

Say something like this to children, *"Close your eyes and imagine that you are in your living room at home. Paint a picture in your mind. Where is the couch? Where*

© Harcourt Achieve Inc. All rights reserved.

Teaching Comprehension in Grades 1–2

Unit

6

No, David!

is the TV? What is some other furniture that is in your living room? What color are the walls? Where is the door or the windows? Put those things in your mind picture. Where are you standing in your living room? See yourself standing in your living room. Now, see yourself with a large crayon in your hand. See yourself holding a crayon. Now, watch yourself as you walk over to a wall. Look carefully and see yourself make long marks on the wall with your crayon. See yourself making lots and lots of marks on the wall with the crayon. You are covering the whole wall with crayon marks. Now, listen carefully. Hear your mother yelling at you. Oh, no, here comes your mother. What will you do? What will she say to you? Here she comes. Oh, no! Oh, no! Now, slowly open your eyes and return to this room. That's O.K., I won't tell your mother what you did. Now, let's listen to a story about David…a story about a boy who always hears the words 'Oh, no!'"

Synthesizing and Summarizing

Invite the youngsters to provide a retelling of the story. You may wish to use some of the following prompts:

- "What should we include in a retelling of this story?"

- "What should we include in an introduction?"

- "Can you be a little more specific?"

- "How can we continue retelling?"

- "What happened next?"

- "If we could keep going, what would happen next in the story?"

Sheep in a Jeep
by
Nancy Shaw
(Boston: Houghton Mifflin, 1986)

Summary In a rollicking, rhyming story, the saga of several sheep and their efforts to maneuver a jeep down a hill and through a mudhole is hilariously presented and illustrated in this fun book. Part of an imaginative series that relies on few words to carry the action, this entry will have kids begging for more "Sheep" books and listening to the playful ways in which the author has skillfully manipulated language.

Mental Imagery

Invite students to gather on the storytelling carpet. Show them the illustration on the cover of the book. Then, ask them to close their eyes and to create a picture in their head as follows: *"Think about the picture on the cover of the book. Now, create a picture in your own head. Paint a picture of a jeep that has lots of sheep in it. Look at all the sheep. They all have white coats. There are some sheep in the front of the jeep. There are some sheep in the back of the jeep. Look at the sheep that is driving the jeep. He can't see very well. He is not sure where he is going. Look at the road. The road is rocky and bumpy. The jeep is moving back and forth and from side to side on the road. The jeep is all over the place. Look at the sheep. They are all holding on. The jeep is going faster and faster. It is a wild ride. Look at the jeep and all the sheep go down the road. Now, very slowly, I would like to have you open your eyes. We will now share this book. This book is* Sheep in a Jeep, *and it's written by Nancy Shaw. Let's listen."*

Synthesizing and Summarizing

Tell students that you would like to have some of them retell the story. But before they retell what happened in this story, you are going to ask them a few questions. They should listen carefully to the questions and try to include answers to these questions in their retellings. Here are a few open-ended questions to get you started:

- "What was the most interesting part of the story?"

- "What did you enjoy most about this story?"

- "What made you laugh?"

- "Tell me how the story turned out."

- "Is this story similar to other stories you have heard?"

These open-ended queries are designed to help students focus on the essential elements that need to be part of their retellings.

The Snowy Day
by
Ezra Jack Keats
(New York: Viking, 1962)

Summary **T**his story stands the test of time. Loved by thousands of youngsters ever since it was first published, this is a wonderful addition to any primary classroom. All about the amazing discoveries a young boy makes on a snowy day, it is also about the strength of imagination and the possibilities of pretending. Read it and feel the magic!

Component	Strategies and Activities	Instruction
Engagement (Schema)	• Gather students together as a whole class or a smaller group. • Present the theme or topic of a forthcoming book. • Talk about the topic. • Ask questions about the theme or topic. • Invite students to share **relevant** experiences (keep the conversation <u>focused</u>). • Talk about any misperceptions or misconceptions. • Provide illustrations or photos that illuminate the theme or concept. • Share (as necessary) other AV resources that stimulate schema development. • Show the book cover and encourage discussion about its topic or theme. • Draw "straight-line" connections between what youngsters know and the book's main idea. • Link the book to a similar story/book.	Invite students to talk about the activities and things that can be done on a snowy day. If you live in an area of the country that gets snow each winter, invite youngsters to discuss some of the things they do whenever it snows. If you live in a part of the country that does not regularly get snow, ask students to speculate on the activities that children can do when it snows. You may wish to create a list on the chalkboard to record all the suggestions and ideas. Afterwards, show students the cover of the book and ask them to make a prediction about some of the activities the young boy on the cover might want to do in the snow.
Modeling	• Introduce the book. • Vocalize your purpose for reading. • Read and discuss the title. • Talk about illustrations.	Read the first page to children. Spend some time talking about the initial illustration. Tell students that you are going to "look inside" Peter's head to

Component	Strategies and Activities	Instruction
Modeling *(continued)*	• Do a "mental walk" through the book. • Demonstrate a talk-aloud (focused on a specific strategy). • Demonstrate a think-aloud (focused on a specific strategy). • Provide multiple opportunities for students to "see" inside your head.	"see" what he might be thinking about. You may wish to share an imaginative talk-aloud with students—taking on the role of Peter. For example, *"Wow, it's snowing outside. That means I can do all sorts of really neat things. Maybe I can go sledding. Maybe I can make some snow angels. Maybe I can have a snowball fight with my friends. Wow! It's snowing. There are all kinds of things that I can do."*
Read Aloud	• Read the selected book out loud to children. • Use expression and intonation as appropriate. • Consider using a big book. • Occasionally "track" the print with your finger or a pointer. • Occasionally use a Shared Book experience with children. • Consider periodic stops (as necessary) to model your thinking. • Demonstrate your enthusiasm for the book while reading.	Read the book aloud to children. Stop at the bottom of page 28. Do a think-aloud for the students. For example, *"Hmmm, I wonder what happened to Peter's snowball. He put it into his pocket and now it's gone. It was there before and now it's not. Hmmm, I wonder what could have happened to his snowball. The book doesn't tell me, so I'm going to have to guess. Hmmm, I wonder if anyone can help me guess."* After youngsters have "helped" you make necessary inferences, complete the rest of the story.
Guided Instruction	• Teacher and students return to text. • Conduct class/group reading conference. • Identify one specific comprehension strategy. • Clarify reading strategy in "kid terms." • Demonstrate the strategy within the context of the book. • Re-model (as necessary) your use of the strategy in that book. • Invite youngsters to "try out" the strategy (by using their own talk-about or think-about conversations).	After completing the initial reading, invite youngsters to make some predictions about what Peter and his friend are going to do. Ask students to think about some of their own experiences in the snow or some things that they have heard people do when it snows. Ask, *"Does that information help you in making predictions about Peter and his friend?"* You may wish to list those predictions on the chalkboard.

Teaching Comprehension in Grades 1–2

Component	Strategies and Activities	Instruction
Guided Instruction *(continued)*	• Encourage retellings. • Discuss transfer of strategy. • Pose open-ended questions. • Reread a portion of the book (as necessary) and talk about how the strategy can be used there. • Provide positive feedback.	
Synthesize and Summarize	• Invite children to talk about what they learned. • Encourage active discussion among all class/group members. • Use open-ended questions. • Students may need thinking time before responding. • Help youngsters focus on 1 or 2 significant points. • Invite students to reflect on the modeling you did throughout the lesson. • Recap (in kid terms) the strategy used.	Invite children to tell you 2–3 important parts of the story. Write those on the chalkboard. Ask selected youngsters to retell the story using some or most of those important parts. You may wish to use some open-ended questions to help youngsters formulate an appropriate retelling. Some possibilities include: *"What do you think was the most important part of the story? Can you tell me something else? What else would you like to add?"*

Recommended Books for First Grade

Ackerman, Karen. (1992). *Song and Dance Man.* New York: Dragonfly.
Grandpa demonstrates for his visiting grandchildren some of the songs, dances, and jokes he performed when he was a vaudeville entertainer.

Ada Alma Flor. (1998). *Yours Truly, Goldilocks.* New York: Atheneum.
Everyone who's anyone will be at the Three Little Pigs' housewarming party. Goldilocks and Little Red Riding Hood have already marked it on their calendars. Unfortunately, so have the wolves—those who've caused the Pigs to build their brick house in the first place!

Addy, Sharon Hart. (2002). *When Wishes Were Horses.* Boston, MA: Houghton Mifflin Co.
While lugging a heavy sack of flour home from the town of Dusty Gulch, Zeb wishes for a horse, and suddenly a buckskin cowpony appears.

Atwater, Richard. (1997). *Mr. Popper's Penguins.* New York: Random House Books for Young Readers.
The story of Mr. Popper, the small-town housepainter who dreamed of exploring Antarctic regions, and Captain Cook, the redoubtable penguin who turned Mr. Popper's world upside down.

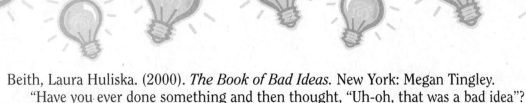

Beith, Laura Huliska. (2000). *The Book of Bad Ideas*. New York: Megan Tingley.
"Have you ever done something and then thought, "Uh-oh, that was a bad idea"?
We thought so.

Bird, Malcolm. (1993). *The School in Murky Wood*. San Francisco: Chronicle Press.
After the children of Murky Wood go home for the night, monsters take over their
school.

Bourgeois, Paulette. (1997). *Franklin Rides a Bike*. New York: Scholastic Press.
At the beginning of spring, Franklin and all his friends have training wheels on
their bikes. But soon Franklin is the only one who can't ride without them.

Brett, Jan. (1985). *Annie and the Wild Animals*. Boston, MA: Houghton Mifflin Co.
When Annie's cat disappears, she attempts friendship with a variety of unsuitable
woodland animals.

Bunting, Eve. (1999). *The Butterfly House*. New York: Scholastic Press.
After saving a caterpillar from a hungry bird, a young girl consults
her grandfather and together they build a butterfly house.

Bunting, Eve. (1993). *Fly Away Home*. New York: Clarion Books.
A homeless boy who lives in an airport with his father, moving
from terminal to terminal trying not to be noticed, is given hope
when a trapped bird finally finds its freedom.

Cain, Janan. (2000). *The Way I Feel*. Parenting Press.
Through simple verses and engaging illustrations, this book gives children the
vocabulary they need to understand and express how they feel.

Carlson, Nancy. (1994). *What If It Never Stops Raining?* London: Puffin Books.
Tim is always worrying about something, but things never turn out as badly as he
thinks they will.

Cazet, Denys. (1990). *Never Spit on Your Shoes*. New York: Orchard Books.
Arnie arrives home exhausted but proud of making it through the first day of first
grade. Greeted by his loving mother, the two sit down for a snack and a good chat.

Charlip, Remy. (1993). *Fortunately*. New York: Aladdin Books.
Good and bad luck accompany Ned from New York to Florida on his way to a
surprise party.

Clements, Andrew. (2001). *Brave Norman*. New York: Simon & Schuster.
Norman is a dog who cannot see. One day, he is at the beach and he hears a girl in
the water calling for help. Can a blind dog save someone's life?

Clements. Andrew. (2002). *Dolores and the Big Fire*. New York: Simon & Schuster.
Dolores is a very timid cat. Her owner, Kyle, keeps a light on all night so she won't
be scared. One night Dolores pokes at Kyle's face while he is sleeping because the
house is on fire! Can Dolores wake Kyle up in time?

Cohen, Miriam. (1983). *Lost in the Museum*. Indiana: Pearson Books.
When he and some other first graders get lost in the museum, Jim decides to be
brave and go find the teacher.

Cole, Joanna. (1990). *Don't Call Me Names*. New York: Random House.
Nell is afraid of Mike and Joe because they always tease her and make fun of her, until the day she stands up to them on behalf of her friend Nicky.

Cowley, Joy. (2003). *Mrs. Wish–Washy's Farm*. New York: Philomel Books.
Tired of being washed by Mrs. Wishy-Washy, a cow, a pig, and a duck leave her farm and head for the city.

Cronon, Doreen. (2000). *Click, Clack, Moo: Cows That Type*. New York: Simon & Schuster.
The literacy rate in Farmer Brown's barn goes up considerably once his cows find an old typewriter and begin typing.

Cronin, Doreen. (2003). *The Diary of a Worm*. New York: HarperCollins.
This is the diary…of a worm. Surprisingly, a worm not that different from you or me. Except he eats his homework. Oh, and his head looks a lot like his rear end.

Cuyler, Margery. (1993). *That's Good, That's Bad*. New York: Henry Holt & Company.
At the zoo a boy is lifted into the sky by his balloon.

Doherty, Berlie. (1995). *The Magic Bicycle*. New York: Random House.
A boy finds that he cannot ride his new bicycle during the day, only in his dreams at night, until one day he finally discovers the magic he needs to ride it in real life.

Dorros, Arthur. (1991). *Abuela*. New York: Dutton.
A child imagines she's rising into the air over the park and flying away with her loving, rosy-cheeked abuela (grandmother).

Fox, Mem. (1992). *Shoes from Grandpa*. New York: Orchard Books.
Jessie, an active girl of nine or so, is growing out of her clothes, and the members of her large and loving family get carried away in their eagerness to provide her with a new wardrobe.

Harper, Isabelle. (2001). *Our New Puppy*. New York: Scholastic Press.
American Book Award-winning artist Barry Moser and his granddaughter invite young readers to spend a not-so-quiet Sunday afternoon with them and their pets, Rosie the dog and newcomer Floyd, a bouncy, curious Rottweiler puppy.

Henkes, Kevin. (1991). *Chrysanthemum*. New York: Greenwillow.
Until Chrysanthemum started school, she believed her parents when they said her name was perfect. But on the first day of school, Chrysanthemum begins to suspect that her name is far less than perfect, especially when her class dissolves into giggles upon hearing her name read aloud.

Heide, Florence Parry. (2000). *Some Things Are Scary*. Boston, MA: Candlewick Press.
The hero demonstrates that some things are scary, and those same things, when they happen to someone else, are darkly funny.

Herold, Ann Bixby. (1991). *The Butterfly Birthday*. New York: Simon & Schuster.
Matt, a collector of caterpillars, expresses his fear of spiders and learns that everyone has fears, even his father.

Himmelman, John. *Amanda and the Magic Garden.* New York: Viking Children's Books.
   Amanda's garden, grown from magic seeds, is a great success until its vegetables
   cause the animals who eat them to grow to giant size.

Hoban, Russell. (1994). *A Birthday for Frances.* New York: HarperTrophy.
   As her little sister Gloria's birthday approaches, Frances wavers between being
   generous and being jealous.

Hoff, Sydney. (1985). *Danny and the Dinosaur.* New York: HarperCollins.
   Danny and the lovable dinosaur, who leaves the museum to play with Danny and
   his friends, are the focus of this story.

Hoff, Sydney. (2002). *The Horse in Harry's Room.* New York: HarperTrophy.
   Harry keeps a horse in his room. A trusty horse only he can see. But then his
   parents take him to the country to see "real" horses. Horses that are free to run,
   kick, and nibble. Now Harry must decide: does his horse need to be free, too?

Hoffman, Mary. (1991). *Amazing Grace.* New York: Dial Books.
   Although a classmate says that Grace cannot play Peter Pan in the school play
   because she is black, Grace discovers that she can do anything she sets her mind
   to do.

James, Simon. (1996). *Dear Mr. Blueberry.* New York: Aladdin Books.
   It is summer, and Emily discovers that a whale is living in the pond in her yard.
   Eager to learn more about this amazing animal, she writes a series of letters to
   her teacher, Mr. Blueberry, asking for information about whales and their habits.

Jones, Maurice. (2003). *Little Bear Finds a Friend.* New York: Oxford University Press.
   Little Bear decides it's time to explore and sets off up the mountain, where he
   hopes to make new friends. On the way he meets chattering monkeys, hungry
   llamas, and sleepy jaguars, but they are all too busy to join him. Or are they?

Kirk, David. (1994). *Miss Spider's Tea Party.* New York: Scholastic Press.
   When lonely Miss Spider tries to host a tea party, the other bugs refuse to come
   for fear of being eaten.

Kotzwinkle, William. (2001). *Walter, the Farting Dog.* California: North
   Atlantic Books.
   When Betty and Billy rescued Walter from the pound, they never
   imagined that such a cute dog was capable of such unpleasant and
   frequent smells.

Kraus, Robert. (1980). *Leo the Late Bloomer.* New York: Wanderer
   Books.
   Leo isn't reading, or writing, or drawing, or even speaking, and his
   father is concerned. But Leo's mother isn't. She knows her son will do all those
   things, and more, when he's ready.

Krensky, Stephen. (1999). *My Teacher's Secret Life.* New York: Aladdin Books.
   Everyone knows that teachers belong in school. But one day, Mrs. Quirk is spotted
   in the supermarket.

Unit 6

Recommended Books for First Grade

Lobel, Arnold. (1979). *Frog and Toad Are Friends.* New York: Scholastic Press.
Frog and Toad are best friends, participating in all elements of life together.

Lobel, Arnold. (1977). *Mouse Soup.* New York: Scholastic Press.
A clever mouse talks his way out of becoming mouse soup for a weasel's dinner.

Long, Melinda. (2003). *How I Became a Pirate.* New York: Harcourt.
When Braid Beard's pirate crew invites Jeremy Jacob to join their voyage, Jeremy jumps right on board.

MacCarone, Grace. (1992). *Itchy, Itchy Chicken Pox.* New York: Scholastic Press.
Bouncy rhymes makes this lively story about coping with chicken pox one that children will love to read long after their itches are gone.

Mayer, Mercer. (1992). *There's an Alligator Under My Bed.* New York: Dial Books.
Mercer tells the tale of a little boy who is sure that there is an alligator under his bed. Getting no sympathy from his parents who "never saw it," he forms a plan of attack.

Mayer, Mercer. (1988). *There's a Nightmare in My Closet.* London: Puffin Books.
At bedtime a boy confronts the nightmare in his closet and finds him not so terrifying after all.

McCully, Emily Arnold. (1997). *Mirette on the High Wire.* New York: Putnam Publishing Group.
A child helps a daredevil who has lost his edge to regain his confidence.

McGovern, Ann. (1986). *Stone Soup.* New York: Scholastic Press.
A clever young man tricks an old woman into believing that soup can be made from a stone. As the pot of water boils with the stone in it, he urges her to add more and more ingredients until the soup is a feast "fit for a king."

McMullan, Kate. (2002). *I Stink!* New York: HarperCollins.
A rowdy, ravenous New York City garbage truck is the unlikely and thoroughly engaging narrator that tells kids what really goes on while they are sleeping.

Meddaugh, Susan. (1998). *Hog-Eye.* Boston: Houghton Mifflin Co.
The hilarious story of how a piglet tells her family how she was caught by a wolf and nearly became soup.

Milich, Melissa. (1995). *Can't Scare Me!* New York: Random House Children's Books.
Two friends often share a special time in the evenings when ghost stories can sometimes be frightening, but a little girl and a special ghost story help Mr. Munroe stop being afraid.

Minarik, Else Holmelund. (1968). *A Kiss for Little Bear.* New York: HarperCollins.
Little Bear's thank-you kiss from grandmother gets passed on to him by many animals and greatly aids the skunks' romance.

Most, Bernard. (1996). *Cock-A-Doodle-Moo.* New York: Red Wagon Books.
When the rooster wakes up with laryngitis, he must quickly think of how to awaken the farm animals. Maybe the cow can take his place.

Munsch, Robert. (1999). *Andrew's Loose Tooth*. New York: Cartwheel Books.
Andrew has a loose tooth. He wants to eat an apple but it hurts. Both of his
parents, the dentist, and even a motorcycle-riding Tooth Fairy try some pretty
drastic measures to help him get rid of the stubborn tooth, but with no success.

Munsch, Robert. (1991). *Show and Tell*. Toronto: Annick Press.
Ben wanted to take something really neat to school for show-and-tell, so he
decided to take his new baby sister.

Noble, Trinka Hakes. (1984). *The Day Jimmy's Boa Ate the Wash*. New York:
Dutton Books.
Jimmy's boa constrictor wreaks havoc on the class trip to a farm.

Numeroff, Laura Joffe.(1996). *If You Give a Mouse a Cookie*. New York: HarperCollins.
What happens if you give a mouse a cookie? Why, he'll need a glass of milk to go
with it! He'll also need a straw, a napkin, a mirror—each item prompts the need
for another.

Olson, Mary. (2000). *Nice Try, Tooth Fairy*. New York: Simon & Schuster.
As if having to collect all the world's unattached baby teeth isn't hard enough, the
Tooth Fairy finds that some children want them back. Young Emma's polite request
to borrow her tooth to show Grandpa brings a succession of not-quite-right
substitutes, from an elephant's tusk to a hedgehog's sand-grain–sized nubbin.

Parish, Peggy. (1992). *Amelia Bedelia*. New York: HarperTrophy.
Amelia Bedelia, the housekeeper with a literal mind, merrily upsets the household
when she "dresses" the chicken and "trims" the steak with ribbons and lace.

Parish, Peggy. (1990). *Play Ball, Amelia Bedelia*. New York: HarperFestival.
Amelia Bedelia, who knows very little about baseball, stands in for a
sick player during a game.

Paterson, Katherine. (2003). *Marvin One Too Many*. New York: Live Oak Media.
Marvin's late on his first day at school and it is hard. Everyone seems to have a
place in class…except Marvin. And everyone seems to know how to read…except
Marvin. But he's too afraid to ask for help.

Peters, Lisa. (1994). *When the Fly Flew In*. New York: Dial Books.
A young boy delays cleaning his room to avoid disturbing his four sleeping pets.
However, a noisy fly appears and irritates one animal after another.

Piper, Watty. (1978). *The Little Engine That Could*. New York: Grosset & Dunlap.
A little engine proves that trying her best can let her accomplish any goal.

Polacco, Patricia. (2001). *The Keeping Quilt*. New York: Aladdin Books.
A family story about a quilt made from an immigrant Jewish family's clothing
from their Russian homeland.

Polacco, Patricia. (2001). *Thank You, Mr. Falker*. New York: Philomel Books.
Trisha could paint and draw beautifully, but when she looked at words on a page,
all she could see was a jumble. It took a very special teacher to recognize little
Trisha's dyslexia: Mr. Falker.

Unit 6

Recommended Books for First Grade

Porte, Barbara Ann. (1989). *Harry in Trouble*. New York: Greenwillow.
Harry put his library card in a very safe place. Now he can't find it! This is the third one he's had this year, and the librarian said she won't give him another. What is Harry going to do?

Rathmann, Peggy. (1995). *Officer Buckle and Gloria*. New York: Putnam Publishing Group.
Officer Buckle, a mustachioed policeman who wears a crossed-out-banana-peel patch on his sleeve, has a passion for teaching students about safety, but his audiences tend to doze off during his lectures.

Reitano, John. (1998). *What If the Zebras Lost Their Stripes?* Paulist Press.
With rhymed couplets and goofy illustrations, this parable attempts to teach that love looks beyond superficial differences

Riddle, Tohby. (1995). *A Most Unusual Dog*. New York: Aladdin Books.
Fletcher, a multitalented dog who can cook, build, decorate, and ride bikes, achieves fame for a while and then vanishes.

Ringgold, Faith. (1995). *Aunt Harriet's Underground Railroad in the Sky*. Connecticut: Dragonfly Press.
Characters fly in a fantastical sky train run by Harriet Tubman that traces a route on the Underground Railroad.

Rylant, Cynthia. (1991). *Night in the Country*. New York: Aladdin Books.
Explores the sights and sounds of the country's nighttime, from an apple falling to the ground to a dog's chain clinking as the animal drinks water.

Rylant, Cynthia. (1993). *The Relatives Came*. New York: Aladdin Books.
In a rainbow-colored station wagon that smelled like a real car, the relatives came. When they arrived, they hugged and hugged from the kitchen to the front room.

Sachar, Louis. (1992). *Marvin Redpost: Kidnapped at Birth*. New York: Random House Books for Young Readers.
Red-haired Marvin is convinced that the reason he looks different from the rest of the family is that he is really the lost prince of Shampoon.

Saller, Carol. (1993). *Pug, Slug, and Doug the Thug*. Minneapolis: Carolrhoda Books.
A humorous Wild West Tale, told in verse, about a dog, a cat, and a lone boy who team up to outwit the villainous bad guys, Pug, Slug, and Doug the Thug.

San Souci, Robert D. (1996). *Sukey and the Mermaid*. New York: Aladdin Books.
Weary of the unreasonable demands of Mister Jones, her new stepfather, Sukey escapes to the water's edge, where she meets "a beautiful, brown-skinned, black-eyed mermaid."

Say, Allen. (1993). *Grandfather's Journey*. Boston, MA: Houghton Mifflin.
Through compelling reminiscences of his grandfather's life in America and Japan, Allen Say gives us a poignant account of a family's unique cross-cultural experience.

Seuss, Dr. (1960). *Green Eggs and Ham*. New York: Random House Books for Young Readers.
Sam-I-Am mounts a determined campaign to convince another Seuss character to eat a plate of green eggs and ham.

Seuss, Dr. (1961). *Ten Apples Up on Top.* New York: Random House Books for Young Readers.
A lion, a dog, and a tiger are having a contest—can they get ten apples piled up on top of their heads?

Sharmat, Marjorie. (1986). *The Big Fat Enormous Lie.* New York: Dutton Books.
A child's simple lie grows to enormous proportions.

Showers, Paul. (1991). *The Listening Walk.* New York: HarperCollins.
We're going on a Listening Walk. Shhhhh. Do not talk. Do not hurry. Get ready to fill your ears with a world of wonderful, surprising sounds.

Simms, Laura. (2002). *Rotten Teeth.* Boston, MA: Houghton Mifflin Co.
Speaking in front of the class isn't easy for small people like Melissa Herman. Especially when there's nothing very special to say about her house or her family or herself. But with the help of her older brother, Melissa borrows a bottle from her father's dental office to take to show and tell.

Slepian, Jan. (2001). *The Hungry Thing.* New York: Scholastic.
One morning a Hungry Thing comes to town, sits on his tail, and says, "I want some shmancakes and tickles and feetloaf and gollipops." The adults simply do not understand. But one little boy thinks he does.

Stewart, Sarah. (1998). *The Gardener.* New York: Live Oak Media.
When the Depression hits her family, Lydia Grace leaves her snug rural home and journeys to a nearby city to live with dour Uncle Jim.

Slobodkina, Esphyr. (1987). *Caps for Sale: A Tale of a Peddler, Some Monkeys, and Their Monkey Business.* New York: HarperTrophy.
"Caps! Caps for sale!" calls the peddler, until one day he wakes up from a nap to find his caps have disappeared.

Tabeck, Simms. (2004). *Joseph Had a Little Overcoat.* London: Puffin Books.
When Joseph's overcoat becomes old and torn, he makes a little jacket out of it. When the jacket becomes tattered, he turns it into a vest. Joseph continues to make something new out of the old until he is left with nothing.

Thomassie, Tynia. (2002). *Mimi's Tutu.* New York: Scholastic Press.
Little Mimi enjoys going to African dance class with her mother, but she longs for a tutu for herself.

Thompson, Kay. (2002). *Eloise Takes a Bawth.* New York: Simon & Schuster.
Ever-irrepressible Eloise absolutely loves taking a "bawth," and her devotees will absolutely love seeing her "splawsh, splawsh, splawsh" her way through a delightfully disastrous—yet ultimately propitious—time in the tub.

Trivizas, Eugene. (1999). *The Three Little Wolves and the Big Bad Pig.* New York: Simon & Schuster.
An altered retelling of the tale about the conflict between the pigs and the wolf—with a surprise ending.

Viorst, Judith. (1999). *Alexander and the Terrible, Horrible, No Good, Very Bad Day.* New York: Bt Bound.
As Alexander's day progresses, he faces many trials and tribulations that make him want to move to Australia.

Waber, Bernard. (1981). *Ira Sleeps Over.* New York: Dutton Books.
Ira is thrilled to spend the night at Reggie's until his sister raises the question of whether he should take his teddy bear.

Watson, Joy. (1990). *Grandpa's Slippers.* New York: Scholastic Press.
Grandmother is determined to get her husband to throw out his old tatty slippers for some new ones. Each day he finds them hidden somewhere different and is getting more and more annoyed.

Wells, Rosemary. (2000). *Max's Dragon Shirt.* New York: Viking Books.
On a shopping trip to the department store, Max's determination to get a dragon shirt leads him away from his distracted sister and into trouble.

Williams, Vera B. (1982). *A Chair for My Mother.* New York: Greenwillow.
After their home is destroyed by a fire, Rosa, her mother, and grandmother save their coins to buy a really comfortable chair for all to enjoy.

Williams, Vera B. (1991). *Cherries and Cherry Pits.* New York: HarperTrophy.
When Bidemmi starts to draw, her imagination takes off. Enter her world, look at her pictures, and watch her stories grow and grow. You will never forget her.

Wilson, Karma. (2003). *A Frog in the Bog.* New York: Margaret K. McElderry.
This imaginative counting book will keep children laughing as a little frog eats his way through a variety of swamp delicacies.

Wood, Audrey. (1985). *King Bidgood's in the Bathtub.* New York: Harcourt Children's Books.
This rollicking tale is the story of an unruly king who refuses to leave his bathtub and attend to his duties.

Wood, Audrey. (1998). *Quick as a Cricket.* London: Egmont Children's Books.
A joyful celebration of a child's growing self-awareness.

Wright, Courtni. (1994). *Journey to Freedom.* New York: Holiday House.
Joshua and his family, runaway slaves from a tobacco plantation in Kentucky, follow the Underground Railroad to freedom.

Yolen, Jane. (1987). *Owl Moon.* New York: Philomel Books.
A girl and her father go owling on a moonlit winter night near the farm where they live.

Yorinks, Arthur. (1986). *Hey, Al.* New York: Farrar Straus & Giroux.
One day, a funny-looking bird sticks its huge head through Al's bathroom window and proposes a journey to a terrific place where there are "no worries" and "no cares."

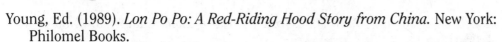

Unit 6

Literature-Based Activities

Young, Ed. (1989). *Lon Po Po: A Red-Riding Hood Story from China.* New York: Philomel Books.
Three little girls spare no mercy to Lon Po Po, the granny wolf, in this version of Little Red Riding Hood where they tempt her up a tree and over a limb, to her death.

Zion, Gene. (1960). *Harry and the Lady Next Door.* New York: HarperCollins.
Harry the dog goes to fantastic lengths to make his neighbor stop singing.

Recommended Books for Second Grade

Aardena, Verna. (1993). *Bringing the Rain to Kapiti Plain.* London: Puffin Books.
A cumulative rhyme relating how Ki-pat brought rain to the drought-stricken Kapiti Plain.

Adler, David. (2004). *Cam Jansen and the Mystery of the Dinosaur Bones.* London: Puffin Books.
Cam is a spunky young heroine whose adventures are told in this story.

Allard, Harry. (1993). *Miss Nelson Is Missing.* Boston, MA: Houghton Mifflin Co.
The kids in Room 207 take advantage of the teacher's good nature until she disappears and they are faced with a vile substitute.

Allsburg, Chris Van. (1985). *The Polar Express.* Boston, MA: Houghton Mifflin Co.
A magical train ride on Christmas Eve takes a boy to the North Pole to receive a special gift from Santa.

Anno, Mitsumasa. (1995). *Anno's Magic Seeds.* New York: Philomel.
A gift from a wizard makes Jack's fortune grow by ones and twos, then threes and fours, then faster and faster, challenging the reader to keep track of his riches.

Auch, Mary Jane. (1996). *Eggs Mark the Spot.* New York: Holiday House.
Pauline is a hen who can reproduce any image on her egg if she concentrates while laying it.

Auch, Mary Jane. (1993). *Peeping Beauty.* New York: Holiday House.
Poulette, the dancing hen, falls into the clutches of a hungry fox, who exploits her desire to become a great ballerina.

Azore, Barbara. (2004). *Wanda and the Wild Hair.* California: Children's Book Press.
Wanda gets a haircut that will shock the whole neighborhood.

Barracca, Debra. (1990). *Adventures of Taxi Dog.* New York: Dial Books.
A stray dog's outlook takes a quick turn for the better when Jim, a New York City taxi driver, offers him a name, friendship, and a place in the front seat.

Teaching Comprehension in Grades 1–2

Unit 6

Recommended Books for Second Grade

Battle-Lavert, Gwendolyn. (1994). *The Barber's Cutting Edge*. California: Children's Book Press.
Rashaad gets his hair cut by the best barber in town who also introduces him to the joy of learning new words.

Berenstain, Stan and Jan. (1968). *The Bear's Vacation*. New York: Random House.
The Bear family goes to the seaside for its vacation and Dad tries to teach his son the rules of water safety.

Berger, Barbara. (1996). *Grandfather Twilight*. New York: Putnam Publishing Group.
At the day's end, Grandfather Twilight walks in the forest to perform his evening task, bringing the miracle of night to the world.

Briggs, Raymond. (1997). *Jim and the Beanstalk*. New York: Putnam Publishing Group.
Jim woke up early one morning to find a plant that was very like a beanstalk growing outside his window. Climbing to the top of the beanstalk, he found a castle and a giant, but with very modern problems that only Jim could help solve.

Brillhart, Julie. (1992). *Story Hour: Starring Megan!* New York: Dial Books.
When Megan's mother, the librarian, cannot read to the children at story hour, beginning reader Megan takes over the job.

Brown, Jeff. (1974). *Flat Stanley*. New York: Scholastic Press.
A bulletin board fell on Stanley. It didn't hurt him; it just made him flat.

Brown, Jeff. (2003). *Stanley in Space*. New York: HarperCollins.
The President of the United States has chosen Stanley Lambchop and his family to become the first humans to fly in the Star Scout, a new top-secret spaceship.

Brown, Marc. (1998). *Arthur's Mystery Envelope*. Boston: Little Brown & Company.
It looks like trouble when the principal asks Arthur to take home a large envelope marked "confidential."

Buehner, Caralyn. (1999). *The Escape of Marvin the Ape*. London: Puffin Books.
One day when the zookeeper wasn't looking, Marvin slipped out. The adventuresome ape proceeds to sample the delights of the city, going to the art museum, the movies, and a ball game.

Buehner, Caralyn. (2000). *I Did It, I'm Sorry*. London: Puffin Books.
Do your words and actions help or hurt? In this humorous guide to good behavior, Ollie Octopus, Bucky Beaver, and their friends help point the way to good behavior.

Bunting, Eve. (1996). *Sunflower House*. New York: Harcourt Children's Books.
Sunflower seeds sown in a circle eventually grow into a beautiful sunflower house with lots of room inside for three friends and their imaginations.

Byars, Betsy. (1996). *My Brother, Ant*. New York: Viking Books.
   Told in the first person, the four short chapters depict a warm, funny relationship between a boy and his sweet but sometimes pesky younger brother.

Byars, Betsy. (1996). *Tornado*. New York: HarperCollins.
   When a doghouse landed in the backyard during a tornado, the family wasn't really surprised. What did surprise them was that there was a dog inside, whom they named Tornado.

Caseley, Judith. (1994). *Dear Annie*. New York: HarperTrophy.
   Letter-writing may be out of style, but this happy chronicle of mail between Annie and her grandfather may reverse the trend.

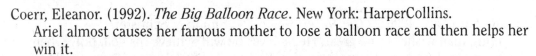

Clements, Andrew. (1991). *Big Al*. New York: Simon & Schuster.
   A big, ugly fish has trouble making the friends he longs for because of his appearance—until the day his scary appearance saves them all from a fisherman's net.

Coerr, Eleanor. (1992). *The Big Balloon Race*. New York: HarperCollins.
   Ariel almost causes her famous mother to lose a balloon race and then helps her win it.

Cohen, Miriam. (1994). *Second-Grade Friends Again!* New York: Scholastic.
   When Jacob says something terrible to Honey after she hits a home run, even Jacob's best friend will not talk to him and he wishes he could take back what he said to Honey.

Cowley, Joy. (1999). *Agapanthus Hum and the Eyeglasses*. New York: Philomel.
   Agapanthus Hum is a whirlwind. She hums, she cartwheels, and she is always running around. Now that Agapanthus has eyeglasses, her parents want her to be careful.

Cresswell, Helen. (1993). *Posy Bates, Again!* New York: Random House.
   Posy Bates and her stray dog, Buggins, seem to get into nothing but mischief no matter how good their intentions are.

Cummings, Pat. (1999). *Clean Your Room, Harvey Moon*. Indiana: Pearson Books.
   Harvey Moon is just settling in to watch his favorite Saturday morning cartoon when his mother tells him to clean his room.

Cushman, Doug. (1992). *Aunt Eater's Mystery Vacation*. New York: HarperCollins.
   A mystery-loving anteater has a chance to solve several mysteries during her vacation at the Hotel Bathwater.

Dadey, Debbie. (1992). *Leprechauns Don't Play Basketball*. New York: Scholastic.
   Melody is certain that her new basketball coach, Mr. O'Grady, is a leprechaun, and soon she and the other children are keeping an eye on him.

Dalgliesh, Alice. (1987). *The Courage of Sarah Noble*. Toronto: Atheneum Books.
   When Sarah Noble was eight years old she had her great adventure—going with her father into the wilds of Connecticut to cook for him while he built a house.

Unit 6

Recommended Books for Second Grade

Danzinger, Paula. (1994). *Amber Brown Is Not a Crayon*. New York: Putnam Publishing Group.
She may not be a crayon, but Amber Brown is certainly blue over the fact that her best friend, Justin Daniels, is moving away.

Demuth, Patricia. (1991). *The Ornery Morning*. New York: Penguin Books.
Farmer Bill wakes up late one morning to find that all of his animals, from the rooster to the cat, refuse to do any work.

dePaola, Tomie. (1979). *Strega Nona*. New York: Aladdin Books.
This Grandma Witch in Italy teaches Big Anthony (her big lug of an assistant) a few lessons in cooking pasta and about life.

dePaola, Tomie. (1996). *Tony's Bread*. New York: Putnam Publishing Group.
A baker loses his daughter but gains a bakery in the grand city of Milano after meeting a determined nobleman and baking a unique loaf of bread.

Ernst, Laura. (1992). *Walter's Tail*. New Jersey: Bradbury Press.
The disasters caused by Walter's wagging tail make him and his owner unwelcome in town until Walter wags a heroic rescue.

Evans, Richard Paul. (2001). *The Tower*. New York: Simon & Schuster.
A young man wishes to be great. He believes he will achieve his goal only when everyone in the village looks up to him. So he constructs a wooden tower that reaches to the clouds, but soon he becomes lonely.

Flack, Marjorie. (1983). *The Story About Ping*. New York: Viking.
The tale of a little duck alone on the Yangtze River is a classic.

Fox, Mem. (1989). *Night Noises*. San Diego: Gulliver Books.
As elderly Lily Laceby dozes by the fire, her dog, Butch Aggie, becomes alarmed by strange noises outside.

Gackenbach, Dick. (1984). *King Wacky*. New York: Knopf Books for Young Readers.
Born with his head on backwards, King Wacky proceeds to do everything in a backward way.

Gackenbach, Dick. (1987). *Mag the Magnificent*. New York: Clarion Books.
When a small boy puts on his Indian suit, magic happens.

Greene, Constance. (1995). *Odds on Oliver*. New York: Penguin Books.
Oliver's attempt to be a hero result in such humorous disasters as going up a tree to rescue a cat and getting stuck himself.

Griffith, Helen. (1997). *Alex and the Cat*. New York: Greenwillow.
The adventures of Alex the dog, who wants to be treated like the family cat, tries to restore a baby bird to a robin's nest, and attempts to migrate to avoid the winter snow.

Guest, Elissa Haden. (2002). *Iris and Walter: The Sleepover*. San Diego: Gulliver Books.
Iris cannot wait to have her first sleepover at her best friend Walter's house.

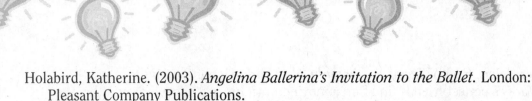

Holabird, Katherine. (2003). *Angelina Ballerina's Invitation to the Ballet*. London: Pleasant Company Publications.
In the story, Angelina finds a large envelope containing two tickets to see Serena Silvertail perform with the Royal Ballet. But each time she asks a friend to attend with her, one of them has other plans!

Horowitz, Ruth. (2001). *Breakout at the Bug Lab*. New York: Dial Books.
What happens when the bug lab your mom works in is having a celebration with TV cameras and big shots—and there's a giant hissing cockroach named Max on the loose?

Howe, James. (1987). *The Day the Teacher Went Bananas*. London: Puffin Books.
A class's new teacher, who leads the children in a number of very popular activities, turns out to be a gorilla.

Howe, James. (1999). *Pinky and Rex*. New York: Aladdin.
Rex thinks his trip to the museum with Pinky is about to be ruined when his grumpy sister, Amanda, decides to join in.

Hutchins, Pat. (1982). *Don't Forget the Bacon*. London: Puffin Books.
A jubilant story about a boy and his attempts to remember the items on his mother's shopping list.

Hutchins, Pat. (1988). *The Very Worst Monster*. New York: HarperTrophy.
Hazel sets out to prove that she, not her baby brother, is the worst monster anywhere.

Kellogg, Steven. (1982). *Pinkerton, Behave*. London: Puffin Books.
His behavior may be rather unconventional, but Pinkerton the dog proves it doesn't really matter.

Kellogg, Steven. (2002). *A Rose for Pinkerton*. London: Puffin Books.
Pinkerton's family decides he needs a friend, but is a cat named Rose really suitable?

Kline, Suzy. (1990). *Horrible Harry in Room 2B*. London: Puffin Books.
Doug discovers that though being Harry's best friend in Miss Mackle's second grade class isn't always easy, as Harry likes to do horrible things, it is often a lot of fun.

Krensky, Stephen. (1993). *Lionel at Large*. London: Puffin Books.
This story includes situations all children go through: eating vegetables (or choosing not to); going to the doctor for a shot; fear of (your sister's) pet snakes; worries about the arrival of a new baby (in your best friend's family); and sleeping away from home for the first time.

Kwitz, Mary. (1997). *Gumshoe Goose, Private Eye*. London: Puffin Books.
Detective Ellery Goose helps his father Inspector Goose solve the case of the hungry kidnapper.

Lawston, Lisa. (1998). *A Pair of Red Sneakers*. New York: Viking Books.
In sometimes-bumpy rhyme, the boy describes his more and more imaginative specifications for sneakers that are equipped to do everything he would like them to do.

Unit 6

Recommended Books for Second Grade

Lester Helen. (1990). *Tacky the Penguin*. New York: Houghton Mifflin.
Tacky's perfect friends find him annoying until his odd behavior saves the day.

Levinson, Nancy. (1992). *Snowshoe Thompson*. New York: HarperCollins.
Danny wishes his dad would come home from Nevada for Christmas and writes him a letter to tell him so

Lexau, Joan. (1997). *Striped Ice Cream*. New York: Scholastic Press.
Becky's hard-working mama and four older brothers and sisters try to surprise her on her eighth birthday.

Leuck, Laura. (2002). *My Monster Mama Loves Me So*. New York: HarperTrophy.
At once tender and funny, this monster bedtime story is guaranteed to generate giggles, tickles, and plenty of monster hugs.

Lindgren, Astrid. (2001). *Lotta on Troublemaker Street*. New York: Aladdin Books.
Angry because everyone at home is so mean, Lotta takes her favorite toy and goes to live in a neighbor's attic.

Little, Jean. (1998). *Emma's Magic Winter*. New York: HarperCollins.
An enjoyable, gentle story about making friends and overcoming fears.

Littledale, Freya. (1987). *The Magic Fish*. New York: Scholastic Press.
A greedy fisherman's wife is granted every wish but can't find happiness.

Marshall, James. (1995). *Fox on the Job*. London: Puffin Books.
Fox tries to earn the money for a new bicycle in several different jobs.

Martin, Bill, Jr. (1996). *Old Devil Wind*. New York: Voyager Books.
On a dark and stormy night one object after another joins in making eerie noises in the old house.

Miller, Sara. (2001). *Three Stories You Can Read to Your Dog*. Boston, MA: Houghton Mifflin Co.
Stories addressed to dogs and written from a dog's point of view, featuring such topics as a burglar, bones, and running free.

Mills, Claudia. (2002). *Gus and Grandpa and Show-and-Tell*. New York: Sunburst.
Everything else about school is good, but for some reason Ryan Mason seems to outdo everyone else when it's his turn to show-and-tell.

Mozelle, Shirley. (1995). *Zack's Alligator*. New York: HarperTrophy.
Zack's alligator, Bridget, is only an alligator key chain when she arrives, but when Zack waters her, Bridget becomes a lively, full-sized gator.

Mosel, Arlene. (1968). *Tiki Tiki Tembo*. New York: Henry Holt & Company.
In this folktale, help is slow in coming when a Chinese boy falls into a well, since the boy's long and difficult name must be pronounced in full.

Munsch, Robert. (1980). *Paper Bag Princess*. Toronto: Annick Press.
The Princess Elizabeth is slated to marry Prince Ronald when a dragon attacks the castle and kidnaps Ronald.

Nolen, Jerdine. (2002). *Raising Dragons.* New York: Voyager Books.
Jerdine Nolen and Elise Primavera team up for the unforgettable story of a young girl and her best friend…a dragon.

Novak, Matt. (1994). *Mouse TV.* New York: Orchard Books.
The mouse family can't agree on what to watch on TV.

Paterson, Katherine. (1993). *Smallest Cow in the World.* New York: HarperCollins.
Rosie is the meanest cow in the world—and Marvin's best friend. When his family moves to a new farm, Marvin is sad and lonely…until he finds Rosie again.

Peet, Bill. (1982). *Big Bad Bruce.* Boston, MA: Houghton Mifflin Co.
Bruce, a bear bully, never picks on anyone his own size until he is diminished in more ways than one by a small but very independent witch.

Perlman, Janet. (1996). *The Emperor Penguin's New Clothes.* New York: Viking Books.
Two scoundrels come into town saying they can make cloth that can't be seen by the dishonest and simpleminded when they really can't do anything of the sort. They trick the emperor into buying a suit of clothes of this imaginary cloth.

Polacco, Patricia. (1992). *Chicken Sunday.* New York: Philomel.
After being initiated into a neighbor's family by a solemn backyard ceremony, a young Russian American girl and her African American brothers determine to buy their gramma Eula a beautiful Easter hat.

Platt, Kin. (1992). *Big Max.* New York: HarperCollins.
Big Max, the world's greatest detective, helps a king find his missing elephant.

Reid, Margarette. (1990). *The Button Box.* New York: Dutton Books.
An imaginative little boy explores the many pleasures that can be found in—and made from—his grandmother's button box.

Rylant, Cynthia. (1987). *Henry and Mudge.* New York: Simon & Schuster.
Henry, feeling lonely on a street without any other children, finds companionship and love with a big dog named Mudge.

Rylant, Cynthia. (2002). *Mr. Putter and Tabby Catch the Cold.* New York: Harcourt Children's Books.
Mr. Putter is feeling a bit—Achoo!—under the weather. And as everyone knows, it's no fun to be old with a cold. Luckily, Mrs. Teaberry and her good dog, Zeke, know just what to do to help Mr. Putter feel better.

Rylant, Cynthia. (2001). *Poppleton in Winter.* Arizona: Blue Sky Press.
Poppleton's fans will need no urging to join in his concern over fallen icicles, his exacting venture into the art of sculpture, and the joys of a surprise birthday party catered by his loving friends.

Schoenherr, John. (1991). *The Bear.* New York: HarperCollins.
Bear awakens one morning to find his mother gone; thus begins this narrative of the coming of age of a wild animal.

Scieszka, Jon. (2002) *The Stinky Cheese Man and Other Fairly Stupid Tales*. New York: Viking Books.
This includes the Really Ugly Duckling, Cinderumpelstiltskin, Little Red Running Shorts, Chicken Licken, and the rest of the hilarious cast of characters loosely based on classic fairy tales.

Scieszka, Jon. (1995). *The True Story of the Three Little Pigs*. New York: Dutton Books.
At long last, the reader has a chance to look past the biased press and (undoubtedly) stacked juries to hear the true story from the lips of Mr. Alexander T. Wolf himself about what really happened to the three little pigs.

Sharmat, Marjorie. (1980). *Gila Monsters Meet You at the Airport*. New York: Simon & Schuster.
A New York City boy's preconceived ideas of life in the West make him very apprehensive about the family's move there.

Sharmat Marjorie. (1984). *Nate the Great and the Snowy Trail*. Indiana: Pearson Books.
When Rosamond's birthday gift for Nate disappears from her sled, the boy detective decides to unravel the mystery.

Sharmat, Mitchell. (1987). *Gregory, the Terrible Eater*. New York: Dial Books.
A very picky eater, Gregory the goat refuses the usual goat diet staples of shoes and tincans in favor of fruits, vegetables, eggs, and orange juice

Smallcomb, Pam. (2002). *Camp Buccaneer*. New York: Simon & Schuster.
Marlon is expecting a boring summer at the cabin her parents have rented for the season—no friends, no adventures, and no fun. That is, until she checks out the last cabin on the lake where she meets three very raffish old salts, proprietors of Camp Buccaneer.

Steig, William. (1971). *Amos & Boris*. New York: Farrar, Straus and Giroux.
Amos the mouse and Boris the whale: a devoted pair of friends with nothing at all in common, except good hearts and a willingness to help their fellow mammal.

Steig, William. (1976). *The Amazing Bone*. New York: Farrar, Straus and Giroux.
Can Pearl, a pig, and her new friend, a small talking bone, outwit a band of robbers and a hungry fox?

Taber, Anthony. (1993). *The Boy Who Stopped Time*. New York: Margaret K. McElderry.
No matter how much fun he is having, Julian has to go to bed when the clock chimes 7:30. So he stops it, making everyone and everything else frozen and motionless in time.

Talbot, John. (1992). *Pins and Needles*. New York: Penguin Books.
Feeling a tingly "pins and needles" sensation in his trunk from having slept on it all night, Jean Pierre the elephant tries different remedies to cure himself.

Thaler, Mike. (1989). *The Teacher from the Black Lagoon*. New York: Scholastic.
On the first day of school, a young boy expects only the worst when he discovers
that his new teacher is the "monstrous" Mrs. Green.

Thomas, Shelley Moore. (2002). *Get Well, Good Knight*. New York: Dutton Books.
The much-heralded Good Knight and his three little dragons are back—only this
time the dragons are sick in bed. They need the Good Knight to come to the
rescue again and tend to their sniffy, drippy noses and fevery heads.

Turner Ann. (1995). *Dust for Dinner*. New York: HarperCollins.
Jake and Maggy lived on a farm where they loved to sing and dance to the music
from Mama's radio. Then terrible dust storms came and ruined the land.

Waber, Bernard. (1973). *The House on 88th Street*. New York: Houghton Mifflin.
The first book in the Lyle series, this tells the story of how the Primms found Lyle
the crocodile in the bathtub of their new home.

Wallace-Brodeur, Ruth. (1989). *Stories from the Big Chair*. New York: Margaret K.
McElderry Books.
Molly tells her parents seven stories about herself and her younger sister,
recounting one story for each day of the week.

Willey, Margaret. (2004). *Clever Beatrice*. New York: Aladdin Books.
Can a very little girl beat a very large giant in feats of strength?

Williams, Linda. (1996). *The Little Old Lady Who Was Not Afraid of Anything*. New
York: HarperCollins.
In this just-spooky-enough tale, an old lady puts to good use some animated
objects that are trying to frighten her.

Wood, Audrey. (1996). *Elbert's Bad Word*. New York: Voyager Books.
A bad word, spoken by a small boy at a fashionable garden party, creates havoc,
and the child, Elbert, gets his mouth scrubbed out with soap.

Wood, Audrey. (2000). *Jubal's Wish*. New York: Blue Sky Press.
It is such a glorious day that Jubal Bullfrog asks Gerdy Toad and Captain Dalbert
Lizard to join him on a picnic.

Ziefert, Harriet. (1986). *A New Coat for Anna*. New York: Knopf Books for Young
Readers.
Even though there is no money, Anna's mother finds a way to make Anna a badly
needed winter coat.

Zion, Gene. (1965). *Harry by the Sea*. New York: HarperCollins.
Harry, a friendly little dog on a visit to the seashore, is mistaken for a sea serpent
when a big wave covers him with seaweed.

Zolotow, Charlotte. (1977). *Mr. Rabbit and the Lovely Present*. New York:
HarperTrophy.
Mr. Rabbit helps a little girl find a lovely present for her mother, who is especially
fond of red, yellow, green, and blue.

Unit 7

Unit 7
Science Literature Activities

Many science programs are designed to give children a large quantity of information, have them memorize that data, and then ask them to recall the information on various assessment instruments. That type of instruction does not allow for the active involvement of students in their own learning, nor does it allow children opportunities to think creatively about what they are learning.

My own experiences as a teacher have taught me that when students, no matter what their abilities or interests, are provided with opportunities to manipulate information in productive ways, learning becomes much more meaningful. I refer to this as a process approach to learning, an approach that allows youngsters to make decisions and solve problems. In so doing, students get a sense that learning is much more than the commission of facts to memory.

A literature-based approach to science is a combination of children's literature, "hands-on, minds-on" projects, and guided instruction used to expand a science concept or idea. A literature-based approach to science offers students a realistic arena within which they can investigate science concepts through an active engagement with text. It is a process approach to learning of the highest magnitude.

This section provides you with relevant and realistic teaching opportunities using Comprehension Circles in concert with science literature. You will discover that Comprehension Circles and quality-based science literature open up innumerable possibilities for instruction and for learning. I hope you will also discover that Comprehension Circles can be a positive element in science as well as each and every dimension of your elementary curriculum.

Around One Cactus: Owls, Bats and Leaping Rats
by
Anthony D. Fredericks
(Nevada City, CA: Dawn Publications, 2003)

Summary **T**his dynamically illustrated book takes children into the heart of the Sonoran Desert to watch the "happenings" that take place in and around a single Saguaro cactus. The young boy in the story doesn't think there is much going on at the cactus and so, near the end of the day, he leaves. But, that's when all the activity begins!

Component	Strategies and Activities	Instruction
Engagement (Schema)	• Gather students together as a whole class or a smaller group. • Present the theme or topic of a forthcoming book. • Talk about the topic. • Ask questions about the theme or topic. • Invite students to share **relevant** experiences (keep the conversation <u>focused</u>). • Talk about any misperceptions or misconceptions. • Provide illustrations or photos that illuminate the theme or concept. • Share (as necessary) other AV resources that stimulate schema development. • Show the book cover and encourage discussion about its topic or theme. • Draw "straight-line" connections between what youngsters know and the book's main idea. • Link the book to a similar story/book.	Provide students with a small cactus (available at most nurseries or garden supply centers). Tell them that the spines on the cactus are very sharp and that they should not touch them. Provide an extended period of time for students to observe the cactus. Then, ask youngsters to share some of their observations with you. You may wish to record their observations on the chalkboard. These can be recorded inside an oversized outline of a Saguaro cactus previously drawn on the board. Afterward, take youngsters on a "picture walk" through the book. Point out the fact that a cactus, although it may be dangerous for humans, is a home for many animals that live in the desert.
Modeling	• Introduce the book. • Vocalize your purpose for reading.	Show students the cover of the book. Talk about the title. Tell students that when you see the

Unit

7

Around One Cactus: Owls, Bats and Leaping Rats

Component	Strategies and Activities	Instruction
Modeling *(continued)*	• Read and discuss the title. • Talk about illustrations. • Do a "mental walk" through the book. • Demonstrate a talk-aloud (focused on a specific strategy). • Demonstrate a think-aloud (focused on a specific strategy). • Provide multiple opportunities for students to "see" inside your head.	title *Around One Cactus*, you begin to think of all the things that might live around one cactus. You think about some of the animals and you think about some of the plants. The title makes you think that there may be many things that live around a cactus. Tell youngsters that when you read this book you will have to pay attention to all the important animals and all the important plants that might be near a cactus plant. In other words, because this story is a true story, you want to pay close attention to the important details of the book.
Read Aloud	• Read the selected book out loud to children. • Use expression and intonation as appropriate. • Consider using a big book. • Occasionally "track" the print with your finger or a pointer. • Occasionally use a Shared Book experience with children. • Consider periodic stops (as necessary) to model your thinking. • Demonstrate your enthusiasm for the book while reading.	Read the book to the end of the page that describes the long-nosed bat. (The pages are unnumbered.) Tell students that you have learned about three important animals so far in the book. You have learned about a rat, an owl, and a long-nosed bat. Tell students that these are important animals in the book because the author used lots of special words to tell about those creatures.
Guided Instruction	• Teacher and students return to text. • Conduct class/group reading conference. • Identify one specific comprehension strategy. • Clarify reading strategy in "kid terms." • Demonstrate the strategy within the context of the book. • Re-model (as necessary) your use of the strategy in that book. • Invite youngsters to "try out" the strategy (by using their own	Tell students that you will continue reading the book and that everyone should listen carefully for any other special creatures that might appear. Remind students that they are listening for "Important Details." Stop at the end of the next two two-page spreads (rattlesnake, scorpions). Inform students that you now know another important detail in the book (due to the number of words used by the author to

Component	Strategies and Activities	Instruction
Guided Instruction (*continued*)	talk-about or think-about conversations). • Encourage retellings. • Discuss transfer of strategy. • Pose open-ended questions. • Reread a portion of the book (as necessary) and talk about how the strategy can be used there. • Provide positive feedback.	describe each creature). Invite them to listen to the next two two-page spreads and to help you identify the selected creatures on each spread (foxes, Gila monster). Finish reading the last page.
Synthesize and Summarize	• Invite children to talk about what they learned. • Encourage active discussion among all class/group members. • Use open-ended questions. • Students may need thinking time before responding. • Help youngsters focus on 1 or 2 significant points. • Invite students to reflect on the modeling you did throughout the lesson. • Recap (in kid terms) the strategy used.	Invite children to think about the various creatures they heard of in this book. Ask them to tell you about some of the thinking you did to figure out the important details in the story. (This is not a memory test. Rather, the emphasis is on significant details identified during reading, not remembered after reading.) Invite selected children to retell the story in their own words.

Happy Birth Day!
by
Robie H. Harris
(Cambridge, MA: Candlewick Press, 1996)

Summary With affection and clarity, the author paints a beautiful picture of the day her own child was born, including the moments just prior to and immediately after the birth. The reader is drawn into one of nature's great events—the birth process. For many children, birth is an event of enormous significance, and both author and illustrator have combined all the wonder, mystery, and joy into a book that will be treasured by teachers and students alike.

Component	Strategies and Activities	Instruction
Engagement (Schema)	• Gather students together as a whole class or a smaller group. • Present the theme or topic of a forthcoming book. • Talk about the topic. • Ask questions about the theme or topic. • Invite students to share **relevant** experiences (keep the conversation <u>focused</u>). • Talk about any misperceptions or misconceptions. • Provide illustrations or photos that illuminate the theme or concept. • Share (as necessary) other AV resources that stimulate schema development. • Show the book cover and encourage discussion about its topic or theme. • Draw "straight-line" connections between what youngsters know and the book's main idea. • Link the book to a similar story/book.	Create a special bulletin board in the classroom. Invite students to bring a photo of themselves just after they were born (if possible). Be sure to bring a photo of yourself as a baby as well. Post all of the photos on the bulletin board. Engage students in a conversation about the events that might take place before, during, and after a baby is born. You may wish to create a master list of suggested events and record those on the chalkboard. Keep the discussion focused on the days and hours just prior to a birth as well as the days and hours just after a birth. If you have children, you may wish to share some of the events that took place prior to and during the birth of one or more of your children.
Modeling	• Introduce the book. • Vocalize your purpose for reading. • Read and discuss the title. • Talk about illustrations. • Do a "mental walk" through the book. • Demonstrate a talk-aloud (focused on a specific strategy). • Demonstrate a think-aloud (focused on a specific strategy). • Provide multiple opportunities for students to "see" inside your head.	Take children on a "book walk" through the pages of this book. Show the pages one by one and do a talk-aloud as you do. Focus on one or two specific details for each illustration. Highlight some of the things you see happening on each two-page spread (without reading the text). Share with students some of the specific details you see on each spread. When you have completed the "walk," summarize the major events/details in a retelling related only to the illustrations. Let students know that you are getting an idea about some of the significant events of the story by just looking at all the illustrations before you actually

Component	Strategies and Activities	Instruction
Modeling *(continued)*		read the book. You may wish to list your "illustration details" on the chalkboard for future reference.
Read Aloud	• Read the selected book out loud to children. • Use expression and intonation as appropriate. • Consider using a big book. • Occasionally "track" the print with your finger or a pointer. • Occasionally use a Shared Book experience with children. • Consider periodic stops (as necessary) to model your thinking. • Demonstrate your enthusiasm for the book while reading.	Read the book aloud to students in two-page spreads. After reading a two-page spread, talk with students about the details that are in the text. As appropriate, spend time talking about the details you determined from the "book walk" and how they may or may not have been supported by the details you discovered as you read the text.
Guided Instruction	• Teacher and students return to text. • Conduct class/group reading conference. • Identify one specific comprehension strategy. • Clarify reading strategy in "kid terms." • Demonstrate the strategy within the context of the book. • Re-model (as necessary) your use of the strategy in that book. • Invite youngsters to "try out" the strategy (by using their own talk-about or think-about conversations). • Encourage retellings. • Discuss transfer of strategy. • Pose open-ended questions. • Reread a portion of the book (as necessary) and talk about how the strategy can be used there. • Provide positive feedback.	Continue the process above, reading each two-page spread and comparing the information discovered in the text with the information previously determined through the illustrations. After each two-page spread, take time to discuss any changes you need to make when comparing illustrative details with textual details. Make sure students understand that this is a process that readers do all the time. They change, modify, and compare information gathered from illustrations with information gathered from the text.
Synthesize and Summarize	• Invite children to talk about what they learned. • Encourage active discussion among all class/group members.	Model for students a think-aloud summary that you might do. Talk out loud about the thought processes that you

Component	Strategies and Activities	Instruction
Synthesize and Summarize *(continued)*	• Use open-ended questions. • Students may need thinking time before responding. • Help youngsters focus on 1 or 2 significant points. • Invite students to reflect on the modeling you did throughout the lesson. • Recap (in kid terms) the strategy used.	might use in reviewing this book for yourself. Do some talk-alouds about specific illustrative details as compared with some specific textual details. Provide students with plenty of opportunities to "see" inside your head as you attempt to reach a satisfactory retelling of important details through illustrative-textual comparisons.

In the Small, Small Pond
by
Denise Fleming
(New York: Henry Holt and Company, 1993)

Summary In a small, small pond there is an incredible variety of creatures. From large to small and from swimming to leaping, these creatures make a delightful range of noises. Punctuated with active verbs and colorful language, this book begs to be read aloud to youngsters. They will want to be part of this engaging and imaginatively illustrated book many times.

Mental Imagery

Say the following to youngsters: *"Close your eyes and imagine that you are a small fish. Imagine that you live in a pond. Paint a picture in your head of a very small pond. Put yourself into that pond. Turn yourself into a fish and put yourself into the pond. Look around you. The water is clear and blue. You can see some other fish swimming nearby. You can see a frog on a nearby lily pad. You can see some ducks resting on top of the water. Look down. You can see some grass growing on the bottom of the pond. There are lots of animals in your pond. But, you are a fish and you just swim around in your pond. See yourself swimming around and around in your small pond. You are very happy to be there. You have lots of friends. There are many things to see. Now, slowly open your eyes. We are now going to listen to a story about some animals that also live in a small, small pond. Listen carefully and see if the animals in this story are similar to the animals you had in the picture in your mind."*

Questioning

Model for students some questions you may ask yourself as you read this book. These may include some of the following:

- "Why am I reading this?"

- "Is this similar to anything I have read before?"

- "Is this interesting to me?"

- "What new things am I learning?"

- "Can I retell the story to someone else?"

- "Is there something else I'd like to learn about the pond?"

Talk about how you would answer some of your own questions.

Important Information

Provide youngsters with a large sheet of newsprint on which you have drawn an outline of a pond. Have a collection of construction paper animals in a large box. Read the book to students a second time. Stop every so often and reach into the box. Select an animal mentioned in the story and tape it inside the outline of the pond. After the page that describes the herons (The pages are unnumbered.), tell students that they will now select a construction paper animal from the box and tape it inside the "pond" as it is mentioned in the story. After this reading, spend time discussing the important "details" that were placed inside the pond outline.

Is This a House for Hermit Crab?
by
Megan McDonald
(New York: Orchard Books, 1990)

Summary Hermit crab needs a new shell. So, he takes a journey across the beach to look for a brand new home. He encounters adventures, mysteries, and a few surprises along the way. Youngsters will discover a delightful story that will engage them and demand their participation. The surprises are many and the illustrations are fascinating.

Predicting and Inferring

Beginning with the fourth page in this book (The pages are unnumbered.), the author poses a question on each succeeding page. The question is "Is this a house for hermit crab?" As you read the book to students, stop each time that question is asked. Model for students the thinking that is taking place in your head relative to any inferences and/or predictions. For example, when the hermit crab encounters the rock, you might say out loud to youngsters, *"Now I need to stop and think about this. I see that the hermit crab has found a rock. I'm looking at that rock and I'm thinking that the rock is bigger than the hermit crab. So, now I'm thinking that the rock might be a heavy rock—one that might be too heavy for hermit crab. Also, since this is the beginning of the book, I don't think that this rock will be the house that hermit crab is looking for."*

Repeat this metacognitive process for the next two events in the story (the rusty tin can and the piece of driftwood). Then, inform students that you would like for them to make their own predictions about hermit crab. Stop after reading the question ("Is this a house for hermit crab?") on the page with the plastic pail. Invite youngsters to make their own predictions. Ask them to discuss reasons why they think their predictions are appropriate. Continue with this process—stopping each time the basic question is asked—until the book is finished. Plan time to talk with students about the value of predictions in helping to understand a story.

Synthesizing and Summarizing

After reading the book to children, invite them to reflect on the modeling that you did. This can be done by reading the book one more time. Stop every so often and ask students to recall the thinking that either you or they did at specific points in the story. Again, focus on the "power" of predicting and inferring as necessary elements in our enjoyment and understanding of any story.

Is Your Mama a Llama?
by
Deborah Guarino
(New York: Scholastic, 1989)

Summary "Is your mama a llama?" Lloyd the baby llama asks various animals that he encounters. Each animal gives Lloyd some hints to help him and the reader guess who each animal's mother really is. But, it's his friend Llyn who finally leads Lloyd to the answer he most wants to hear.

Unit

7

Science
Literature
Activities

Predicting and Inferring

Model the types of predictions you might make as you read the story. Here are a few examples:

At the end of the fourth page, with the baby llama peering into the cave: *"Hmmm, I wonder what kind of animal is being talked about. I think there might be some clues in the words. They are talking about an animal that hangs by her feet. Hmmm, I wonder what kinds of animals do that. They are also talking about an animal that lives in a cave. Hmmm, I wonder what kinds of animals live in a cave? I guess I'll have to turn the page to find out."*

At the end of the eighth page, with the baby duck floating on the pond surface: *"Hmmm, I wonder what kind of animal is being talked about. I think there might be some clues in the words. They are talking about an animal that has a long neck. They are also talking about an animal that has white feathers and wings. Hmmm, I wonder what kind of animal has those features? Oh, look, maybe there's a clue in the word at the end of this sentence—the word is 'on.' Maybe the answer is a word that rhymes with 'on.' Let me read the next page to find out."*

At the end of the twelfth page, with the baby calf walking through the fence: *"Hmmm, I wonder what kind of animal is being talked about here. I think there might be some clues in the words. They are talking about an animal that eats grass and that says 'Moo.' And, I think there's another clue at the end of this sentence—the one that ends with the word 'now.' I think that the word on the next page is one that rhymes with 'now'…a word like 'cow.' Let me read the next page and find out."*

Synthesizing and Summarizing

Invite one or two students to retell the story. Ask them to recall as many animals (and their mothers) as possible. It is not necessary for youngsters to name all the animals, so you might want to focus on some of the most significant animals. Talk about why some animals and their mothers were more memorable than others. What helped in recalling the different animals? Was it the rhyming words? Was it the illustrations? Was it some of the funny things that happened? Discuss some of the factors that help in recalling specific events or creatures in the book.

 Teaching Comprehension in Grades 1–2

Under One Rock:
Bugs, Slugs and Other Ughs
by
Anthony D. Fredericks
(Nevada City, CA: Dawn Publications, 2001)

Summary In this creatively illustrated book, youngsters journey with a young boy as he lifts up a single rock to find an amazing collection of creatures that take up residence on and in the ground. Using a rhythmic verse, this book introduces children to some delightful inhabitants of this community of creatures.

Engagement (Schema)

Take children on a "walking field trip." Go outside and walk around the playground or along a path. Look for any flat stones or rocks. Invite students to stand around you as you lift up a rock. Ask them to note any and all creatures that may be living under the rock. As students make these discoveries, record their observations in a notebook (to be transcribed upon your return to the classroom). If possible, try to locate several rocks; you may need to do a preliminary search a day or two in advance of the "field trip." Invite children to note as many animals as possible. Upon returning to the classroom, construct a master list of "rock creatures" on the chalkboard. Plan sufficient time to talk about each creature as well as the entire community that typically lives under a rock.

Important Information

Post a large sheet of newsprint on a wall. List the following animals from the book in addition to the adjective that describes each one. Read the book one more time and ask students to listen carefully to the words that are used to tell about each animal. Invite students to contribute one more adjective for each creature. Invite students to suggest additional words from their own first-hand experiences (via the "field trip") with these animals.

Animal	Details
Earthworm	squiggly, _____
Ant	tiny, _____
Spider	8-legged, _____
Beetle	shiny, _____
Field cricket	noisy, _____
Millipede	crawly, _____
Slug	slimy, _____

Synthesize and Summarize

Provide students with a collection of illustrations and photographs of various animals (including some of the ones included in the book) cut from old magazines. Provide small groups with construction paper and paste. Invite each group to make a collage of the animals that were included in the book. Inform students that their collage is a summary of the important information (animals) they learned about in the story.

The Very Lonely Firefly
by
Eric Carle
(New York: Philomel, 1995

 **Summary** This is a book sure to light up any classroom! A very lonely firefly goes off to look for some companionship. Along the way it discovered a light bulb, a candle, a flashlight, a lantern, some animals, a car's headlights, and some fireworks. In the end, however, it found what it was looking for—and the results are sparkling!

Engagement (Schema)

Invite students to suggest a list of objects that make or create light. You may wish to "get the ball rolling" by suggesting things such as light bulbs, candles, and car headlights. As suggestions are made, record them on the chalkboard. Depending on the experiential background of students, you may also wish to generate an alternate list of animals that produce or create their own light. These would include fireflies, lightning bugs, certain types of squid, and some deep sea fish.

Teaching Comprehension in Grades 1–2

Predicting and Inferring

This is an excellent book to demonstrate the comprehension strategy of predicting and inferring. Begin by reading the first three pages out loud to students. In the middle of the third page, stop reading after the first sentence ("…saw a light and flew toward it."). Invite students to look at the accompanying illustration and to make a prediction as to the source of the light. Record their prediction on the chalkboard. Then, read the remainder of the page. If there was a "match" between the prediction and the text, place a check mark next to the prediction. Read the first sentence on the next page ("…and flew toward it."). Stop the reading and ask students to look at the illustration. Invite them to make a prediction about the source of the light. Record the prediction on the chalkboard. Finish reading the page. If the prediction was correct, place a check mark next to it on the chalkboard. Continue with this procedure through the remainder of the book. Plan time to talk about how the illustrations and text in a book help readers make predictions and confirm those predictions as they continue reading.

Recommended Science Literature for First and Second Grade

Aardena, Verna. (1993). *Bringing the Rain to Kapiti Plain.* London: Puffin Books.
A cumulative rhyme relating how Ki-pat brought rain to the drought-stricken Kapiti Plain.

Andreae, Giles. (2001). *Commotion in the Ocean.* New York: Orchard Books.
There's a curious commotion at the bottom of the ocean; I think we ought to go and take a look. You'll find every sort of creature that lives beneath the sea swimming through the pages of this book.

Andreae, Giles. (2001). *Rumble in the Jungle.* New York: Orchard Books.
There's a rumble in the jungle; there's a whisper in the trees; the animals are waking up and rustling the leaves!

Bash, Barbara. (2002). *Desert Giant: The World of the Saguaro Cactus.* San Francisco, CA: Sierra Club.
A story about the mighty saguaro cactus. It's a plant and an apartment house all rolled into one.

Berkes, Marianne. (2002). *Seashells by the Seashore.* Nevada City, CA: Dawn.
There's a lot of seashells at the seashore—some large, some small, some with a palette of colors…all wonderful!

Branley, Franklyn. (1999). *Flash, Crash, Rumble, and Roll.* New York: HarperTrophy.
Explains how and why a thunderstorm occurs and gives safety steps to follow when lightning is flashing.

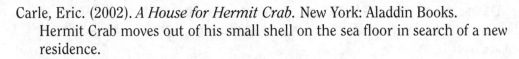

Carle, Eric. (2002). *A House for Hermit Crab*. New York: Aladdin Books.
Hermit Crab moves out of his small shell on the sea floor in search of a new residence.

Carle, Eric. (1991). *The Tiny Seed*. New York: Simon & Schuster.
Dazzling colorful collage illustrations and a simple but dramatic text tell the fascinating story of the life cycle of a flower in terms of the adventures of a tiny seed.

Cherry, Lynne. (1992). *A River Ran Wild*. San Diego: Gulliver Books.
Tells a story of restoration and renewal.

Cherry, Lynne. (1998). *The Great Kapok Tree: A Tale of the Amazon Rainforest*.
New York: Harcourt Big Books.
Exhausted from his labors, a man chopping down a great kapok tree in the Brazilian rain forest puts down his ax, and, as he sleeps, the animals who live in the tree plead with him not to destroy their world.

Cole, Joanna. (1990). *The Magic School Bus Lost in the Solar System*. New York: Scholastic.
On a special field trip in the magic school bus, Ms. Frizzle's class goes into outer space and visits each planet in the solar system.

Cowley, Joy. (2003). *Where Horses Run Free*. Honesdale, PA: Boyds Mills Press.
When people try to capture the wild horses, they are led to safety by the lead mare. But the danger is not over.

dePaola, Tomie. (1984). *The Cloud Book*. New York: Holiday House.
Introduces the ten most common types of clouds, the myths that have been inspired by their shapes, and what they can tell about coming weather changes.

Dorros, Arthur. (1991). *Animal Tracks*. New York: Scholastic Press.
Introduces the tracks and signs left by various animals, including the raccoon, duck, frog, black bear, and human.

Falwell, Cathryn. (2001). *Turtle Splash!* New York: Greenwillow.
There's a lot of action down at the pond. One by one, the animals are counting down until…

Fleming, Denise. (1991). *In the Tall, Tall Grass*. New York: Holt.
Captivating illustrations and a fast-paced text make this a read aloud book that will be shared again and again.

Fowler, Allan. (1998). *Inside an Ant Colony*. Connecticut: Children's Press.
Describes how these social insects live and work together in organized communities that are like bustling cities.

Fowler, Allan. (1995). *It Could Still Be a Butterfly*. Connecticut: Children's Press.
Describes how butterflies and caterpillars change from one form to another.

Frasier, Debra. (1991). *On the Day You Were Born*. San Diego, CA: Harcourt.
A most magical book that celebrates birth and all the special events surrounding it. A "must have" for any classroom!

Unit 7

Recommended
Science
Literature for
First and
Second Grade

Frasier, Debra. (1998). *Out of the Ocean*. San Diego, CA: Harcourt.
There's much to discover and much to find at the edge of the sea. Look, what do you see over there?

Fredericks, Anthony D. (2003). *Around One Cactus: Owls, Bats and Leaping Rats*. Nevada City, CA: Dawn.
A saguaro cactus is a haven for all sorts of creatures, most of whom come out at night to "play and prey."

Fredericks, Anthony D. (2002). *In One Tidepool: Crabs, Snails and Salty Tails*. Nevada City, CA: Dawn.
A young girl peers into a tidepool by the side of the ocean and finds a magical world of critters and creatures.

Fredericks, Anthony D. (2000). *Slugs*. Minneapolis, MN: Lerner Books.
To some they're disgusting. But these are amazing creatures that will awe and amaze the youngest of readers.

Fredericks, Anthony D. (2001). *Zebras*. Minneapolis, MN: Lerner Books.
Students will thrill to the incredible photographs and engaging text that fill the pages of this book.

Fredericks, Anthony D. (2001). *Under One Rock: Bugs, Slugs and Other Ughs*. Nevada City, CA: Dawn
A young boy takes a peek under a single rock and discovers an entire community of creatures living together.

Gelman, Rita. (1992). *Body Battles*. New York: Scholastic.
An introduction into the body's immune system.

Gibbons, Gail. (1987). *Dinosaurs*. New York: Holiday House.
Gibbons introduces one or two dinosaurs per page, providing a few brief bits of information about each creature, along with a pronunciation guide.

Guiberson, Brenda. (1996). *Into the Sea*. New York: Holt.
A tiny sea turtle climbs out of a hole in the sand, scurries down to the waiting waves and into a life full of adventures and dangers!

Harris, Robie. (2000). *Hi New Baby!* Cambridge, MA: Candlewick.
A new baby comes into the family, which means that someone is going to have to get used to his new brother.

Horowitz, Ruth. (2000). *Crab Moon*. Cambridge, MA: Candlewick.
One night in June, Daniel sees the extraordinary sight of hundreds of horseshoe crabs spawning on the beach.

Johnston, Tony. (2000). *The Barn Owls*. Watertown, MA: Charlesbridge Publishing.
Describes the lives of generations of owls, who have lived in a redwood barn for one hundred years.

Johnston, Tony. (2000). *Desert Song*. San Francisco, CA: Sierra Club.
The desert is filled with wonder, many animals, and lots of mysteries just waiting to be discovered.

Kalan, Robert. (1981). *Jump, Frog, Jump*. New York: Greenwillow.
A perfect cumulative tale that will have listeners singing along as the frog encounters one adventure after another.

Karas, G. Brian. (2002). *Atlantic*. New York: Putnam's.
Fun-filled illustrations along with a light text make this book a wonderful introduction to the Atlantic Ocean and life in the sea.

Lawrence, Elizabeth. (2002). *Busy, Buzzy Bees*. New York: Barron's Books.
Buzzy bee is busy. He visits every flower. Working hard from dawn to dusk, no matter what the hour.

Locker, Thomas. (1995). *Sky Tree*. New York: HarperCollins.
This wonderful tale about one year in the life of a tree celebrates the powers of observation and quiet discovery.

London, Jonathan. (2002). *Mustang Canyon*. Cambridge, MA: Candlewick.
A little mustang that begins its life in the harshness of a desert canyon has many adventures and many things to learn in order to survive.

London, Jonathan. (1999). *Baby Whale's Journey*. San Francisco, CA: Chronicle Books.
Life for a baby whale can be challenging. But with the help of his mother he is able to survive and thrive.

Miller, Debbie S. (1997). *Disappearing Lake*. New York: Walker.
The seasons change and so does one vernal lake in the heart of Alaska's Denali National Park.

Most, Bernard. (2000). *ABC T-Rex*. New York: Harcourt Children's Publishing.
T-Rex loves the alphabet so much, he wants to eat it up.

Pow, Tom. (2000). *Who Is the World For?* Cambridge, MA: Candlewick.
Baby animals all over the world ask who the world is for. Their parents provide the perfect answer every time.

Pringle, Laurence. (2003). *Come to the Ocean's Edge*. Honesdale, PA: Boyds Mills Press.
Twenty-four hours in the life of the seashore—there's lots to see and lots to hear. Take time and enjoy!

Ray, Mary. (2001). *Mud*. New York: Voyager Books.
An ode to muddy hands and feet, brown earth, and new grass.

Reigot, Betty. (1988). *A Book About Planets and Stars*. New York: Scholastic Books.
Allows children to explore the great outer space.

Rogers, Paul. (1990). *What Will the Weather Be Like Today?* New York: HarperCollins.
Animals and humans discuss, in rhyming verse, the possibilities of the day's weather.

Unit 7

Recommended Science Literature for First and Second Grade

Rose, Deborah. (2000). *Into the A, B, Sea: An Ocean Alphabet.* New York: Scholastic Books.
An eye-catching look at the diverse, colorful, and unique creatures that inhabit the world's oceans.

Ross, Tony. (2000). *Wash Your Hands!* New York: Dutton Books.
When the little princess hears about the germs and nasties living all around her, she understands the importance of washing her hands.

Sayre, April Pulley. (1998). *Home at Last: A Song of Migration.* New York: Holt.
Many animals migrate, and this wonderful book chronicles their journeys and adventures with sparse text and invigorating illustrations.

Sayre, April Pulley. (2001). *Dig, Wait, Listen.* New York: Greenwillow.
A spadefoot toad leads a solitary life buried under the desert sand. But, then the rains come and things really begin jumping!

Simon, Mary. (1998). *Drip! Drop!* New York: Concordia Publishing House.
A fun-loving book that explains the water cycle.

Wallace, Karen. (1996). *Imagine You Are a Tiger.* New York: Henry Holt.
Just imagine you are a tiger. What kind of adventures would you have? What kinds of things would you learn?

Ward, Helen. (2002). *Old Shell, New Shell.* Brookfield, CT: Millbrook.
Hermit Crab loves his shell, but there's a problem—he has grown too big for it.

Wilhelm, Hans. (2002). *I Love My Shadow!* New York: Scholastic Books.
A little dog has fun playing with his shadow at the beach, where he learns how it's made.

Unit 8
Social Studies Literature Activities

Traditional approaches to social studies instruction rely primarily on packaged materials, usually in the form of commercial social studies series and the ubiquitous teacher's manual and student textbooks. A major disadvantage is that students often perceive social studies as textbook-based or as taking place at a certain time in the school day. Literature-based instruction in social studies, however, provides students (and teachers) with an expanded curriculum that has no limits or boundaries. Compare some of the differences between literature-based instruction in social studies and more traditional forms of classroom organization such as textbooks and school/district curriculum guides:

Literature-based instruction facilitates the teaching of social studies as much as it does the learning of social studies. Equally important, the inclusion of literature within your primary social studies curriculum allows the integration of necessary and appropriate comprehension strategies through the use of Comprehension Circles. A quick review of the chart will reveal that the benefits of a literature-based social studies curriculum are also the benefits of explicit comprehension instruction via Comprehension Circles.

In this section you will discover a range of appropriate social studies literature for use in first- and second-grade classrooms. You will also discover intriguing ways in which this literature can be effectively used to promote, extend and underscore the importance of comprehension instruction above and beyond the reading curriculum.

Literature-Based Instruction	Textbook-Based Instruction
Facilitates responsible learning.	Students are told what to do, but not always why.
Encourages risk taking.	Emphasis is on the accumulation of "right" answers.
Promotes inquiry and reflection.	Teacher asks most of the questions and has most of the answers.
Breaks down artificial curricular boundaries; integrates the entire curriculum.	Segmented and divided curriculum is imposed.
Encourages collaborative and cooperative learning.	Students attempt to get high marks or good grades (vis-à-vis tests and exams).
Has teacher model appropriate learning behaviors.	Teacher dictates learning behaviors.
Encourages self-direction and individual inquiries.	Everyone must learn the same body of knowledge.
Helps students understand the WHY of what they're learning.	Students are told what to learn.
Allows students to make approximations of learning.	Students must learn absolutes.

Amazing Grace
by
Mary Hoffman
(New York: Dial, 1991)

Summary Grace loves stories, and she especially loves to act out stories. When there's an opportunity to play a part in the school play, *Peter Pan*, Grace wants to be the lead character. Everyone tells her she can't; but with the loving support of her mother and wise grandmother, Grace learns that she can be anything she wants to be, and the results are amazing.

Engagement (Schema)

Invite youngsters to create a personal list of special talents or qualities. Encourage children to each make up a separate list of items that they feel make each one of them special. Each child may wish to dictate or write his or her own list entitled "Amazing Me." These lists can be combined into one large list or chart to be posted in the classroom. You may elect to refer to the wide variety of traits that students have that make them very special. [NOTE: If youngsters are reluctant to share special traits or have difficulty suggesting personal qualities, you may wish to model by using yourself as an example. Another strategy would be to inform each child that she/he should think about three (or any other specified number) special traits to share with the class.]

Questioning

Model for students some of the questions that you might ask yourself as you read this story. You may wish to stop at designated parts of the story as you read it aloud to demonstrate how each question is related to a selected section of the book. Here are a few possible questions you may choose to model for students:

- "I wonder why nobody believed in Grace."

- "I wonder why the students thought that a girl couldn't be Peter Pan."

- "I wonder why the students thought that a black girl couldn't be Peter Pan."

- "I wonder if Grace's grandmother had something happen to her when she was young."

- "I wonder how the students will act towards Grace after the play."

- "I wonder if Grace will try out for other plays."

A Chair for My Mother
by
Vera B. Williams
(New York: Greenwillow, 1982)

Summary Josephine and her mother live simply. Her mother works as a waitress in a diner and Josephine helps her grandmother at home. They are all saving money to buy a new chair—something they've wanted for a long time. Then disaster strikes—a fire rages through their apartment. But, all is not lost. With the help of friends and family a new chair, a new place and a new life bring a most satisfactory conclusion to this endearing tale of hope and persistence.

Questioning

Model for students some of the questions you would ask yourself as you read this book. Do a think-aloud for students using some of the following examples:

- "Do I have any questions about this story before I read?"

- "What do I like about the cover of this book?"

- "What can I do if I don't understand something?"

- "Am I enjoying the story so far?"

- "Can I retell this story to someone else?"

- "Would I want to read another book like this?"

As you do an initial read-aloud, slip some of the questions above into the storytelling. Pause each time and allow students to "see inside your head" as you model each question and as you think about how you might respond to each one. For example, if you asked yourself (in a "talk-aloud"), *"What can I do if I don't understand something?"* you could make up the following response, *"Well, I guess if I don't understand something, I could continue reading and hope that the author gives me some more information. Or, maybe I could ask a friend to help me figure out what is going on in the story."* The scenarios don't have to be long, just illustrative of the thinking you might do as you ask and answer your own thought processes.

How to Make an Apple Pie and See the World
by
Marjorie Priceman
(New York: Knopf, 1994)

Summary From gathering cinnamon in the jungles of Sri Lanka to picking apples in Vermont orchards, the heroine of this book searches far and wide to locate all the necessary ingredients for the ideal apple pie. Along the way there are discoveries to be made and people to meet. In the end, she gathers all the ingredients and creates a wonderfully delicious concoction. Filled with whimsy and a light touch of humor, this is an ideal read-aloud for any primary classroom.

Engagement (Schema)

Obtain a map of the world and lay it on the floor of the classroom or on top of a large table. [NOTE: Do not use a pull-down wall map with young students. Many students in the primary grades, who have not yet fully developed their sense of spatial relationships, conceive of north as being "up" and south as being "down" as the result of pull-down maps. It is more proper (and spatially correct) for youngsters to use maps in a horizontal, rather than vertical, dimension.] Use the map to point out the United States, Canada, and Mexico. Point out the locations mentioned in the book. These include Italy, France, Sri Lanka (Madagascar), England, Jamaica, Vermont, and your home town.

Determining Important Information

Use the world map as before. On 3 x 5 index cards write the name of locations mentioned in the book. For each location, invite students to suggest the food item obtained from that location (as mentioned in the book). These cards can then be posted around the edge of the map. Read the book aloud again and stop each time a food/location is mentioned. Invite students to point to the appropriate index card as the items are shared in the book.

The Island-Below-the-Star
by
James Rumford
(Boston: Houghton Mifflin, 1998)

Summary **A** magical tale with rich, dynamic illustrations, this story tells of five brothers and their journey across the vastness of the Pacific Ocean in search of the Island-Below-the-Star—Hawaii. Understated watercolors and a compelling text highlight this book about adventure, brotherly love, and the importance of people working together for a common goal. This story will be told and retold many times.

Component	Strategies and Activities	Instruction
Engagement (Schema)	• Gather students together as a whole class or a smaller group. • Present the theme or topic of a forthcoming book. • Talk about the topic. • Ask questions about the theme or topic. • Invite students to share **relevant** experiences (keep the conversation <u>focused</u>). • Talk about any misperceptions or misconceptions. • Provide illustrations or photos that illuminate the theme or concept. • Share (as necessary) other AV resources that stimulate schema development. • Show the book cover and encourage discussion about its topic or theme. • Draw "straight-line" connections between what youngsters know and the book's main idea. • Link the book to a similar story/book.	Plan an open-ended discussion with children about selected times when they have taken a trip, journey, or vacation. Keep the conversation focused and relevant. You may wish to guide the discussion with some focused questions such as: "What did you have to take on your trip?" "How long did it take to plan the trip?" "Did the whole family participate in putting the trip together?" It is important to keep the conversation focused on the planning and execution of the trip (not what they saw, how they felt, souvenirs they purchased, etc.).
Modeling	• Introduce the book. • Vocalize your purpose for reading.	Tell youngsters that whenever you read a story, you are always asking questions of yourself.

Unit

8

**The Island-
Below-the-Star**

Component	Strategies and Activities	Instruction
Modeling *(continued)*	• Read and discuss the title. • Talk about illustrations. • Do a "mental walk" through the book. • Demonstrate a talk-aloud (focused on a specific strategy). • Demonstrate a think-aloud (focused on a specific strategy). • Provide multiple opportunities for students to "see" inside your head.	These questions help you look for information and they help you understand the story better. Say to the students, *"I have questions about this story as I read it. I'm going to read part of the story to you and let you 'see' inside my head."* Read the book from the beginning to the bottom of the page ending with "The brothers left just before dawn." *"Now, as I read this story, here are the questions that came into my head: I wonder why the brothers decided to sail to the bright star? I wonder what they thought they would find under the star. I wonder if they were scared. I wonder if they had ever taken any long journeys before? I wonder how long they thought their trip would take. These are some questions I might ask."*
Read Aloud	• Read the selected book out loud to children. • Use expression and intonation as appropriate. • Consider using a big book. • Occasionally "track" the print with your finger or a pointer. • Occasionally use a Shared Book experience with children. • Consider periodic stops (as necessary) to model your thinking. • Demonstrate your enthusiasm for the book while reading.	Demonstrate your enthusiasm for the book while reading. Say to the students, *"Now, I want you to think about some questions that you might like to ask yourself before we read the next part of the story. I'll record your questions on the chalkboard, and we'll leave them there as we share the next part of the story."* Solicit 4–5 questions from students and record them. Then continue reading the book to the bottom of the page ending with "...dear life as they rode out the storm."
Guided Instruction	• Teacher and students return to text. • Conduct class/group reading conference. • Identify one specific comprehension strategy.	Say to the children, *"Do you remember when I asked myself some questions before we read the story? I didn't find the answers to all of my questions in the book, but those questions*

Component	Strategies and Activities	Instruction
Guided Instruction *(continued)*	• Clarify reading strategy in "kid terms." • Demonstrate the strategy within the context of the book. • Re-model (as necessary) your use of the strategy in that book. • Invite youngsters to "try out" the strategy (by using their own talk-about or think-about conversations). • Encourage retellings. • Discuss transfer of strategy. • Pose open-ended questions. • Reread a portion of the book (as necessary) and talk about how the strategy can be used there. • Provide positive feedback.	*helped me look for information in the story and those questions helped me enjoy the story more. Well, did we discover some answers to one or more of the questions we had for the second part of the story? Maybe we did and maybe we didn't, but that's O.K. The important thing is that we asked some questions and then we thought about those questions and some possible answers as we continued reading the story."*
Synthesize and Summarize	• Invite children to talk about what they learned. • Encourage active discussion among all class/group members. • Use open-ended questions. • Students may need thinking time before responding. • Help youngsters focus on 1 or 2 significant points. • Invite students to reflect on the modeling you did throughout the lesson. • Recap (in kid terms) the strategy used.	Read the remainder of the book to students. Invite one or two students to do a brief and focused retelling of the story. Invite youngsters to review the questions posed throughout the story and to identify those that were answered within the context of the story and those that were not. Plan some time to talk about the fact that sometimes readers find all the answers to their questions as they read and sometimes they find only some of the answers. What is important is that questions were asked before reading and while reading.

The Summer My Father Was Ten
by
Pat Brisson
(Honesdale, PA: Boyds Mills Press, 1998)

Summary This is a touching story about trust and responsibility. It tells of the bond between an old man and a young boy—a boy who unwittingly destroys one of the most sacred things in the old man's life—his garden. With affecting prose and a delightful insight into the feelings of youngsters and the sensibilities of old men, the author weaves a timeless tale that will spark wonderful discussions in any classroom.

Engagement (Schema)

Invite youngsters to share specific instances in their lives when their feelings were hurt. As always, it is critical that this discussion remain sharp and focused. Don't allow it to stray into long-winded scenarios or historical dramas. Encourage students to share episodes, but inform them that these memories should be "short and sweet." You may wish to model by sharing a personal experience. For example, "I remember when I was seven and my sister called me "four eyes" when I got my first pair of glasses. I didn't like that." You may wish to inform students that they may relate no more than two sentences each. Ask students for permission to briefly record their experiences on the chalkboard.

Predicting and Inferring

Read the story to the students. Stop at the bottom of the page ending with "…my father turned and saw his neighbor." Invite students to predict what will happen next in the story. Record their predictions on the chalkboard. Then, invite students to create (as a whole class or as individuals) an imaginary diary entry as though they were taking on the role of Mr. Bellavista. How would he have recorded his perceptions or feelings about the tomato-throwing incident? How did he feel? What did he want to do with the boys? Encourage students to share their various diary entries with each other.

Synthesize and Summarize

Invite students to create a prequel or sequel to the story. What could have taken place before the story began? What could have happened after the story concluded? Encourage students to discuss differences or changes they might add to the story if the author had invited them to do so.

Tar Beach
by
Faith Ringgold
(New York: Crown, 1991)

Summary Cassie Lightfoot has a dream: to be free to go wherever she wants for the rest of her life. One night, up on "Tar Beach"— the rooftop of her family's Harlem apartment building—her dream comes true. The stars lift her up, and Cassie is flying. Magical artwork and a personally enriching story make this a book that will be shared again and again in any primary classroom.

Component	Strategies and Activities	Instruction
Engagement (Schema)	• Gather students together as a whole class or a smaller group. • Present the theme or topic of a forthcoming book. • Talk about the topic. • Ask questions about the theme or topic. • Invite students to share **relevant** experiences (keep the conversation <u>focused</u>). • Talk about any misperceptions or misconceptions. • Provide illustrations or photos that illuminate the theme or concept. • Share (as necessary) other AV resources that stimulate schema development. • Show the book cover and encourage discussion about its topic or theme. • Draw "straight-line" connections between what youngsters know and the book's main idea. • Link the book to a similar story/book.	Invite youngsters to observe or look for apartment buildings in your town, neighborhood, or nearby city. Ask students to note some of the details about those apartment buildings. They may want to look for the height of some buildings, how many apartments (estimate) are in a specific building, and how many families might live in an apartment building. Plan time to discuss both the similarities and differences in living in a "stand-alone" house as compared to an apartment building. Keep the conversation focused on exactly what they saw on their various "field trips." You may want to jot down some of their observations or thoughts on the chalkboard.
Modeling	• Introduce the book. • Vocalize your purpose for reading.	Model some questions that you might pose to yourself as you look at this book. Without

Unit

8

Tar Beach

Component	Strategies and Activities	Instruction
Modeling *(continued)*	• Read and discuss the title. • Talk about illustrations. • Do a "mental walk" through the book. • Demonstrate a talk-aloud (focused on a specific strategy). • Demonstrate a think-aloud (focused on a specific strategy). • Provide multiple opportunities for students to "see" inside your head.	reading the text, take students through a "book walk" and highlight some questions you would ask in your head as you look at just the pictures. Here are some examples: *"I wonder why people are having a party on the roof (cover)." "I wonder why the girl is flying." "I wonder why the man is standing over the water." "I wonder why there are small pictures at the bottom of each page." "I wonder why there is another party on the roof of the building."* and/or *"I wonder why the girl flies all the time."*
Read Aloud	• Read the selected book out loud to children. • Use expression and intonation as appropriate. • Consider using a big book. • Occasionally "track" the print with your finger or a pointer. • Occasionally use a Shared Book experience with children. • Consider periodic stops (as necessary) to model your thinking. • Demonstrate your enthusiasm for the book while reading.	Read the book from beginning to end to the class.
Guided Instruction	• Teacher and students return to text. • Conduct class/group reading conference. • Identify one specific comprehension strategy. • Clarify reading strategy in "kid terms." • Demonstrate the strategy within the context of the book. • Re-model (as necessary) your use of the strategy in that book. • Invite youngsters to "try out" the strategy (by using their own talk-about or think-about conversations). • Encourage retellings.	Reread the book to children. Stop periodically and ask yourself the same questions you asked during the "modeling" stage. Then, provide yourself with a possible answer to your own questions by extracting the necessary information from the text. For example, one of the initial questions was "I wonder why the man is standing over the water." Point out to students that you were able to find the answer to your own question as you read that specific part of the story. Go through the rest

Component	Strategies and Activities	Instruction
Guided Instruction *(continued)*	• Discuss transfer of strategy. • Pose open-ended questions. • Reread a portion of the book (as necessary) and talk about how the strategy can be used there. • Provide positive feedback.	of the book and point out how you could locate answers to your pre-reading questions by paying attention to the information in the book. Let students know that readers (and listeners) are always asking themselves questions and are always looking for answers in the books they read.
Synthesize and Summarize	• Invite children to talk about what they learned. • Encourage active discussion among all class/group members. • Use open-ended questions. • Students may need thinking time before responding. • Help youngsters focus on 1 or 2 significant points. • Invite students to reflect on the modeling you did throughout the lesson. • Recap (in kid terms) the strategy used.	Invite youngsters to talk about the modeling you did while sharing the book. Encourage them to summarize how you were able to ask your own questions and how you were able to find answers to those questions when you read the book. Invite students to recall specific questions (it is not necessary to remember all of them) and to tell where in the book (approximately) the answers were located.

Train Song
by
Diane Siebert
(New York: HarperCollins, 1981)

Summary This is a book that begs to be read aloud. The cadence of the train ("clickety-clack, clickety-clack") reverberates across each page and will inspire an active participation from any audience. This is a book about trains of all sorts—those that move freight and those that move people. It touches on the various geographical areas visited by trains as well as the various cars that make up a train. Read this once and you'll read it many times over.

Engagement (Schema)

Obtain some photographs of trains. Share these with youngsters and invite them to talk about what they know about trains—what they look like, how they move, the sounds they make, etc. If possible, obtain a video or DVD of moving trains and show it to your students. Talk about places trains travel to and about how train travel is different from other forms of transportation.

You may be able to invite a train enthusiast into your classroom to talk about trains or share some photos of trains—both past and present. Invite youngsters to create their own "Train Dictionary" of train terminology and vocabulary.

Mental Imagery

Show students a photo or illustration of a moving train. Lead them through the following activity: *"I want everyone to close their eyes. Imagine yourself on the train I just showed you. You are sitting in the train as it is moving along the track. Make a picture in your mind of you sitting inside the train as it begins to pick up speed and move faster down the track. The train is puffing smoke. The train is going faster and faster. You are sitting inside a passenger car looking out the window. Make a picture in your head of you sitting and looking out a train window. You can see lots of grass outside the window. You can see some animals moving slowly through the grass. They are eating the grass. They look up at you as you speed by in the train. Listen to the sounds of the train. Listen carefully and hear the train. Listen—clickety-clack, clickety-clack, clickety-clack. You are riding in a train. Make a mind picture of you and the train. Now, very slowly, I want everyone to open their eyes. I'm going to read you a book called Train Song by Diane Siebert. As you listen to the book, try to make a picture in your mind of a train going down the track—clickety-clack, clickety-clack."*

Recommended Social Studies Literature for First and Second Grade

Aardema, Verna. (1981). *Bringing the Rain to Kapiti Plain*. New York: Dial.
   An engaging poetic text and rich illustrations make this book an ideal read-aloud and read-along for any primary classroom.

Aardema, Verna. (1975). *Why Mosquitoes Buzz in People's Ears*. New York: Dial.
   The classic tale that never loses its impact on listeners young and old.

Bates, Katherine Lee. (2003). *America the Beautiful*. New York: Live Oak Media.
   Discover the magic and wonder America has to offer.

Brenner, Martha. (1994). *Abe Lincoln's Hat*. New York: Random House Books for Young Readers.
  The book begins with his purchase of a tall black hat. Later, a group of boys rig up a high wire and knock it off his head, scattering the important papers he kept inside.

Bridges, Shirin Yim. (2002). *Ruby's Wish*. San Francisco: Chronicle Books.
  Ruby is unlike most little girls in old China. Instead of aspiring to get married, Ruby is determined to attend university when she grows up, just like the boys in her family.

Bunting, Eve. (1993). *Fly Away Home*. New York: Clarion Books.
  A homeless boy who lives in an airport with his father, moving from terminal to terminal trying not to be noticed, is given hope when a trapped bird finally finds its freedom.

Bunting, Eve. (1994). *Smoky Night*. San Diego, CA: Harcourt.
  With bright and creative illustrations, this affecting story tells the tale of riots and a neighborhood's struggle to come together.

Bunting, Eve. (1994). *The Wall*. New York: Clarion Books.
  A boy and his father have come to the Vietnam War Memorial to look for the boy's grandfather's name among those who were killed in the war.

Bunting, Eve. (1989). *The Wednesday Surprise*. New York: Clarion.
  A young girl and her grandmother plan a very special surprise for the girl's father…a timeless surprise!

Coleman, Evelyn. (1999). *White Socks Only*. Connecticut: Albert Whitman and Company.
  Approaching a water fountain, the thirsty girl mistakes its "Whites Only" sign to mean that she should take off her shoes so that only her white socks will touch the step stool.

Cooney, Barbara. (1982). *Miss Rumphius*. New York: Puffin.
  Miss Rumphius must do something to make the world a little better. Listeners will find inspiration and possibilities in this story.

Donnelly, Judy. (1989). *Moonwalk: The First Trip to the Moon*. New York: Random House Books for Young Readers.
  More than 20 years after Apollo 11 blasted off on the longest, most famous trip ever, Judy Donnelly captures all the thrills and danger of that first voyage to the moon.

Geisert, Bonnie and Arthur. (2001). *Desert Town*. Boston: Houghton Mifflin.
  The desert can be a harsh environment, but the people who live in a desert town have learned to adapt and survive.

Geisert, Bonnie and Arthur. (2000). *Mountain Town*. Boston: Houghton Mifflin.
  There's lots happening on a mountain throughout the year. Come and see!

Geisert, Bonnie and Arthur. (1999). *River Town*. Boston: Houghton Mifflin.
  The seasons change, and so does life by the river. It's an active place in summer, but the pace slows in the winter.

Unit

8

Recommended
Social Studies
Literature for
First and
Second Grade

Grifalconi, Ann. (1986). *The Village of Round and Square Houses.* Boston: Little, Brown. In the village of Tos, the men live in square houses and the women live in round houses. But, this was not always so.

Hamanaka, Sheila. (1994). *All the Colors of the Earth.* New York: Morrow. People come in many colors as does nature. This magical book celebrates our similarities and common experiences. Be sure to share this one with students!

High, Linda. (1998). *Beekeepers.* Honesdale, PA: Boyds Mills Press. Gathering honey is a special time for a young girl and her grandfather. There are many lessons to learn.

Hopkinson, Deborah. (1995). *Sweet Clara and the Freedom Quilt.* New York: Knopf. Clara is a young slave girl living on a plantation. She devises a secret code for the Underground Railroad that is quilted onto blankets.

Kalman, Maira. (2002). *Fireboat: The Heroic Adventures of the John J. Harvey.* New York: Putnam's. In an inspiring true story, a vintage fireboat plays an important role in the rescue of many people during the events of September 11, 2001.

Kay, Verla. (2000). *Covered Wagons, Bumpy Trails.* New York: Putnam's. A lyrical and poetic journey along the Oregon Trail will have listeners captivated and entranced.

Key, Francis Scott. (2002). *The Star-Spangled Banner.* Carmel, Indiana: Quarry Press. A creatively illustrated rendition of "The Star-Spangled Banner" will invite lots of inspection and discussion. A must-have book!

Leedy, Loreen. (2000). *Mapping Penny's World.* New York: Henry Holt and Company. In simplistic and colorful ways, this book shows children how to create maps of their familiar surroundings.

Leighton, Maxinne Rhea. (1992). *An Ellis Island Christmas.* New York: Viking Books. Krysia and her family leave Poland to meet her father in America. She experiences a variety of emotions on their voyage across the ocean and makes friends with other passengers on the ship.

Littlesugar, Amy. (2001). *Freedom School, Yes!* New York: Philomel Books. This story is based on the 1964 Mississippi Freedom School Summer Project.

Lorbiecki, Marybeth. (2000). *Sister Anne's Hands.* London: Puffin Books. An African-American nun challenges the beliefs of her second-grade students in this thought-provoking picture book set in the 1960s.

Lundell, Margo. (1999). *A Girl Named Helen Keller.* Minneapolis: Sagebrush Education Resources. An easy-to-read version of the remarkable story of Helen Keller and her special teacher, Ann Sullivan.

Mathis, Sharon Bell. (1993). *The Hundred Penny Box.* New York: Scholastic Press. Michael's relative uses her collection of pennies to teach him about life during the Depression.

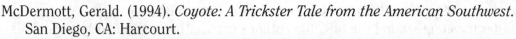

McDermott, Gerald. (1994). *Coyote: A Trickster Tale from the American Southwest.*
San Diego, CA: Harcourt.
Coyote gets himself into all kinds of trouble, but he eventually learns a most
important lesson—one he carries with him to this day.

McDermott, Gerald. (2001). *Jabuti the Tortoise.* San Diego, CA: Harcourt.
Rich illustrations and an engaging tale about a tiny turtle make this one
book that will be read again and again.

Miller, William. (1994). *Zora Hurston and the Chinaberry Tree.*
New York: Lee and Low.
Young Zora learned an important lesson from her mother.
This book emphasizes nature, family, and community with
touching prose.

Murphy, Frank. (2001). *Ben Franklin and the Magic Squares.* New York:
Random House Books for Young Readers.
A funny, entertaining introduction to Ben Franklin and his many inventions,
including the story of how he created the "magic square."

Polacco, Patricia. (1991). *Appelemando's Dream.* New York: Philomel Books.
Appelemando has many amazing dreams. When it rains, his vivid dreams stick to
surfaces and brighten up the drab village. With the linked lesson plan, students
can learn about how rules can help them to achieve their dreams.

Polacco, Patricia. (2001). *Mr. Lincoln's Way.* New York: Philomel Books.
Mr. Lincoln is the "coolest" principal: he is Santa at Christmas, lights the menorah
at Chanukah, and wears a dashiki for Kwanza and a burnoose for Ramadan.

Polacco, Patricia. (1990). *Thunder Cake.* New York: Putnam and Grosset.
Making a Thunder Cake with Grandma is the only way to deal with the fear of an
approaching thunderstorm…and it works!

Priceman, Marjorie. (1994). *How to Make an Apple Pie and See the World.* New York:
Knopf Books for Children.
In this whimsical, geographical shopping journey, a young baker thinks of how to
proceed if the market is closed.

Ransom, Candice. (1999). *The Promise Quilt.* New York: Walker.
Addie makes a very special quilt to honor her father who was killed in the Civil
War. A great read-aloud.

Ringgold, Faith. (1991). *Tar Beach.* New York: Crown Books.
As Cassie lies on the roof of her apartment building, which is known as Tar Beach,
she imagines herself flying over famous New York City landmarks. In her
daydream the beautiful sites belong to her, a reward for the injustices her family
has suffered.

Rylant, Cynthia. (1985). *The Relatives Came.* New York: Bradbury.
Yes, the relatives came and all kinds of wonderful and delightful things began to
happen.

Teaching Comprehension in Grades 1–2

Unit 8

Recommended Social Studies Literature for First and Second Grade

Say, Allen. (1992). *Grandfather's Story*. New York: Dutton Books.
After traveling around the U.S., the author's grandfather returns to Japan and his family. He tells his grandson Allen tales of California, and eventually the young man moves there.

Sharmot, Marjorie. (1980). *Gila Monsters Meet You at the Airport*. New York: Aladdin.
This is a humorous tale about geographical misconceptions and misperceptions that will bring smiles to the faces of any listeners.

Siebert, Diane. (1992). *Mojave*. New York: HarperCollins.
This epic poem is great for reading out loud. The author uses the text and illustrations to describe the beauty of the Mojave desert and the story of its people's history.

Siebert, Diane. (1991). *Sierra*. New York: HarperCollins.
A rich and engaging poem about life in the great Sierra Mountains of eastern California, this books rings with visual imagery.

Vaughan, Marcia. (2001). *The Secret to Freedom*. New York: Simon and Schuster.
In the days before the Civil War, a young enslaved girl and her older brother help slaves escape to freedom using the Underground Railroad quilt code.

Viorst, Judith. (1971). *The Tenth Good Thing About Barney*. New York: Aladdin.
A small boy grieves over the death of his favorite cat. But he discovers something about death and the cycle of life in this affecting tale.

Weinberger, Kimberly. (2001). *Let's Read About...Christopher Columbus*. New York: Scholastic Press.
A simple biography of the Italian explorer who became the first European to discover the West Indies islands in three historic voyages sponsored by Spain's monarchy.

Wiles, Deborah. (2001). *Freedom Summer*. Toronto: Atheneum.
"John Henry Waddell is my best friend," begins the narrator of this story, set during a summer of desegregation in the South.

Winter, Jeanette. (1992). *Follow the Drinking Gourd*. New York: Dragonfly Books.
Colorful pictures based on American folk tradition complement a text that weaves history and song to describe how runaway slaves used song to guide them to the Ohio River and the Underground Railroad.

Woodson, Jacqueline. (2001). *The Other Side*. Philadelphia: Penguin Books.
Clover, the young African-American narrator, lives beside a fence that segregates her town. Her mother instructs her never to climb over to the other side because it isn't safe.

Wyeth, Sharon. (1995). *Always My Dad*. New York: Knopf.
For a girl whose daddy doesn't live at home, times can be tough. But then he visits and something magical happens.

Unit 9

Math Literature Activities

As you have discovered, literature across the elementary curriculum offers an abundance of teaching and learning opportunities. This is certainly true in the reading program and equally so in the science and social studies programs. Not surprisingly, the utility of children's literature also extends into the math curriculum. Through literature, children begin to see and understand the practical applications of math concepts into their everyday lives.

Here are some of the advantages (for both teachers and students) of a literature-rich math curriculum for first- and second-grade students:

- Underscores the utility of math concepts, rather than just the facts.

- Reduces and/or eliminates the artificial barriers that often exist between math and the other subjects.

- Provides an integrated approach to learning.

- Promotes a child-centered math curriculum—one in which they are encouraged to make their own decisions and assume a measure of responsibility for learning.

- Stimulates self-directed discovery and investigation both in and out of the classroom.

- Assists youngsters in developing relationships among math concepts, thus enhancing comprehension.

- Math instruction does not have to be crammed into limited, artificial time periods, but can be extended across the curriculum and throughout the day.

- The connections that can and do exist between math and other subjects, topics, and themes can be logically and naturally developed. Teachers can demonstrate relationships and assist students in comprehending those relationships.

- Teachers can extend math learning into many areas of students' lives.

- Teachers can place more emphasis on teaching students and less on telling students.

- Teachers can promote problem solving, creative thinking, and critical thinking within all dimensions of a topic.

     Teaching Comprehension in Grades 1–2

The use of Comprehension Circles in tandem with math literature provides learning opportunities of considerable value. Children begin to understand the significance of comprehension, not just as a corollary of the reading program, but as a necessary ingredient of each and every subject and each and every topic. With Comprehension Circles, you and your students can set your sails for some magical and incredible scholastic adventures.

Alexander, Who Used to Be Rich Last Sunday
by
Judith Viorst
(New York: Aladdin Books, 1978)

 **Summary** Last Sunday, Alexander's grandparents gave him a dollar and he was rich. There were so many things that he could do with all that money. He could buy as much gum as he wanted or even a walkie-talkie. But, somehow, mysteriously the money began to disappear. Try as he might, Alexander soon found himself right back where he started… except, he still had some bus tokens. This is a wonderful book for teaching money concepts to youngsters.

Component	Strategies and Activities	Instruction
Engagement (Schema)	• Gather students together as a whole class or a smaller group. • Present the theme or topic of a forthcoming book. • Talk about the topic. • Ask questions about the theme or topic. • Invite students to share **relevant** experiences (keep the conversation <u>focused</u>). • Talk about any misperceptions or misconceptions. • Provide illustrations or photos that illuminate the theme or concept. • Share (as necessary) other AV resources that stimulate schema development.	Obtain toy coins or real coins. Gather the children around you and describe each of the coins for them. This can be part of a planned math lesson on coins and their values. Plan time to describe the name of each coin (these can be posted on a special chart on a classroom bulletin board) and the value of each. Provide some activities that will allow students to manipulate the coins into various groups and categories. For example, manually demonstrate how five pennies equal one nickel. Or, show how five nickels equal one quarter. Be

Component	Strategies and Activities	Instruction
Engagement (Schema) *(continued)*	• Show the book cover and encourage discussion about its topic or theme. • Draw "straight-line" connections between what youngsters know and the book's main idea. • Link the book to a similar story/book.	sure youngsters have sufficient opportunities to handle and manipulate the coins into a variety of groups and clusters. Students may wish to create their own posters to illustrate the equivalents of various amounts and denominations.
Modeling	• Introduce the book. • Vocalize your purpose for reading. • Read and discuss the title. • Talk about illustrations. • Do a "mental walk" through the book. • Demonstrate a talk-aloud (focused on a specific strategy). • Demonstrate a think-aloud (focused on a specific strategy). • Provide multiple opportunities for students to "see" inside your head.	Say the following to youngsters, *"When I think about stories, I like to make some predictions about what might happen. In this story, I know that someone is going to get some money. Everyone tells him to save his money. But, like many kids, he finds it hard to do. So, I predict that he will probably want to spend his money on something. I predict that he will slowly use up most or all of his money. I got a clue from the title of the book. I also got a clue from the illustration on the cover of the book—the one where he is holding his pockets inside out. So, my prediction is that he will have some money at the start of the story, but he won't have any money at the end of the story."*
Read Aloud	• Read the selected book out loud to children. • Use expression and intonation as appropriate. • Consider using a big book. • Occasionally "track" the print with your finger or a pointer. • Occasionally use a Shared Book experience with children. • Consider periodic stops (as necessary) to model your thinking. • Demonstrate your enthusiasm for the book while reading.	Demonstrate your enthusiasm for the book while reading. Read the entire book to students. You may choose to read it again, this time using some coin manipulatives to demonstrate how Alexander slowly began to lose his dollar.

Component	Strategies and Activities	Instruction
Guided Instruction	• Teacher and students return to text. • Conduct class/group reading conference. • Identify one specific comprehension strategy. • Clarify reading strategy in "kid terms." • Demonstrate the strategy within the context of the book. • Re-model (as necessary) your use of the strategy in that book. • Invite youngsters to "try out" the strategy (by using their own talk-about or think-about conversations). • Encourage retellings. • Discuss transfer of strategy. • Pose open-ended questions. • Reread a portion of the book (as necessary) and talk about how the strategy can be used there. • Provide positive feedback.	Say to children, *"You know, I guess I was right with my first prediction. I predicted that Alexander would have some money at the start of the story, but he wouldn't have any money at the end of the story. I based my prediction on the title of the story and the illustration on the cover of the book. Let's see if we can work together to make some more predictions. What else do you think might happen to Alexander?"* Invite youngsters to make a few new predictions and record them on the chalkboard.
Synthesize and Summarize	• Invite children to talk about what they learned. • Encourage active discussion among all class/group members. • Use open-ended questions. • Students may need thinking time before responding. • Help youngsters focus on 1 or 2 significant points. • Invite students to reflect on the modeling you did throughout the lesson. • Recap (in kid terms) the strategy used.	Invite children to talk about some of the predictions that they may make during the course of the day (e.g., what the weather will be like, what they will be having for lunch, etc.). Share with them the value of making predictions before listening to any story. Reflect on the predictions you made as you read the book and how the predictions helped you understand the story better. Invite youngsters to talk about some other predictions that could be made throughout the school day.

Teaching Comprehension in Grades 1–2

Chicka Chicka 1, 2, 3
by
Bill Martin, Jr., and Michael Sampson
(New York: Simon and Schuster, Inc., 2004)

Summary **O**ne hundred and one numbers climb to the top of the apple tree in this fun-filled and joyous book. As more and more numbers gather in the tree, they are threatened by a swarm of bumblebees. But, one number will save the day—which one is it? This is a book that will be read again and again as it celebrates all the fun that can be had with numbers of any size or dimension.

Component	Strategies and Activities	Instruction
Engagement (Schema)	• Gather students together as a whole class or a smaller group. • Present the theme or topic of a forthcoming book. • Talk about the topic. • Ask questions about the theme or topic. • Invite students to share **relevant** experiences (keep the conversation <u>focused</u>). • Talk about any misperceptions or misconceptions. • Provide illustrations or photos that illuminate the theme or concept. • Share (as necessary) other AV resources that stimulate schema development. • Show the book cover and encourage discussion about its topic or theme. • Draw "straight-line" connections between what youngsters know and the book's main idea. • Link the book to a similar story/book.	Provide children with a collection of plastic or manipulative numbers. Invite them to play with the numbers, arranging them in different patterns, on top of one another, in groups, or any other fun activities. Ask students to describe some of their experiences with numbers. "Where have you seen this number before?" "Does this number look familiar to you?" Later, invite 2–3 children to pretend they are each a number. Ask them to make up a short story about themselves. For example, *"I'm the number 5 and you can find me in the fingers (5) on one hand and the toes (5) on one foot."*
Modeling	• Introduce the book. • Vocalize your purpose for reading. • Read and discuss the title.	Take children on a "book walk" through the pages of this book. Show the pages one by one and do a "talk-aloud" as you do.

Unit
9

**Chicka Chicka
1, 2, 3**

Component	Strategies and Activities	Instruction
Modeling *(continued)*	• Talk about illustrations. • Do a "mental walk" through the book. • Demonstrate a talk-aloud (focused on a specific strategy). • Demonstrate a think-aloud (focused on a specific strategy). • Provide multiple opportunities for students to "see" inside your head.	Highlight some of the things you see happening on each two-page spread (without reading the text). Share with students some of the predictions you have about the action taking place in the story. When you have completed the "walk," make a final prediction about the whole story. Let youngsters know that you are giving them an opportunity to "see inside your head" as you make some predictions about this story.
Read Aloud	• Read the selected book out loud to children. • Use expression and intonation as appropriate. • Consider using a big book. • Occasionally "track" the print with your finger or a pointer. • Occasionally use a Shared Book experience with children. • Consider periodic stops (as necessary) to model your thinking. • Demonstrate your enthusiasm for the book while reading.	Read the story aloud to children. Stop at the page where all the numbers tumble out of the tree. The pages are un-numbered. Tell youngsters this is the midpoint of the story and that it seems that more things might happen in the rest of the story. Invite youngsters to assist you in making a prediction about the remainder of the story.
Guided Instruction	• Teacher and students return to text. • Conduct class/group reading conference. • Identify one specific comprehension strategy. • Clarify reading strategy in "kid terms." • Demonstrate the strategy within the context of the book. • Re-model (as necessary) your use of the strategy in that book. • Invite youngsters to "try out" the strategy (by using their own talk-about or think-about conversations). • Encourage retellings.	Read the rest of the story to youngsters. Take time to discuss some of your prior predictions as well as the prediction they made at the middle of the story. Share with youngsters the fact that not all predictions will be correct, but that predictions help us understand and enjoy a story more. Invite children to make a prediction about the end of the story: *"What do you think will happen after the 'zero' climbs to the top of the tree?"*

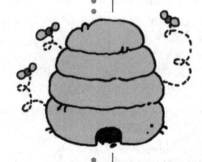

Component	Strategies and Activities	Instruction
Guided Instruction (*continued*)	• Discuss transfer of strategy. • Pose open-ended questions. • Reread a portion of the book (as necessary) and talk about how the strategy can be used there. • Provide positive feedback.	
Synthesize and Summarize	• Invite children to talk about what they learned. • Encourage active discussion among all class/group members. • Use open-ended questions. • Students may need thinking time before responding. • Help youngsters focus on 1 or 2 significant points. • Invite students to reflect on the modeling you did throughout the lesson. • Recap (in kid terms) the strategy used.	Provide students with the plastic or manipulative numbers again. Invite them to retell the story in their own words using the numbers as props. It is not necessary for them to use every number, only that they get the gist of the story. If necessary, you may want to share the story one more time, using the plastic numbers and a toy tree prop in concert with the retelling.

The Doorbell Rang
by
Pat Hutchins
(New York: Greenwillow, 1986)

Summary **M**a has made a dozen cookies for Victoria and Sam to share. Then, the doorbell rings and two friends are welcomed in to share the cookies. The doorbell rings again and more friends arrive and the cookies are divided between them. Again, the ringing doorbell signals fewer and fewer cookies for each person until finally the doorbell rings and…. This is a delicious story about division and sharing—a terrific introduction to a direct application of a mathematical concepts in everyday life.

Engagement (Schema)
Prior to reading this book aloud to students, engage them in a simulation of the events of the story. Invite two youngsters to sit in front of the class. Provide them with twelve similar objects (e.g., manipulatives, blocks, fake cookies, etc.) and ask that they divide these objects equally between them. Then, invite two more

Unit

9

The Doorbell Rang

youngsters to join the group and ask that the four students now divide the twelve objects equally among them. Repeat the process (following the script in the story) until there are twelve youngsters in the group (each having one of the manipulatives). Ask students to speculate the results if one or two more people were to join the group (making a total of 13 or 14 individuals).

Mental Imagery

Invite students to create a mental image of two children sitting in a kitchen with their mother. *"I would like everyone to close their eyes. Paint a picture in your mind of a kitchen. Put a stove in the kitchen. Put a refrigerator in the kitchen. Where is the sink? Where is the table? Now, I want to put a mother in the kitchen. The mother has an apron on. She has just finished baking some cookies. Look at the cookies on the tray. Smell the cookies. They are your favorite cookies. They are chocolate chip cookies. The mother has just taken them out of the oven. Ummm, they smell sooooo good! Look and you will see two children sitting at the table. They are waiting to eat the cookies that have just come out of the oven. The mother walks over and sets the cookie tray on the table. Look closely and you will see twelve cookies on the tray. That means that the two children will each get six cookies each."*

Read the story aloud to youngsters, but stop at the end of the page where Tom and Hannah arrive.]

"Now look at the picture in your head. Now there are four children at the table and twelve cookies…four children and twelve cookies. Keep your eyes closed and watch as the mother puts three cookies on one plate, three cookies on another plate, three cookies on a third plate, and three cookies on the last plate. That means that each child will get three cookies. Three delicious cookies. Now, listen as I read the next part of the story."

Read to the end of the page where Peter and his little brother come in. Repeat the preceding process until you come to the end of the story. Invite youngsters to craft a mental image of the events of the story as you slowly read it to them and engage them in "mentally dividing" the cookies among all the characters.

Questioning

Reread the story to students. As you do, stop at appropriate places and model some of the following questions for youngsters:

- "I wonder how many cookies each child will get."
- "I wonder how many cookies each child will get now that there are two more children."
- "I wonder how the mother is going to divide up the cookies now."
- "I wonder why the children keep mentioning grandma and her cookies."
- "I wonder what will happen at the end of the story."

The Grouchy Ladybug
by
Eric Carle
(New York: HarperCollins, 1996)

Summary   **O**nce upon a time there was this grouchy ladybug…I mean, it was really GROUCHY. In fact, it wanted to pick a fight with everyone it met and everyone it saw. At each hour of the day, it encountered a creature who was larger and bigger than the one before. Finally it met a big blue whale and learned a very important lesson. At 6:00 it returned to where it started and decided to start anew. A classic Eric Carle tale, this is a book that begs to be read aloud to children. Besides several math lessons about time, size, and shape, it also will stimulate discussions about manners and respect.

Engagement (Schema)

This book would be a delightful follow-up to any lesson about time. Make sure students are acquainted with analog clocks and how to tell time using those instruments. If possible, obtain a teaching clock (yellow plastic face with two blue plastic "hands"). Review for students various times during the day. Be sure to focus on hourly times, for example, 1:00, 2:00, 3:00, 4:00, etc. Invite students to create their own personal "clocks" using paper plates and construction paper "hands."

Predicting and Inferring

Read the story up to the page that describes the encounter with the yellow jacket (6:00). Invite children to arrange their homemade clocks with the "hands" in the appropriate positions. Before reading the following page, invite students to predict the next time period. Ask each one to place the "hands" on their personal clocks in the correct positions. Then, read the page about the stag beetle (7:00). Ask students to move the "hands" on their clocks into the correct positions. Repeat this process throughout the remainder of the book, inviting students to move their clock "hands" into a predicted position prior to reading the next page in the story. Afterwards, take time to talk with students about how predicting the times in this story is very similar to predicting events in other stories.

Turtle Splash!
Countdown at the Pond
by
Cathryn Falwell
(New York: Greenwillow, 2001)

Summary Ten turtles were lounging on a log at the pond. Startled by a bullfrog, one swam away. Then there were nine. A rustling rabbit causes another to seek safety in the water. The diminishing sequence continues until, at the end of the day, the ten original turtles gather at the bottom of the pond for a most relaxing evening. This is a magical read-aloud book that introduces youngsters to the "art" of counting backwards. The story is complemented by Field Notes about each of the creatures featured in the book.

Engagement (Schema)

Use magnetic letters or numbers and place ten of them on a magnetic chalkboard or other vertical surface for youngsters to see. Engage the class in counting the objects up from one several times. Then, show them how to count downwards with the objects by removing one object each time. "First there are ten, and we take away one. Now there are nine. Now there are nine, and we take away one. Now there are eight." (and so on) Invite one or two youngsters to come to the front and physically remove one object at a time while the class chants the appropriate "result." You may wish to repeat this process with ten similar objects from the classroom (ten chairs, ten desks, ten crayons, ten pushpins, etc.).

Predicting and Inferring

Read the first two pages and the first three words on the third page of text ("Then there are _____."). Model for youngsters how you would be able to predict the word that would go in the blank (for example, do a "talk-aloud" about how you think it might be a word that rhymes with the word "line" and/or that it might also be a word that is one less than the number ten.). Read that fourth word ("nine") so that you can confirm your original prediction. Then, read the remainder of the third page of text and the first three words on the next page ("Now there are _____."). Again, model your thought processes by doing a similar "talk-aloud" for youngsters (e.g. "I heard the word "late" on the previous page, so I think that the missing word might rhyme with "late." Also, because another turtle left the log and jumped into the pond, I think that the word might be one that is one less than nine."). After students have gotten a "feel" for the

pattern of the text, invite them to make appropriate predictions as you continue to read (and stop at appropriate places) the rest of the book. Afterwards, confirm and congratulate students for using their predictive powers to help themselves figure out the numbers in the story.

Synthesizing and Summarizing

Invite one or two selected youngsters to retell the story in their own words. This can be done by listing the numbers 10–1 vertically on the chalkboard and asking students to point to each one as they relate the sequence of events in the book. It's not important that a specific animal is associated with each number, rather that children see how the book focuses on the progression (from high to low) of a number sequence.

Recommended Math Literature for First and Second Grade

• • • • • • • • • • • • • • •

Axelrod, Amy. (1997). *Pigs Will Be Pigs: Fun with Math and Money*. New York: Aladdin Books.
   The Pigs are very hungry, and there's no food in the house. Mr. Pig suggests eating out, but oh, no! The Pigs are out of money!

Buckless, Andrea. (2002). *Too Many Cooks!* New York: Cartwheel Books.
   Wouldn't it be nice to surprise the family with a delicious, super-duper soup? Cara, Jay, and Marcos think so! Cara takes charge of the cookbook. As she reads the recipes, Marcos adjusts the ingredients for six people. But what does the recipe mean?

Burningham, John. (1980). *The Shopping Basket*. New York: HarperCollins.
   Steven's mother sends him to the store to buy groceries, but on the way back he is accosted by a series of animals, each with a demand for a goodie.

Burns, Marilyn. (1997). *Spaghetti and Meatballs for All: A Mathematical Story*. New York: Scholastic Books.
   When Mrs. Comfort's guests rearrange all of her carefully placed tables and chairs, dinnertime at the family reunion becomes a complete mess.

Burns, Marilyn. (1995). *The Greedy Triangle*. New York: Scholastic Books.
   In this introduction to polygons, a triangle convinces a shapeshifter to make him a quadrilateral and later a pentagon, but discovers that where angles and sides are concerned, more isn't always better.

Canizares, Susan. (1998). *How Many Can Play?* New York: Scholastic Books.
   A counting book presenting children engaged in various sports, including swimming, football, and rollerblading.

Canizares, Susan. (1998). *Numbers All Around.* New York: Scholastic Books.
Simple text and photographs depict the numbers one to twelve in interesting places.

Carle, Eric. (1996). *The Grouchy Ladybug.* New York: HarperCollins.
The arrangement of the book introduces concepts of comparative size and telling time.

Cave, Kathryn. (1989). *Just in Time.* Clarkson Potter.
This telling time storybook will help young readers discover the magic of the clock.

Cristaldi, Kathryn. (1996). *Even Steven and Odd Todd.* New York: Scholastic Books.
The arrival of Cousin Odd Todd greatly upsets Even Steven who likes everything to come in even numbers: his pets, his library books, and even his pancakes.

Duke, Kate. (1998). *One Guinea Pig Is Not Enough.* New York: Dutton Books.
One lonely guinea pig plus one other lonely guinea pig make two smiling guinea pigs.

Feelings, Muriel. (1971). *Moja Means One: Swahili Counting Book.* New York: Dial.
Presents cardinal numbers in both English and Swahili.

Hutchins, Pat. (1986). *The Doorbell Rang.* New York: Greenwillow.
Ma has made a dozen delicious cookies. It should be plenty for her two children. But then the doorbell rings—and rings and rings.

MacCarone, Grace. (1997). *Three Pigs, One Wolf, and Seven Magic Shapes.* New York: Cartwheel Books.
Tells the story of three pigs who acquire some magic shapes, which they use for various purposes, some smart and some not so smart.

Mahy, Margaret. (1987). *17 Kings and 42 Elephants.* New York: Dial Books.
The story is simple: 17 kings sing and dance their way through the jungle on the backs of 42 elephants until the "deep dark jungle" swallows them.

Merriam, Eve. *12 Ways to Get to 11.* New York: Simon and Schuster.
Introduces familiar situations that demonstrate how a single number can be made up of many number combinations.

Murphy, Stuart. (1996). *A Pair of Socks.* New York: HarperTrophy.
Young children learn about the concept of matching when a lonely striped sock, searching the house for its mate, wonders if it matches a polka-dotted sock and the other socks it encounters along the way.

Myller, Rolf. (1991). *How Big Is a Foot?* New York: Yearling Books.
Thrown in jail because the bed he made for the Queen is too small, an apprentice comes up with a more accurate way of measuring size.

Neuschwander, Cindy. (1997). *Sir Cumference and the First Round Table: A Math Adventure.* Watertown, MA: Charlesbridge Publishing.
Assisted by his knight, Sir Cumference, and using ideas offered by his wife and son, King Arthur finds the perfect shape for his table.

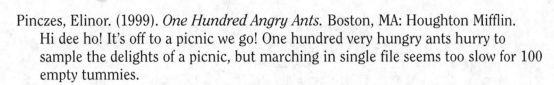

Pinczes, Elinor. (1999). *One Hundred Angry Ants*. Boston, MA: Houghton Mifflin.
Hi dee ho! It's off to a picnic we go! One hundred very hungry ants hurry to
sample the delights of a picnic, but marching in single file seems too slow for 100
empty tummies.

Pinczes, Elinor. (1995). *A Remainder of One*. Boston, MA: Houghton Mifflin.
Here, an army of insects is planning a parade, but each formation that the
squadron comes up with for its 25 members, two lines of twelve, three of eight,
four of six, leaves Joe Bug standing alone, a remainder of one.

Scieszka, John. (1995). *Math Curse*. New York: Viking Books.
Did you ever wake up to one of those days where everything is a problem? You
have 10 things to do, but only 30 minutes till the bus leaves. Is there enough
time? You have 3 shirts and 2 pairs of pants—can you make 1 good outfit? Don't
worry—it's just the Math Curse striking!

Schwartz, David. (1985). *How Much Is a Million?* New York: HarperCollins.
This book reveals how big a bowl would be needed to hold a million goldfish, or
how many years it would take to count to a million.

Tang, Greg. (2001). *The Grapes of Math*. New York: Scholastic Books.
By looking for patterns, symmetries, and familiar number combinations displayed
within eye-catching pictures, math will become easier and quicker and much
more fun than anyone could have ever imagined!

Tompert, Ann. (1997). *Grandfather Tang's Story*. Connecticut: Dragonfly Books.
Two competitive fox fairies go through rapid physical transformations until a
hunter's arrow reminds them of their true friendship.

Wells, Rosemary. (2000). *Bunny Money*. New York: Viking Books.
When Max and Ruby head into town to get presents for Grandma's birthday, they
run into nothing but trouble!

Viorst, Judith. (1978). *Alexander Who Used to Be Rich Last Sunday*. New York:
Aladdin Books.
Although Alexander and his money are quickly parted, he comes to realize all the
things that can be done with a dollar.

Zimelman, Nathan. (1992). *How the Second Grade Got $8,205.50 to Visit the Statue of
Liberty*. Illinois: Albert Whitman & Company.
Chronicles the triumphs and setbacks of the second
grade as they try a variety of schemes to raise
money for a trip to the Statue of Liberty.

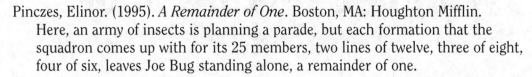

Unit 10
Wordless Picture Books

Wordless picture books offer you and your students some marvelous opportunities to use comprehension strategies in a host of unique learning situations. Without the constraints of text, children are free to allow their imaginations to soar. They can create their own stories to match the illustrations in a book. They can predict story lines, endings, and character actions. They can make inferences about what is taking place on a page or throughout the plot of a story. They can engage in vivid mental images that elucidate images on the pages of a book or expand those images. In short, wordless picture books are a treasure trove of learning opportunities for any primary-level teacher.

Benefits of Wordless Picture Books

- Focusing on sequence
- Teaching left to right patterns
- Emphasizing important details
- Enhancing oral language development
- Noting cause and effect relationships
- Making judgments
- Understanding plot
- Stimulating active participation
- Determining main ideas
- Making inferences
- Making predictions

Not only can wordless picture books be used as an aid in developing comprehension, they are also appropriate in helping children develop language and thinking skills. The chart presents other benefits of wordless picture books as a valuable element of the primary classroom.

One of the major advantages of wordless picture books (particularly for young children) is that they gently "nudge" youngsters into stories. They invite students to contribute ideas or imagine possibilities—and the possibilities can be diverse and wildly varied every time you use a book with a different group of students.

Wordless picture books are an ideal tool for stimulating creativity and helping children develop the building blocks of language. Children learn how stories are constructed and how illustrations are tools that help us appreciate and comprehend the author's message. Best of all, imaginations are stimulated and creativity is promoted.

A lesson plan using a wordless picture book follows. Notice how a comprehension strategy can be used with "text-less books" just as effectively as with "word-rich" books. Please consider this plan as an example of some languaging opportunities for your own classroom.

Pancakes for Breakfast
by
Tomie dePaola
(New York: Harcourt, 1978)

Summary **A** woman wakes up and thinks about having some pancakes for breakfast. She checks her recipe book and then begins to gather all the necessary ingredients. The process becomes more and more complicated when she realizes all that she needs to do. On her way home from purchasing the pancake syrup, she discovers that all her pets have eaten the ingredients. Undeterred, she goes to her neighbor's house and has a delicious breakfast of pancakes.

Component	Strategies and Activities	Instruction
Engagement (Schema)	• Gather students together as a whole class or a smaller group. • Present the theme or topic of a forthcoming book. • Talk about the topic. • Ask questions about the theme or topic. • Invite students to share **relevant** experiences (keep the conversation <u>focused</u>). • Talk about any misperceptions or misconceptions. • Provide illustrations or photos that illuminate the theme or concept. • Share (as necessary) other AV resources that stimulate schema development. • Show the book cover and encourage discussion about its topic or theme. • Draw "straight-line" connections between what youngsters know and the book's main idea. • Link the book to a similar story/book.	Gather all the children together into a large circle. Invite the children to think of a time when they had pancakes for breakfast. Ask them to think about all the things that were necessary in order to have pancakes. *"What were some of the ingredients necessary to make pancakes?"* *"What types of tools were needed?"* Make a chart on the chalkboard that lists the ingredients on one side and tools on the other side. Spend a little time talking about all the different things that are needed in order to make pancakes.

Unit 10

Pancakes for Breakfast

Component	Strategies and Activities	Instruction
Modeling	• Introduce the book. • Vocalize your purpose for reading. • Read and discuss the title. • Talk about illustrations. • Do a "mental walk" through the book. • Demonstrate a talk-aloud (focused on a specific strategy). • Demonstrate a think-aloud (focused on a specific strategy). • Provide multiple opportunities for students to "see" inside your head.	Model the following mental imagery activity for children. *"When I think about having pancakes, I sometimes make a picture in my head. In my picture I can see the breakfast table at my house. I can see the stove and the refrigerator in the kitchen. I can see some kitchen cabinets. I can see someone walking into the kitchen. They are opening up the cabinets and taking out bowls, spoons, mixers, measuring cups, and other things. I can see them reaching into the refrigerator and taking out some eggs, some milk, and some butter. I can see them standing at a counter and putting all those ingredients into a bowl. Then, I can see them mixing the ingredients together with a spoon. Then, I see them walk over and turn on the stove and put a frying pan on the top to get it hot. I can see lots of things happening in the picture that I have in my head."*
Read Aloud	• Read the selected book out loud to children. • Use expression and intonation as appropriate. • Consider using a big book. • Occasionally "track" the print with your finger or a pointer. • Occasionally use a Shared Book experience with children. • Consider periodic stops (as necessary) to model your thinking. • Demonstrate your enthusiasm for the book while reading.	With a wordless picture book, there is no true read aloud. However, you can share each of the individual pages with children silently. It is not necessary to tell youngsters what they see on the pages, nor is it necessary at this point to discuss the details of the illustrations. This should simply be a quiet sharing time together. "Pause" the sharing time at the page where the old woman is taking eggs from the chicken.

Component	Strategies and Activities	Instruction
Guided Instruction	• Teacher and students return to text. • Conduct class/group reading conference. • Identify one specific comprehension strategy. • Clarify reading strategy in "kid terms." • Demonstrate the strategy within the context of the book. • Re-model (as necessary) your use of the strategy in that book. • Invite youngsters to "try out" the strategy (by using their own talk-about or think-about conversations). • Encourage retellings. • Discuss transfer of strategy. • Pose open-ended questions. • Reread a portion of the book (as necessary) and talk about how the strategy can be used there. • Provide positive feedback.	Say, *"O.K. I would like each of you to create a mind picture in your own head. Think about some of the things we saw the woman do in this story. Use those events to help you create a picture of the story in your head. Make sure you have some of the details about the woman's house in your picture. Make sure you also have some details from the outside, too. Let's take a few moments to describe some of our mental images with each other. Some of our mind pictures might be similar and some may be different. That's O.K. What is most important is that we all get to make a picture in our own head."*
Synthesize and Summarize	• Invite children to talk about what they learned. • Encourage active discussion among all class/group members. • Use open-ended questions. • Students may need thinking time before responding. • Help youngsters focus on 1 or 2 significant points. • Invite students to reflect on the modeling you did throughout the lesson. • Recap (in kid terms) the strategy used.	Finish the entire story. Afterwards, invite the youngsters to draw or illustrate their own versions of the story. They may wish to focus on a single event from the story or create a series of events (similar to cartoon panels) to illustrate some of the events in sequence. Upon completion, plan time to talk about how their mental images may have been similar to or different from the illustrations in the book. Be sure to post their illustrations in an appropriate location.

Following are some examples of other wordless picture books and some suggested comprehension strategies for each. As in the book above, you will see that even wordless texts have the potential for helping youngsters engage in the dynamics of comprehension.

Rain
by
Peter Spier
((New York: Doubleday, 1982))

Summary A brother and sister venture into a downpour to explore their neighborhood. They have all kinds of delightful adventures and make some wonderful discoveries about their "wet world." Later they scamper home and awake the next day to a sunshine day. It has been a magical experience.

Engagement (Schema)

Invite youngsters to talk about rainy days. What are some of the activities they like to do outside whenever it rains? What games do they play? What do they like to discover? How is a rainy day different from a sunny day? Take time to engage children in a lively discussion about all the activities that are possible when it rains. You may wish to have some oversize raindrops cut out of construction paper posted on a bulletin board. For each of the rainy day activities suggested by students, write one on a construction paper raindrop and post it.

Important Information

As you share the illustrations in this book, stop every so often and ask children to volunteer a word or sentence about an important detail; this should be limited to no more than 4–5 significant details. Write each detail volunteered on one of the construction paper raindrops (prepared earlier) and post it on the bulletin board. Plan time to talk about the similarities between their "prior knowledge raindrops" and the "story raindrops." Be sure there are 3–4 of each posted on the bulletin board.

Questioning

Model for children some of the types of questions you might ask yourself as you share this book. Focus on those questions that establish a "connection" between prior experiences and the experiences of the brother and sister in the story. For example, you might ask (out loud) these questions: "I wonder if the two kids will jump into some puddles like I used to do?" "Will their clothes get all wet like mine do when I go out in the rain?" Or "I wonder if they will have some hot chocolate like I do when I come in from a rainy day?"

Carl Goes Shopping
by
Alexandra Day
(New York: Farrar, Straus and Giroux, 1992)

Summary **C**arl the dog is left alone with the baby while the mother goes upstairs in a department store. Carl and the baby make many discoveries in the toy section of the store. They find some books and share them together. They meander through the ladies department, the electronics section, the rug department, fine foods, and even the pet center. Finally they scamper back to the waiting carriage just before the mother returns.

Engagement (Schema)

Invite youngsters to participate in a role-playing experience. Tell them that you are going to take on the role of a large dog (similar to Carl). Ask one of the children to take on the role of a small baby. As appropriate (with the assistance of an aide), place the child on your back as you are on your hands and knees. Tell everyone that you and the child are inside a large store. "Walk" around on your hands and knees with the child on your back (ensure the safety of the "volunteer"). Ask students to suggest some of the things that you and your rider might see in a large department store (toys, books, clothes, etc.). Ask them to imagine that they are "riders" on the back of a large dog. What would be some things they might discover?

Predicting and Inferring

As you share the book, stop 2–3 times and invite children to make predictions about some of the future "adventures" Carl and the baby might get into. Here are some suggested stopping points (The pages of the book are unnumbered.):

- The page where the baby is reaching out for the small toy elephant

- The page with the word "Electronics"

- The page where the baby is riding on Carl's back in the pet section

- The page where Carl is "dumping" the baby back into the carriage

Do You Want to Be My Friend?
by
Eric Carle
(New York: Philomel Books, 1988)

Summary A little mouse asks the question, "Do you want to be my friend?" So, he follows a tail and finds an unfriendly horse at the other end. But there's another tail, and another, and another. Each time, there is a surprise at the end of the tail. Finally, a very long and very green tail appears. When the mouse gets to the other end of this tail, he must do something very, very quickly.

Engagement (Schema)

Invite children to participate in a discussion about animals that have tails. Ask students to brainstorm all the animals they can think of that have tails. They may wish to start with more familiar animals (dogs, cats) and move to animals at the zoo (kangaroos, zebras, lions) and even to various creatures they may have seen on TV (e.g., Discovery Channel, Animal Planet). Make a list on the board with their ideas. If possible, have a collection of illustrations or photos depicting various animals with tails.

Predicting and Inferring

As you share this book with youngsters, stop at the end of each two-page spread. (The pages are unnumbered.) Show the tail on the second page of the spread and invite youngsters to predict the animal (to be featured on the next page) that belongs to that tail. Ask them to share any clues (shape, size, color) that might help them figure out the animal "attached" to that tail.

• • • • • • • • • • • • • • • •

As you can see, wordless picture books can offer your students a wonderful array of comprehension activities that can excite and stimulate all sorts of thinking. Unencumbered by text, these books provide magical journeys that foster imagination, involvement, and lots of predictions. Use them throughout your literacy program to enhance children's involvement and participation.

Following is a list of some recommended wordless picture books. Consider these as positive additions to your classroom library.

Wordless Picture Books for Your Classroom

Anderson, Lena. (1991). *Bunny Box*. New York: Farrar, Straus and Giroux.
As a small boy gets ready for bed, his mother tries to soothe him by pushing a box full of toys into his bed. Nothing helps until the young bunny discovers his friend's blanket at the bottom of the box.

Anno, Mitsumasa. (1978). *Anno's Journey*. New York: Philomel.
A journey through small towns and villages of Europe is depicted though a series of pictures.

Anno, Mitsumasa. (1986). *Anno's Counting Book*. New York: HarperTrophy.
Over the course of a year (each picture represents a different month and time of day), a little town grows up with viewers witnessing the building of bridges, streets, and railroads.

Baker, Jeannie. (2004). *Home*. New York: Greenwillow.
When baby Tracy is first brought to her new home, the view of the urban neighborhood as seen through her window is not a pleasant one. She and her family decide to help clean it up, and they do a magnificent job.

Baker, Jeannie. (1991). *Window*. New York: Greenwillow.
A mother, holding her newborn son, gazes out the window of his room at lush vegetation, tropical birds, a pond, a kangaroo, and more.

Bang, Molly. (1996). *The Grey Lady and the Strawberry Snatcher*. New York: Aladdin Books.
The Grey Lady loves strawberries. But so does the Strawberry Snatcher, and unfortunately for the Grey Lady, he is not far away and getting closer all the time.

Banyai, Istvan. (2000). *Re-Zoom*. New York: Viking Publishers.
Viewers are shown something that turns out to be just a piece of something larger, and thus not at all what they saw (or thought they saw) in the first place.

Bartlett, T.C. (1997). *Tuba Lessons*. New York: Harcourt Children's Publishing.
While walking through the forest, a young boy meets up with a bear and uses his tuba to make friends.

Blake, Quentin. (1996). *Clown*. New York: Henry Holt and Company.
Follow the fortunes of Clown, who starts in a garbage can and ends up in a happy family.

Briggs, Raymond. (1987). *The Snowman*. New York: Random House Children's Books.
When his snowman comes to life, a little boy invites him home and in return is taken on a flight high above the countryside.

Bullock, Kathleen. (1993). *Rabbits Are Coming!* New York: Simon and Schuster.
A score of rabbits, each with a balloon, leave Mom and their home in the woods for a joyous escapade, hopping over the fields and into the house of an astonished family.

Butterworth, Nick. (1991). *Amanda's Butterfly*. New York: Random House Children's Books.
Net in hand, Amanda sets off in search of butterflies, but has no success. When rain starts to fall, she takes shelter in a backyard tool shed.

Carle, Eric. (1987). *1, 2, 3 To the Zoo*. New York: Philomel Books.
As a band of animals travel to the zoo by train, children can count the occupants of each car.

Carle, Eric. (1988). *Do You Want to Be My Friend?* New York: Philomel Books.
A little mouse is looking for a friend but always seems to be one step behind.

Chesworth, Michael. (1992). *Rainy Day Dream*. New York: Farrar, Straus and Giroux.
The traveler's imagination takes him from the local stream out to a rushing river and then a mighty ocean, passing over city, town, ship, and train as he flies.

Day, Alexandra. (1992). *Carl Goes Shopping*. New York: Farrar, Straus and Giroux.
Carl is told to "take good care of baby" while the mother shops for curtains. Of course, a department store offers too much adventure for Carl and baby to stay in one place.

Day, Alexandra. (1993). *Carl Goes to Daycare*. New York: Farrar, Straus and Giroux.
The lovable Rottweiler returns, this time accompanying his young owner on a visit to a daycare center. When the teacher accidentally gets locked outside, Carl takes charge.

Day, Alexandra. (1994). *Carl Makes a Scrapbook*. New York: Farrar, Straus and Giroux.
Mom started a scrapbook years ago, but when she leaves the house, Carl and baby Madeleine decide to update it with their own mementos.

Day, Alexandra. (1997). *Carl's Birthday*. New York: Farrar, Straus and Giroux.
Beloved from many previous escapades, Carl, the gentle Rottweiler, and Madeline, the mischievous toddler, are sent to nap at the neighbors' while Mom prepares for the surprise birthday party.

dePaola, Tomie. (1981). *The Hunter and the Animals: A Wordless Picture Book*. Boston, MA: Houghton Mifflin Company.
When the discouraged hunter falls asleep, the forest animals play a trick on him.

dePaola, Tomie. (1978). *Pancakes for Breakfast*. New York: Harcourt Children's Books.
A little old lady's attempts to have pancakes for breakfast are hindered by a scarcity of supplies and the participation of her pets.

Drescher, Henrik. (1987). *The Yellow Umbrella*. New York: Simon and Schuster.
A visitor and his little girl lose their yellow umbrella in the monkeys' arena at the local zoo.

Dupasquier, Philippe. (1990). *I Can't Sleep*. New York: Orchard Books.
It is not only the winsome girl on the cover of this book who can't sleep, but her father, brother, mother, and cat as well.

Euvremer, Teryl. (1987). *Sun's Up*. New York: Random House Children's Books.
Depicted as a rather jolly, colorful character, the sun awakens and has breakfast
before proceeding to brighten the day of the rural folks below.

Florczak, Robert. (2003). *Yikes!!* New York: Blue Sky Press.
A young boy who appears to be on safari is pictured on each spread, alongside the
world's most fearsome and exotic creatures—cobras, gorillas, and crocodiles, oh my!

Gladstone, Lise. (1980). *The Inside Kid*. New York: McGraw-Hill.
A story where many unexpected magic things can happen…and do.

Goffin, Josse. (2000). *Oh!* New York: Harry N. Abrams.
A visual surprise that literally unfolds before your eyes. Each fold-out spread
contains a simple image—a cup, a fish, an apple—which is transformed into
an entirely new image by lifting a flap.

Goodall, John S. (1977). *The Surprise Picnic*. New York: Macmillan.
Two kittens and their mother meet with scary and unexpected adventures
on a summer's day.

Hutchins, Pat. (1987). *Changes, Changes*. New York: Aladdin Books.
Two wooden dolls rearrange wooden building blocks to form various objects.

Jonas, Ann. (1990). *Two Bear Cubs*. Boston, MA: Houghton Mifflin Company.
Two adventurous cubs love to wander, but when frightened, appreciate
having Mother close by.

Keats, Ezra Jack. (1999). *Clementina's Cactus*. New York: Viking Press.
Clementina and her father are out for a walk in the desert when Clementina
discovers a lone cactus, all shriveled and prickly. But Clementina discovers there
is something beautiful hiding inside that thick skin.

Maizlish, Lisa. (1996). *The Ring*. New York: Greenwillow Books.
The boy finds a yellow plastic ring that changes his black-and-white winter world
into a colorful summer panorama.

Mayer, Mercer. (1987). *A Boy, a Dog, a Frog, and a Friend*. New York: Dutton Books.
First came a boy and his dog. Then they found a frog. Can a new turtle be a good
friend, too?

Mayer, Mercer. (1987). *Frog, Where Are You?* New York: Dial Books for Young Readers.
Follow a young boy as he romps through the woods, making mischief and new
friends along the way.

Mayer, Mercer. (1992). *One Frog Too Many*. London: Puffin Books.
A boy's pet frog thinks that the new little frog the boy gets for his birthday is one
frog too many.

McCully, Emily Arnold. (1984). *Picnic*. New York: Harper and Row.
A young mouse is lost on the day of the family picnic.

Unit 10

Wordless Picture Books for Your Classroom

McCully, Emily Arnold. (2001). *Four Hungry Kittens*. New York: Dial Books for Young Readers.
While the mama cat searches for dinner on the farm (and gets trapped in the feed room by the unknowing farmer), her four kittens pass the time engaged in various exploits: looking yearningly at a nursing calf, falling into a milk can, and narrowly escaping a hungry hawk.

Milich, Zoran. (2003). *The City ABC Book*. New York: Kids Can Press.
Features dramatic black-and-white photographs of urban landscapes with hidden letters boldly highlighted in red.

Mogensen, Jan. (1991). *The Forty-Six Little Men*. New York: HarperCollins.
This is the story about forty-six miniature people who make their home in a painting on a nursery wall.

Ormerod, Jan. (1984). *Moonlight*. New York: Walker Books.
As her parents attempt to help a child fall asleep at bedtime, they themselves become more and more sleepy.

Ormerod, Jan. (1988). *Sleeping (Dad and Me)*. New York: Walker Books.
A baby does his best to get his sleeping father's attention.

Peddle, Daniel. (2000). *Snow Day*. New York: Doubleday Books for Young Readers.
One sunny winter day, a child has a wonderful time building a snowman. But what happens to the snowman after the child goes home?

Popov, Nikolai. (1998). *Why?* New York: Michael Neugebauer Books.
A frog dressed in long johns sits on a rock, peacefully smelling flowers. Out of the ground pops a mouse (in overalls) with an umbrella. A new friend? Hardly.

Schories, Pat. (1991). *Mouse Around*. New York: Farrar, Straus and Giroux.
A young mouse falls from his safe nest in the cellar into a plumber's pocket. From there he journeys via doughnut, slipper, and toy truck.

Schubert, Dieter. (2000). *Where's My Monkey?* Connecticut: Front Street.
Unusual events happen when a toy monkey is separated from his young owner.

Spier, Peter. (1977). *Noah's Ark*. New York: Doubleday.
The classic story is punctuated by detailed illustrations.

Spier, Peter. (1982). *Rain*. New York: Doubleday.
This book captures the wonder and beauty of a brother and sister's fun in the rain as they splash through puddles, see where the animals hide, and make footprints in the mud.

Tafuri, Nancy. (1987). *Do Not Disturb*. New York: HarperCollins.
It is the first day of summer, and each member of a family enjoys all sorts of activities, from swimming to camping to flying a kite. But the family is oblivious to all of the forest animals they are disturbing until night falls.

Unit

10

Wordless
Picture Books

Tafuri, Nancy. (1999). *Have You Seen My Duckling?* New York: Dial Books for
   Young Readers.
   A mother duck leads her brood around the pond as she searches for one missing
   duckling.

Turkle, Brinton. (1987). *Deep in the Forest.* London: Puffin Books.
   A curious bear explores a cabin in the forest with disastrous results.

Vincent, Gabrielle. (2000). *A Day, A Dog.* Connecticut: Front Street.
   A series of adventures leads a dog from abandonment at the side of the road to
   acceptance by a young boy who smiles and invites the dog into his world.

Ward, Lynd. (2001). *The Silver Pony.* New York: Houghton Mifflin.
   Told only in pictures, this is the story of a lonely farm boy who confuses his
   dreams of adventure on a winged pony with reality.

Wiesner, David. (1991). *Free Fall.* New York: HarperTrophy Publishing.
   When he falls asleep with a book in his arms, a young boy dreams an amazing
   dream about dragons, castles, and an uncharted, faraway land.

Wiesner, David. (1991). *Sector 7.* New York: Clarion Books.
   The adventure begins with a school trip to the Empire State Building. There a boy
   makes friends with a mischievous little cloud, who whisks him away to the Cloud
   Dispatch Center for Sector 7 (the region that includes New York City).

Wiesner, David. (1991). *Tuesday.* New York: Clarion Books.
   The unpredictable events of a particular Tuesday unroll before the reader with the
   precision and clarity of a silent movie.

Unit II
Literacy Centers

The Importance of Literacy Centers

One of the issues many primary-level teachers struggle with is the quality of instructional time for students when they were not engaged in explicit instruction. Their concerns center on the time when they are working with a small group of students in a planned comprehension lesson. "How can I develop powerful independent activities and practices that will reinforce strategies taught in group situations?" is a question often asked. The question is not unusual—it is one being asked in one form or another by many teachers. It revolves around the development of literacy centers—or those opportunities for youngsters to work apart from the teacher.

> "*How can I develop powerful independent activities and practices that will reinforce strategies taught in group situations?*"

It is apparent from a survey of the research (Baumann, Hoffman, Duffy-Hester, and Ro, 2000; Ford and Opitz, 2002), as well as in conversations with teachers across the United States and Canada, that student time AWAY from the teacher is a significant concern of many educators. In many classrooms teachers have used literacy centers (or Learning Centers) as a practice and part of their overall literacy programs. But creating literacy centers and effectively implementing them into the overall structure of the reading program are constant and continuing challenges for many teachers.

Ford and Opitz (2002) have presented five important considerations that will ensure the success of literacy centers. These are summarized below:

1. Students cannot be assigned to literacy centers without adequate instruction on how to be independent learners. One teacher interviewed for this book indicated that she spends the first two months of school teaching her students how to work by themselves on independent activities. She uses that time to carefully assess children's skills as well as their needs as they relate to the use of literacy centers. For example, these might include learning how to work with a partner, learning how to operate a tape player and headphones, learning how to use a pocket chart, or learning how to record ideas in a personal journal. As teachers identify these needs (individually and collectively) in their students, it

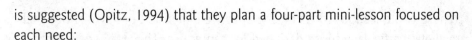

is suggested (Opitz, 1994) that they plan a four-part mini-lesson focused on each need:

- A focus (purpose for the lesson);

- An explanation, in which children are provided with the information related to the stated purpose;

- Role playing, which gives students opportunities for guided practice; and

- Direct application, which provides children with time to use the information as they complete their center activities for the day.

2. Teachers need to consider the specific types of activities for independent work. The critical question becomes, "What specific activities do children need that will advance their knowledge about literacy?" Embodied within that larger question is a series of mini-questions that can help in formulating appropriate centers. These may include one, some, or all of the following:

- Do students need to write a response to something they have read?

- Do students need to listen to a story on tape as they follow along in a book?

- Do students need to work with a classmate to practice and refine a comprehension strategy?

- Do students need to engage in sustained silent reading activities?

- Do students need to expand their concepts of print skills?

- Do students need to develop speaking/reading skills with readers' theater?

- Do students need to understand the relationship between illustrations and text through art activities?

The fundamental question that needs to be addressed as you respond to these questions is: *What activities will require students to become actively engaged in their literacy development?*

3. One operational plan that can help you in designing appropriate centers can be your state or district standards. Centers can be constructed that focus on designated competencies as outlined in these curricular guides. Obviously, not all standards can be easily translated into the literacy center, nor should they be. However, a thoughtful and careful perusal of those standards (and their conversion into possible centers) can be a productive component of your overall reading plan.

4. Two key considerations for the development of literacy centers revolve around the perception of those centers by youngsters. That is, students must have the answers to two questions both prior to and during their engagement in a specific center. These are:

- Will I be successful in this activity?

- Will my participation in this activity be valued?

Unit 11

The Importance of Literacy Centers

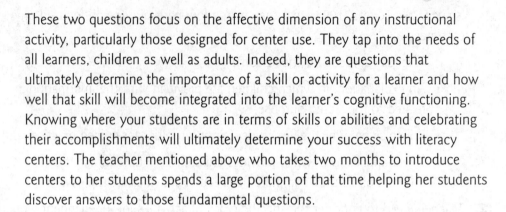

These two questions focus on the affective dimension of any instructional activity, particularly those designed for center use. They tap into the needs of all learners, children as well as adults. Indeed, they are questions that ultimately determine the importance of a skill or activity for a learner and how well that skill will become integrated into the learner's cognitive functioning. Knowing where your students are in terms of skills or abilities and celebrating their accomplishments will ultimately determine your success with literacy centers. The teacher mentioned above who takes two months to introduce centers to her students spends a large portion of that time helping her students discover answers to those fundamental questions.

5. Ford and Opitz (2002) offer some final guidelines that will ensure the success of literacy centers:

- Consider centers that will cause the least disruption to your instructional activities.

- Operate centers with minimal transition time.

- Encourage equitable use of activities by all students.

- Include a simple accountability form for each center.

- Consider simple centers rather than elaborate ones.

- Build the centers around established classroom routines and expectations.

It is clear that the establishment, implementation, and ultimate success of literacy centers are the result of careful planning and an attention to the needs and routines of students in your classroom. Literacy centers are an important part of any classroom literacy program and can offer youngsters significantly meaningful opportunities to utilize their developing reading competencies in worthwhile activities and processes.

Suggested Literacy Centers

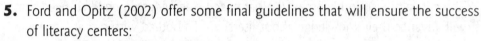

Two key factors (mentioned above) that will assist you in developing appropriate centers for your classroom are simplicity and routines. The centers suggested below are based on a successful formula shared by scores of teachers. That is, each center serves as a structure for the activities within it. In other words, the centers stay the same (routine), but the activities that are "housed" in a particular center can be changed, modified, replaced, or added to throughout the school year (simplicity).

Each of the following center ideas is divided into five subsections. These include: 1) a brief description of the center, 2) the value of the center to the reading program, 3) some design considerations, 4) suggested activities, and

Additional Considerations

- Start the school year with a few centers (3–4). As students become comfortable with routines, gradually increase the number of centers (depending on available classroom space, 7–8 may be the maximum).

- The ultimate success of your centers can be assured by "imprinting" your students with a series of familiar routines (how to move between centers, how to work cooperatively, how to cause minimal disruption to others). Plan to devote several weeks at the beginning of the year to teaching these routines. Sufficient time spent early in the year will ensure success throughout the remainder of the year.

- Consider the physical placement and arrangement of centers in your room. Students need to be able to move to and between centers with minimal disruption and time.

- Post a set of directions in each center. Plan time to share and discuss each set of directions and/or routines with students as part of your introductory mini-lesson (see above).

- Create a daily schedule of activities (see below) as well as center monitoring devices (see below) and spend time regularly reviewing these plans with students.

- Consider "assigning" students to selected centers as well as offering students opportunities to select centers on their own.

- Talk with students about the amount of time necessary to engage in or complete the activities within a center. Establish flexible time frames for various centers in line with students' abilities and the tasks available.

- Establish a procedure or routine that will allow students to signal when they are having difficulty with a specific center activity.

- Provide regular opportunities for students to "debrief." Invite them, on a regular or daily basis, to discuss what went well at one or more centers, as well as what might be done to improve a center.

- As you finish with a reading group and before you move to another group, take a few minutes to "walk the room" to observe students working at center activities.

- Centers should not be comprised of "busy work" activities, rather extending activities related directly to the books shared during reading lessons.

- It is not critical for students (particularly in the beginning stages of reading) to complete all the activities within a center. You may elect to carry over activities for several days or for an entire week.

5) directions and/or routines (to be discussed and shared with students). For the last subsection, invite your students to state these directions in their own words. These "student-to-student" directions can then be posted in each literacy center.

It is important to remember that the suggested activities are only possibilities—ideas that have been successfully used in a variety of primary classrooms. It is not necessary (or even productive) to use all of the centers or all of the instructional suggestions. You are encouraged to continuously assess the needs of your students throughout the year and determine the appropriateness of any series of centers (or the activities within a center) in concert with students' developing reading abilities. Obviously, centers should not be "thrown into" the reading program without adequate instruction (see the mini-lesson above) and familiarity.

Listening Center

A listening center offers youngsters a unique opportunity to integrate two of the language arts. Reading and listening are combined into an enjoyable and productive format that supports and extends the guided reading program. Students can begin to make a "match" between the sounds of language and the written form of that language.

Value

• Stimulates active involvement with text
• Improves listening comprehension and, ultimately, reading comprehension
• Brings books and stories to life
• Allows for personal interpretations of text
• Supports the integrated language arts
• Provides opportunities for students to *do* something with what they hear
• Students can hear models of good reading

Design Considerations

• Select an area that is farthest away from the reading instructional area.
• Provide a simple and easy-to-operate tape player.
• Provide multiple headphones for students to use.
• Thoroughly train students in the operation of the tape player and positioning of headphones.
• Record stories in your own voice (rather than using commercial tapes).
• Record stories at a rate commensurate with students' reading fluency.
• Record stories and books that will be part of future reading lessons.

Suggested Activities

• Invite students to "warm up" with a book at the listening center.
• Invite students to review a book at the listening center.
• Invite students to listen to a book after receiving instruction on specific reading strategies.

- Students can listen to a story several times over a period of several days.
- Students may wish to orally read and record their own stories for others to listen to.
- Students can listen just for pleasure.
- Students can listen to a story and then retell it to another student.

Directions/Routines (to be discussed and shared with students)

- Select a tape and a book from the box.
- Put a recorded tape in the player.
- Put on and adjust a set of headphones.
- Turn on the player and adjust the volume.
- Listen to the story and follow along in the book.
- Point to the words as you listen to them on the tape.
- At the end of the tape, rewind it.
- Remove the tape from the player.
- Turn off the tape player and return the tape to the box.
- Talk about the story with someone else.

ABC/Spelling Center

An ABC/Spelling Center provides a unique opportunity for students to work independently on visual/graphophonic skills. Students can engage in various matching activities in which they manipulate both the sounds and letters of the English language.

Value

- Students can work independently on specific phonics skills.
- Students manipulate the basic elements of language.
- Students learn to match phonemes and graphemes.
- Students "take charge" of learning spelling conventions.

Design Considerations

- Provide appropriate manipulation space on a table or desk.
- Provide a variety of letter sizes (uppercase, lowercase).
- Provide a variety of letter materials (cardboard, plastic, wood, etc.).
- Provide magnetic letters and a magnetic surface.
- Provide words from a book for students to duplicate.
- Provide opportunities for students to work in teams.

Suggested Activities

- Encourage students to spell their names.
- Invite students to spell or reconstruct words from a selected book or story.
- Students can work with various affixes (suffixes, prefixes).
- Each day designate a letter or word of the day for students to duplicate in the center.

Teaching Comprehension in Grades 1–2

- Invite students to "spell the room."
- Invite students to create their own letters for inclusion in the center.
- Invite students to share a favorite word from a story and then to spell it in the center.

Directions/Routines (to be discussed and shared with students)

- Please work quietly.
- If you need help, please ask.
- Share your work with someone else.
- Talk about what you are learning.

Art Center

An art center encourages youngsters to focus on one of the most important beginning reading strategies—the match between text and illustrations. As youngsters engage in a variety of books and a variety of genres, they begin to develop understanding about the cues inherent in pictures, illustrations, and photographs. Providing creative outlets for students to express themselves through art assists them in making the transition from visual cues to spoken cues to written cues.

Value

- Allows students to develop personal responses to literature
- Enhances the development of the visual/spatial multiple intelligence
- Creates "connections" between pictures and words
- Extends reading activities in imaginative ways
- Is personally fulfilling and enriching

Design Considerations

- Provide a wide variety of art materials.
- Assemble the materials in well-labeled boxes or baskets.
- Instruct students on how to obtain and replace materials.
- Allow children free choice of materials.
- Provide smocks, aprons, and other protective wear as necessary.
- Provide examples of text/illustration matches for display.
- Post student work prominently in the center.
- Little pre-planning or teacher intervention is necessary for this center to be successful.

Suggested Activities

- Invite students to duplicate illustrations from a favorite book.
- Provide the text from a book and invite students to create a matching illustration.
- Invite students to label pictures and illustrations.
- Ask students to include "talking bubbles" for book characters.

- Invite students to write descriptive sentences (from a book) on their illustrations.
- Bind student illustrations into a class book.
- Consider developing students' illustrations into a PowerPoint presentation (with accompanying text).
- Invite students to work together to create "Buddy Books."

Directions/Routines (to be discussed and shared with students)

- Work with a quiet voice.
- Put a smock on before you begin.
- Remember: Neatness counts.
- Take only the materials you need.
- When you are done, put everything back.
- Clean up any messes.
- Share your work with others.

Writing Center

One of the most valuable parts of the classroom literacy program is the multiple opportunities there are to integrate writing into the curriculum. Writing allows children another form of expression—a way to describe their world, their thoughts, their imaginations, and their "learnings." Writing is a natural and normal corollary to reading in that youngsters have multiple opportunities to use some of their reading strategies in another context. Writing is also a personal response to one's world that can be valued and celebrated.

Value

- Fosters critical thinking
- Demonstrates the interrelationships between all language arts
- Promotes organization of ideas
- Allows for expressive thought
- Places a personal value on words and their use
- Stimulates application of print conventions
- Highlights Process Writing (pre-writing, drafting, revising, editing, publishing)

Design Considerations

- Provide a large expansive area.
- Offer a wide variety of writing tools (pencils, markers, pens, crayons, colored pencils, etc.).
- Provide journals or notebooks as necessary.
- Offer many types of recording possibilities (paper, cardboard, construction paper, etc.).
- Provide writing-related tools (stapler, paper clips, scissors, glue, data stamp, etc.).
- Put all materials in labeled trays or baskets for ease of use.
- Provide a "check out/check in" system for all materials.

Suggested Activities

(NOTE: There are many excellent resources available for teachers with a host of suggested writing activities for beginning readers.)

- Invite students to retell favorite stories/books.
- Students can create labels for various classroom items.
- Students can create a set of directions for a game.
- Students can write their name using various materials and devices for posting in the room.
- Students can create lists.
- Invite students to write a letter.
- Students can create their own poetry.
- Invite students to rewrite a story and read it aloud.
- Students can write alphabetic letters and post them.
- Students can keep a journal or diary.
- Students can create vocabulary lists.
- Students can add to a Word Wall.

Directions/Routines (to be discussed and shared with students)

- Write something every day.
- Share your work with someone else.
- Use different writing tools (pencils, markers, crayons).
- Think about words and letters in the books you read.

Reading Around the Room Center

This particular center is less a center than it is an opportunity for students to become more aware of their surroundings (particularly in a print-rich classroom suffused with letters, words, sentences, and other examples of language). You are encouraged to "flood" your classroom with signs, posters, bulletins, letters, words, sentences, and items to be read of every shape, size, and dimension.

Value

- Students are immersed in the sights and sounds of language.
- Supports the "immersion" principle of language learning.
- Students appreciate the various ways in which language is used.
- Students see language "in action."
- Students begin to make connections between the language in a book and the language that is/can be used in normal everyday activities.

Design Considerations

- Provide a central location for students to begin.
- Provide appropriate writing materials.
- Post/use words selected from specific reading texts.
- Use the students' own language.

- Cover every available classroom space with words and letters.
- Invite students to create their own signs and postings for the classroom.
- Provide students with pointers (long and short) to use.

Suggested Activities

- Invite students to work with a partner to locate specific words/letters.
- One student can point to a word while the other reads the word.
- Reverse the roles on a regular basis.
- Invite students to "write the room," copying down selected letters and/or words.
- Students can read LEA stories.
- Students can read selected sentences from a story posted on a wall.
- Invite students to "read" alphabet charts.
- Invite students to read several different versions of their own names posted throughout the room.
- Students can read appropriate materials posted in pocket charts.

Directions/Routines (to be discussed and shared with students)

- Work with a partner.
- Work with quiet voices.
- Use the pointer very carefully. It is not a weapon.
- Share what you discover.
- Write down what you find.

Pocket Chart Center

Pocket charts allow you to focus on the structure of language for the youngsters in your class. You may wish to devote attention to the various language patterns that exist in the books and stories you share with students and compare those patterns with the oral language used by individuals. Pocket charts allow for a great deal of flexibility and can enhance the teaching of the ways in which language works.

Value

- Enhances cooperation
- Engages students in a "hands-on, minds-on" activity
- Promotes student independence
- Provides students with opportunities to "see" the relationships between oral and written language

Design Considerations

- If possible, provide several pocket charts for students to use.
- Post one or more pocket charts on the wall (where they cannot be pulled down).
- Provide one or more pocket charts for students to use at a table, desk, or other flat area.

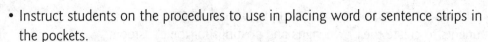

- Instruct students on the procedures to use in placing word or sentence strips in the pockets.
- Provide opportunities for students to work independently as well as in small groups.
- Provide pre-printed strips as well as blank strips for students to construct their own words and/or sentences.

Suggested Activities

- Students can reconstruct the words in a story sentence.
- Students can reconstruct a sentence from the story.
- Students can reconstruct a favorite poem or song.
- Students can dictate a sentence to the teacher. The teacher prints each word on a separate card for the student to reconstruct in a pocket chart.
- One student can read a sentence from a book while another places the pre-printed words in a pocket chart.
- A small group of students can place words in a pocket chart to create a sentence and then locate that sentence in the accompanying book.
- Students can construct rebus (picture) sentences.
- Students can build words from a book using specific phonic elements.

Directions/Routines (to be discussed and shared with students)

- Work with a quiet voice.
- Practice putting letter or word cards in the pockets first.
- Think about what makes sense.
- Ask for help if you need it.
- Talk with someone and share what you did.

Free Reading Center

The ultimate goal of reading instruction is to assist children in becoming independent readers. Students who have opportunities to select books on their own and to read those books using the skills and strategies taught them in the classroom reading program are provided with a genuine gift. Not only do they see the value of reading instruction, but they also have valid opportunities to utilize those newfound abilities in meaningful ways.

Value

- Students become independent readers.
- Students are able to use reading strategies in a variety of self-selected texts.
- Children have easy access to texts.
- Students can extend comprehension strategies in various ways.
- Reading is seen as a personal endeavor.
- Students have time, by themselves, to read.

Design Considerations

- Flood the center with books from all genres.
- Provide carpet squares, rugs, chairs, or other forms of seating.
- Offer pillows and/or stuffed animals as appropriate.
- Provide a quiet space away from the hustle and bustle of the classroom.
- Provide a timer (egg timer, small travel alarm, etc.) so that students can read for a set period of time.
- Make the center as colorful and as print-rich as possible with signs ("Our Favorite Authors"), lists (books, genres), posters ("Good Readers Gather Here"), and other indicators.

Suggested Activities

- Students can read silently.
- Students can read with a buddy.
- Students should free-select books from the classroom library.
- Students can read softly to themselves or to a partner.
- Students can "warm up" for reading instruction with a matching book.
- Students can extend a reading lesson with a similar book (theme, level, author, genre, etc.).
- Invite students to read with an older student or an adult volunteer.
- Invite students to keep a list of books read in a journal or individual notebook.

Directions/Routines (to be discussed and shared with students)

- Choose your own book.
- Get a carpet square and find a quiet place.
- Read in your quiet voice.
- Read by yourself or to a buddy.
- Please respect others.
- Put the name of the book in your notebook.

Drama/Storytelling Center

Drama provides youngsters with opportunities to bring the books and stories they read to life. It is an opportunity to share with children the divergent and creative interpretations possible with literature. Youngsters begin to understand reading as a personal interpretation that can be "colored" by one's experiences and imagination.

Value

- Enables students to interpret literature in a variety of ways
- Enhances cooperative learning skills
- Allows children to use their imaginations in a host of activities
- Enhances and facilitates students' oral language skills

Unit

11

Suggested Literacy Centers

- Enhances students' listening skills
- Encourages appreciation of stories through multiple sharing activities
- Allows students to cultivate personal interpretations of reading materials
- Provides opportunities for students to be creative, imaginative, and inventive
- Integrates speaking and listening skills

Design Considerations

- Provide students with a variety of materials for the construction of puppets.
- Offer lots of props and supplies (paper, pencils, magazines, etc.).
- Provide a variety of costumes (hats, masks, old clothing, shoes, etc.).
- Provide boxes that can be turned into houses, buildings, and related structures.
- Provide drawing, marking, and coloring tools (crayons, paints, markers, etc.) for students to design props, scenes, or book settings.
- Encourage students to work together to interpret a story or book.
- Recruit an older student or adult volunteer to assist with the construction of materials.
- Provide opportunities for student groups to share their "productions" with others.

Suggested Activities

- Invite students to use one or more puppets.
- Invite students to create their own original puppets.
- Create a staging set (e.g., simple: the bottom cut out of a cardboard box; complex: a plywood puppet stage that has been painted and hung with curtain material).
- "Productions" can be videotaped for later showing.
- Invite students to turn the traditional "Show and Tell" into a dramatic sharing of a favorite book.
- Invite students to develop a favorite book into a readers' theater production.

Directions/Routines (to be discussed and shared with students)

- Choose a favorite book.
- Think about how you would like to "produce" it.
- Work with a buddy.
- Make one or more puppets for the characters.
- Share your production with others.
- Return all supplies to their proper places.

Buddy Reading Center

Buddy reading allows children to work together in pairs to share and discuss a favorite story or book. Its advantage is that youngsters begin to understand that reading, speaking, and listening are all related and can all be integrated into meaningful and purposeful literacy activities. Students get to share their developing competencies with a member of their peer group in a highly supportive environment.

Value

- Listening skills are enhanced.
- Cooperative learning techniques can be taught and practiced.
- Students are actively engaged in discussing text.
- Students assume a measure of independence in language learning.
- Students find an eager and receptive audience.

Design Considerations

- Provide a quiet area for students to work.
- Train students in advance about the importance of sharing and listening.
- Fill the center with books appropriate for students' reading levels.
- Students can be randomly assigned to the center.
- Students can select their own reading buddies.
- A special rug or several carpet squares can be used.
- Provide pillows as warranted.
- Provide one or two stuffed animals to be used as alternate "reading buddies."

Suggested Activities

- Students can read a story or book to a stuffed animal.
- Students can have identical copies of a book and read it to each other.
- Students can have two different books and share them with each other.
- One student can read the first page of a book, the other student can read the second page, the first student then reads the third page, and so on.
- One student can read a book aloud while the other points to the accompanying illustrations.
- One student can read a book aloud while the other points to the matching words.
- Reading buddies can read a book together out loud.
- Reading buddies can read a book together silently.

Directions/Routines (to be discussed and shared with students)

- Select a book to share with a buddy.
- Practice reading the book by yourself.
- Read to your buddy in a "quiet voice."
- Invite your buddy to read to you.
- Talk about the book together.

 ## Big Book Center

This center is an extension of the activities and processes that take place during comprehension lessons. However, in this center the role of the teacher can be taken over by one or more students. Thus, students have a unique opportunity to use "teacher materials" (e.g., big books) and emulate the teacher or replicate the activities shared during other forms of reading instruction.

Value

- Students use familiar materials.
- Students use and practice familiar routines.
- Students have unique opportunities to extend reading concepts through independent work.
- Students use large-print materials that can be seen by all members of a group.
- Students engage in cooperative learning activities.

Design Considerations

- Provide a wide assortment of big books.
- Provide opportunities for students to practice using the big books using "teacher skills" (e.g., opening the cover of the book, turning a page, pointing to selected words, etc.).
- Provide small pointers (pullers, short lengths of dowels, pencils) for children to use.
- In lieu of big books, consider reproducing text on acetate sheets and projecting them on a wall (in large font) for students to read.
- Provide students with a set of laminated cards on which you have outlined the things you do during reading instruction so that students may emulate them.
- Provide books with which students are familiar or have used in reading sessions.
- Reinforce the spines of books with library tape to ensure long life.

Suggested Activities

- Encourage students to work in small groups to discuss a book shared during reading instruction.
- Ask students to focus on a specific literary feature of the story (e.g., character, setting, point of view, theme, plot).
- Invite students to share and discuss what they enjoyed about a book.
- Ask students to retell the story in their own words.
- Invite students to compare and contrast two big books.
- Invite students to use word frames to highlight selected words.
- Invite students to use sticky notes to mask selected words, phrases, punctuation, illustrations, etc.

Directions/Routines (to be discussed and shared with students)

- Select a big book.
- Work with a group of buddies.
- Share the book just as your teacher does.
- Follow the instructions on the cards.
- Talk about the book and what you liked.
- When you are finished, put back all the materials.

Unit 12

Plans and Schedules

There is no ideal plan for scheduling Comprehension Circles. There are as many ways of presenting comprehension instruction to students as there are teachers. Each classroom is unique. The needs of children and the competencies of the teacher must be balanced against the time available for instruction and the other elements of a well-rounded instructional program.

Following are some considerations that you may wish to keep in mind as you begin developing schedules for Comprehension Circles. These considerations are framed as questions simply because the answers will determine the structure of a routine that works in your particular classroom for your particular students:

- How many students do you have in your class?

- Do you have instructional assistance (aides, volunteers)?

- What is the largest group you can manage? (This will be determined by students' pre-reading competencies outlined earlier in this book.)

- How many students would you like to have in a Comprehension Circle? (This can range from an entire class down to the ideal size of 4–5.)

- How much time do you have available in the schedule for Comprehension Circles? (The ideal is 10–15 minutes per session.)

- How often do you want to meet with youngsters in Comprehension Circles? (Five meetings in a 2-week period is suggested.)

- How much "down time" or transition time between groups and activities is necessary?

> *"The needs of children and the competencies of the teacher must be balanced against the time available for instruction . . ."*

The answers to these questions will help you construct a workable schedule of literacy activities that respects the needs of individuals and offers a support structure for students and for you.

Suggested Formats

It is important to remember that Comprehension Circles are one element in the overall instruction program. They should be structured in such a way that youngsters see them as a natural and normal outgrowth of their encounters with books. Since it is assumed that you will be engaging students in regular and daily encounters with literature through read alouds, Comprehension Circles should be "placed" into the schedule to offer children authentic extensions of the books and stories you share on a daily basis. In so doing, you will help to promote the idea that thinking about what is read is just as important as the pleasurable experience of listening to a story read aloud.

Following are examples of daily schedules collected from several teachers who have embraced the concept of Comprehension Circles. They are provided as examples of the wide variety of instructional schedules that support comprehension instruction and children's developing literacy abilities. Use them as models for your classroom design and scheduling. Feel free to modify or adjust these schedules in accordance with school practices, schedules, and conventions. Make these your own: change them to suit the needs of your classroom, the needs of your students, and your own philosophy about teaching reading and the other areas of your first- and second-grade schedule.

Daily Schedule #1

8:20 – 8:45	**Table Activities**	Children play games at tables and talk quietly with their classmates.
8:45 – 9:15	**Morning Meeting**	Children shake hands and greet friends; pledge; sing song; calendar; weather activities; Morning Message.
9:15 – 9:30	**Journals**	Children record stories (with accompanying illustrations) in their own personal journals.
9:30 – 10:15	**Specials**	Art, Music, Gym, Health, Library
10:15 – 10:35	**Snack/Book Time**	
10:35 – 11:00	**Shared Reading**	Read a big book together (student selected or teacher selected).
11:00 – 11:15	**Comprehension Circle**	Teacher works with a group of students on a specific comprehension strategy. This may be an extension of the Shared Reading experience or a new book.
11:15 – 12:15	**Lunch and Recess**	
12:15 – 12:45	**Math**	Math activities using unifix cubes, pattern blocks, tiles, links, and various counters.
12:45 – 1:10	**Shared Reading**	Read a big book together (student selected or teacher selected).
1:10 – 1:25	**Comprehension Circle**	Teacher works with a group of students on a specific comprehension strategy. This may be an extension of the Shared Reading experience or a new book.
1:25 – 1:55	**Literacy Centers**	Children work in various centers including ABC Center, Pocket Chart Center, Poetry Center, and Writing Center.
1:55 – 2:15	**Interactive Writing**	Students (with teacher assistance) write a sentence about something that happened during the day.
2:15 – 2:35	**Phonemic Awareness**	Using the book *The Complete Phonemic Awareness Handbook* (Rigby, 2001), the teacher provides students with various activities at the five stages of phonemic awareness.
2:35 – 2:45	**Ready to Go Home**	

Daily Schedule #2

7:55 – 8:20	Math Tubs	Children use math manipulatives.
8:20 – 8:35	Class Meeting	Daily activities; calendar; weather; sing-alongs.
8:35 – 8:55	Math Board	Whole class math lesson and follow-up activities.
8:55 – 9:10	Phonemic Awareness	Whole class and small group phonemic awareness activities (assisted by aide).
9:10 – 9:20	Daily News Chart	
9:20 – 9:50	Shared Reading	Read a big book together (student selected or teacher selected).
9:50 – 10:05	Comprehension Circle	Teacher works with a group of students on a specific comprehension strategy. This may be an extension of the Shared Reading experience or a new book.
10:05 – 10:20	Language Arts Centers	Children work in various centers including ABC Center, Pocket Chart Center, Poetry Center, and Writing Center.
10:20 – 10:35	Morning Recess	
10:35 – 10:50	Alphabet/ Phonics Lesson	
10:50 – 11:10	Reading Workshop	
11:10 – 11:20	Picture and Word Chart	Students match illustrations with sight vocabulary words.
11:20 – 11:40	Writing Workshop	Students record a sentence in their individual journals.
11:40 – 12:20	Lunch and Recess	
12:20 – 12:50	Computer Lab	
12:50 – 1:10	Shared Reading	Read a big book together (student selected or teacher selected).
1:10 – 1:25	Comprehension Circle	Teacher works with a group of students on a specific comprehension strategy. This may be an extension of the Shared Reading experience or a new book.
1:25 – 1:40	Afternoon Recess	
1:40 – 2:10	Science/ Social Studies	
2:10 – 2:50	Special Classes	Art, Music, Library, Gym
2:50 – 3:05	Show and Tell	
3:05 – 3:15	Getting Ready and Dismissal	

Daily Schedule #3

8:30 – 8:45	**Greet Children**	Put backpack and lunch kit away; Morning reading.
8:45 – 8:55	**Morning Announcements**	
8:55 – 9:10	**Calendar**	
9:10 – 9:30	**Theme Work**	One of four annual themes (e.g., Bears, Growing Up, Holidays, Measuring) is pursued by children using a variety of language arts activities.
9:30 – 10:00	**Math**	Youngsters use a variety of math manipulatives.
10:00 – 10:15	**Phonemic Awareness**	Using the book *The Complete Phonemic Awareness Handbook* (Rigby, 2001), the teacher provides students with various activities at the five stages of phonemic awareness.
10:15 – 11:00	**Writing**	Modeled writing; Journal writing
11:00 – 11:15	**D.E.A.R./Restrooms**	
11:15 – 11:45	**Lunch**	
11:45 – 12:15	**Recess**	
12:15 – 12:45	**Storytelling**	
12:45 – 1:00	**Read Aloud**	The teacher selects a book to share orally with all students.
1:00 – 1:15	**Comprehension Circle**	Teacher works with the whole class on a specific comprehension strategy. This is an extension of the Read Aloud book.
1:15 – 1:45	**Literacy Centers**	Students select from 8 different centers positioned around the room.
1:45 – 2:15	**Science/ Social Studies**	
2:15 – 2:35	**Free Play**	
2:35 – 2:45	**Clean room; Pack backpacks**	
2:45	**Dismissal**	

Unit 12

Suggested Formats

Daily Schedule #4

8:30 – 8:50	**Opening**	Students arrive and put away their book bags. They gather in small groups to read the room or engage in independent reading activities.
8:50 – 9:15	**Whole Class Instruction**	A structured and planned lesson is presented to the entire class. The emphasis may be on a reading strategy or concept.
9:15 – 9:45	**Writing Process**	The class is divided into various groups to participate in a wide variety of writing activities.
9:45 – 10:30	**Guided Reading Groups**	Students are assigned to various learning centers arranged throughout the classroom. The teacher works with each of two separate guided reading groups on specific reading strategies.
10:30 – 11:30	**Science/ Social Studies**	Students participate in textbook readings and complementary "hands-on, minds-on" activities that extend and expand the concepts in the text.
11:30 – 12:00	**Lunch**	
12:00 – 12:30	**Sustained Silent Reading**	Students and the teacher read self-selected books throughout the room. Quiet pervades.
12:30 – 1:15	**Math**	Students work in their math textbooks and accompanying workbooks on various math concepts and principles.
1:15 – 1:35	**Storytelling/ Read Aloud**	A selection of authors, genres, and books is shared with students in the Town Center.
1:35 – 2:10	**Art/Music**	Students go with either the Art teacher or Music teacher.
2:10 – 2:40	**Comprehension Circle**	Students work with the teacher in Comprehension Circles using familiar literature.
2:40 – 3:00	**Responding to Literature**	Students complete book-related activities and projects in self-selected literacy centers.
3:00 – 3:15	**Daily Closure**	Students gather in the Town Center to discuss the days' activities and plan for the next day's lessons.
3:15	**Dismissal**	

Daily Schedule #5

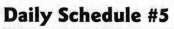

8:45 – 9:00	Arrival Prepare for the Day	
9:00 – 9:20	Sustained Silent Reading	Students each select their own book to read, crawl under a desk, flop in a bean bag chair, or sprawl on the floor to read by themselves.
9:20 – 9:45	Class Meeting	Students and the teacher meet to plan the day's activities, discuss any "leftover" material from the day before, and outline the goals and objectives for various lessons.
9:45 – 10:25	Reading	Students are assigned to various guided reading groups. The teacher works with two separate groups on pre-selected strategies. Other students are engaged in learning center activities.
10:25 – 10:45	Comprehension Circle	The teacher works with the entire class on a Comprehension Circle strategy.
10:45 – 11:45	Writing	Stages of the writing process are taught or reinforced. Students are provided with authentic opportunities to use those stages in a variety of writing projects.
11:45 – 12:15	Lunch	
12:15 -12:30	Read Aloud	The teacher reads a book to the students that they have selected.
12:30 – 1:15	Math	Students use a variety of manipulatives to reinforce various math concepts.
1:15 – 1:45	P.E.	Students go with the P.E. teacher to the gym.
1:45 – 2:45	Science	Students work in an "Oceans" unit, reading ocean-related books, cleaning the classroom aquarium, and designing an interactive bulletin board.
2:45 – 3:15	Technology	Students work on the classroom computers.
3:15	Dismissal	

Daily Schedule #6

8:50 – 9:30	Calendar Math; Math	Students work with the daily calendar identifying days, working with ordinal numbers, and engaging in manipulative activities.
9:30 – 10:30	Word Work	Students engage in a wide variety of literacy activities, including reading the room, searching for words in books, and learning structural analysis skills.
10:30 – 10:45	Recess	
10:45 – 11:45	Guided Reading	Students are grouped (and regrouped) for various guided reading activities with leveled books.
11:45 – 12:30	Lunch	
12:30 – 1:15	Writing Block	Students participate in process writing activities that originate with the literature shared in the classroom.
1:15 – 1:30	Self-Sustained Reading	Students are provided an extended period of time to read books of their own choosing.
1:30 – 2:00	Comprehension Circle	The teacher works with two separate Comprehension Circle groups (1:30 – 1:45 and 1:45 – 2:00).
2:00 – 2:45	Special Subject (Art, Music, P.E., Library)	
2:45 – 3:05	Recess	
3:05 – 3:25	Story Time	The teacher reads a book to the students that is tied into a current theme they are studying.
3:25	Dismissal	

Suggested Frequencies

Many schools follow a five-day, six-day, or seven-day schedule (e.g., Day 1, Day 2, Day 3, etc.). As a result, schedules cannot always be configured for a normal Monday through Friday schedule. This sometimes presents some scheduling challenges. In assembling a schedule for your classroom, keep in mind these basic principles. These have been gathered from teachers in a wide range of classrooms and underscore the basic principles of literacy development discussed earlier in the book.

Literacy Practice	Frequency
Read Aloud	Daily
Think-Aloud	Daily
Shared Reading	Daily
Comprehension Circles	3–4 times per cycle
Independent Reading	Several times per cycle
Phonemic Awareness	Daily (as appropriate)
Kid Writing	Several times per cycle
Shared Writing	Several times per cycle

Note: A "cycle" is one complete sequence of instructional days. This may include 1) a Monday through Friday schedule, 2) a Day #1 through Day #6 schedule, 3) a Day #1 through Day #7 schedule, 4) a Day "A" through Day "F" schedule, or any other possibility used by your school or district.

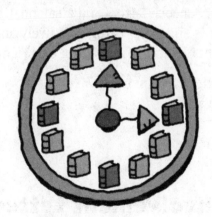

Unit 13

Parent Involvement Activities

The Importance of Parent Involvement

It has often been said that parents are a child's first and best teachers. Without question, parents provide children with the basic foundation on which successful learning experiences can be built. The support, encouragement, patience, and understanding of parents have a profound effect on both the academic and social development of children.

During the first five years of life, when children spend a majority of their time at home, more than 60 percent of their intellectual development takes place. It is during this time that children learn to walk, talk, eat by themselves, develop a sense of independence, and seek to explore the world around them. Children learn more at this time than at any other time in their lives. These foundational skills serve as the basis for the learning and social experiences a child encounters in the more formal atmosphere of the classroom.

The three sections that follow have been designed to provide you with a selection of relevant and meaningful suggestions to share with parents. These suggestions, in the form of special letters and a calendar to be sent home on a periodic basis, offer parents and other caregivers lively and fun activities that stimulate the development of successful reading experiences.

The following sections are included:
• Involvement Letters
• Literature Letters
• Family Reading Time Letters

Involvement Letters

This section provides you with several reproducible letters to send home to parents. Each of the letters focuses on direct and easy-to-implement activities that

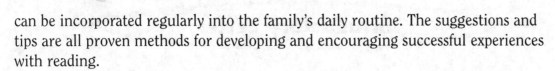

can be incorporated regularly into the family's daily routine. The suggestions and tips are all proven methods for developing and encouraging successful experiences with reading.

You are encouraged to send these letters to the parents of your students on a regular basis. The following ideas are suggested:

1. Photocopy one letter and sign your name in the space provided at the bottom of the letter. Add the date at the top of the letter.

2. Photocopy the letter in a quantity sufficient for the number of students in your class.

3. Send the letter home with your students on a selected day (every other Tuesday is "Letter Day" or every third Thursday is "Letter Day").

4. Encourage students to ask their parents to work with them on the activities and suggestions on each letter. Emphasize that these letters are not "homework" assignments, rather an opportunity for families to work and learn together.

5. You may wish to encourage students to bring in and share selected family activities with other members of the class.

The following strategies may help to facilitate a two-way communication of the letters between home and school:

• Include a letter as part of a regular newsletter/newspaper sent home by the school.

• Clip the letters to school bulletins or other announcements sent home to parents.

• Write a brief, personalized note at the bottom of each letter commenting on something positive about the student.

• Schedule workshops at school at which parents can share some of their favorite activities, books, or songs.

• Ask the principal or superintendent to prepare a special introductory letter to parents explaining the letters and their value.

• You may wish to have translations of these letters made for parents who don't speak English.

> "*P*arents provide children with the basic foundation on which successful learning experiences can be built."

This section and the ones that follow have been designed to serve as convenient resources for you as you seek to involve parents in the education of their children. Used throughout the course of your reading comprehension program, these letters can help ensure that everyone is working toward a common goal and that the best interests of all children are being provided for in an atmosphere of mutual trust, support, and encouragement.

Introductory Letter

Date: _____

Dear Parents:

Our class will be learning many new skills this year. Students will be learning many things about books and reading. Your child will be learning some important reading skills that will help her/him understand and appreciate books.

I would like to invite you to become a partner in your child's learning experiences this year. I believe your involvement will help your child attain a higher level of academic success. This partnership between home and school can provide your child with a wealth of learning opportunities that will positively affect her or his reading performance.

In order to help reinforce the work we are doing in the classroom, I will be sending home prepared parent letters regularly with activities for you and your child to share. These letters are designed to provide you with ideas that can help your child become a successful reader. Each letter contains several choices of activities to share—activities that will reinforce the work we are doing in school without disrupting your family schedule. There are no special materials to buy; no expensive equipment or electronic gadgets are required. Your only investment is a few moments of your time each day—a few moments that can make a world of difference in your child's education. I look forward to your participation in our learning experiences this year. If you have any questions about these letters or calendars, please feel free to contact me. Let's work together this year to help your child succeed in school!

Sincerely,

Sharing Reading Time

Date: _____

Dear Parents:

Reading stories to your children is a most valuable activity. When children listen to adults read, it helps them develop an appreciation for written material and for the ideas and thoughts that books can convey. Many experts in the field of reading have determined that parents who read to their children on a regular basis are more likely to have children who are good readers. Children who have been read to will undoubtedly be eager to read for themselves because they know of the pleasures to be found in books. Here are some suggestions:

1. Before reading to your child, practice reading aloud by yourself the first few times to feel more comfortable.

2. Establish a relaxed atmosphere with no radios, TV, or other distractions. Try setting aside a family reading time when everyone reads.

3. Encourage your child to stop to ask you questions. This shows that your child is interested in what you are reading.

4. You may want to stop from time to time in your reading to ask questions about the characters or events in the story. Ask questions like "Why do you think she/he did that?"

5. Be sure to check with the school librarian, children's librarian at your local public library, and bookstore personnel for suggested books. Provide opportunities for your child to select books she or he would enjoy hearing.

Your child will enjoy the time you spend together. Together we are sending your child on the road to academic success.

Sincerely,

Reading Aloud with Your Child

Date: _____

Dear Parents:

Learning to read is one of the most valuable skills your child can ever learn. To help your child on the road to reading success, set aside a special time each day to read with your child. This sharing time is important since it demonstrates to your child that reading can be fun, exciting, and informative. Best of all, when parents and children share a book, they have a special time together. Plan to take a few moments each day to share the joy of literature with your child. Here are some ideas:

1. Give your child plenty of opportunities to choose the reading materials to share together. Let her or him pick books based on special interests, favorite characters, hobbies, or the illustrations on the front of a book.

2. Read aloud with lots of expression. You may wish to take on the role of one of the characters in a book and adjust your voice accordingly.

3. As you read an old familiar story to your child, occasionally leave out a word and ask your child to suggest the missing word or a substitute word.

4. Make reading a regular part of your family activities. Take books along on family outings or trips. Read to your child every chance you get.

Thank you for being an important part of your child's learning. Working together, we can help your child become a great reader.

Sincerely,

Making Reading Fun

Date: _____

Dear Parents:

In order for children to become good readers, they must be actively involved in all the fun and magic of good books. We know that children who are motivated to learn to read are those who are surrounded by the fun of reading. When children know that reading can be a fun, enjoyable, and satisfying activity, they will be actively engaged in all of the skills and activities designed to help them on the road to reading success. Just as important is the fact that children will help develop positive attitudes towards reading and learning in general when parents share some fun reading-related activities. Try these motivators:

1. Take lots of photographs of your child with books—for example, taking a book off a shelf, sharing a book with another family member, or looking at a book in a bookstore. Paste these on sheets of paper and ask your child to suggest titles for each one. Then display them.

2. After you and your child finish reading a book together, create a puppet or model of one of the characters. These can be displayed on top of the bookcase or refrigerator.

3. After you have read a book to your child, ask her or him to tell you a word from the story that she or he especially liked. It can be a funny word, a sad word, a rhyming word, or a strange word. Write the word on an index card and place the card inside the front cover of the book. The next time you share the book with your child, talk about the word on the card and why your child selected that word after the previous reading.

4. Invite your child to draw an illustration or picture of her or his favorite character or favorite part of the story. Post these on the refrigerator or family bulletin board.

The time you spend with your child is important. Thank you for all your contributions.

Sincerely,

Story Questions

Date: _____

Dear Parents:

Questions help children discover more about the world in which they live—whether that world is their living room, a community park, or a large city. Questions help children acquire new knowledge and gain an appreciation of the "how" and "why" of life. Parents, too, can participate in asking their children questions, not to test how much children know, but rather to help their children focus on important points of discovery. Try 2 or 3 of these questions each time you read a book to your child:

1. What do you think this story will be about?

2. Do you know about any other books on this topic? Tell me about them.

3. Where do you think this story might take place?

4. How do you think this story will end?

5. Did the story turn out as you expected?

6. What made this an interesting story?

7. What might be some new ideas we could add to this story?

8. Is the main character someone you would enjoy as a friend?

9. What did you like most?

10. What would you like to say to the author/writer?

Thank you for helping your child get ready for reading. I really appreciate all your assistance.

Sincerely,

Making Predictions

Date: _____

Dear Parents:

One of the skills all good readers use is the skill of making predictions or "educated guesses." When readers look at the title of a book, for example, they make a prediction about the characters ("Who are they?"), the plot ("What is this story all about?"), or the setting ("Where does this story take place?"). Adults do this all the time when they read the headlines in a newspaper or scan the shelves in a bookstore. Making predictions is one of the most important skills any reader can have.

You can help your child make predictions while she/he is learning how to become a successful reader. You can do this by modeling, or showing, your child how you think when you read something. This can be done very easily by talking to your child about the thinking that is going on in your head when you read. In other words, let your child "see" what goes on inside your head when you read. Here are some examples to get you started:

- "From this title, I think this story is about a haunted house."
- "When I look at this picture, I think that this book is about cowboys."
- "The picture on this page makes me think that (the main character) is having a good time."
- "I think the next page will tell us where the dragon lives."
- "The picture on the front of the book makes me think that the story takes place on the ocean."
- "This picture makes me smile, so I think that this will be a funny book."

You can offer your child opportunities to "look inside your head" whenever you read a book to her/him. You can do this before you read the book ("This title makes me think that we are going to read a sad story.") or while you are in the middle of a story ("Since the dog ran away, I think that Jamie will go after it."). Talking about how you think when you read a book (especially when you read a book with your child) is important to your child's success as a reader. Together we can help ensure a lifetime of reading enjoyment for your child.

Sincerely,

Mind Pictures

Date: _____

Dear Parents:

In school we are learning about some of the skills that readers use to appreciate and understand stories. One of those skills is the creation of mind pictures when we read. In other words, all readers, including you and me, create pictures in our heads when we read. If we are reading an adventure story, we often create an adventure scene in our mind as we read. If we read a story about the ocean, we frequently create a picture of a beach in our mind. This is something all readers do, and it is one of the keys to successful reading experiences—even for youngsters who are just learning to read.

You can help your child with this important skill by showing your child how you create pictures in your own mind when you read. To do this, just talk out loud about the pictures you "see" inside your head either before you read a story with your child or while you are reading a story with your child. Here are some examples:

- "When I read this title, I can see a picture of a boy playing with his dog."

- "I'm getting a picture in my head of a ship sailing on the ocean."

- "The picture I have in my mind is of a group of whales."

- "I can see a picture in my head of a pond filled with frogs and fish."

After you and your child finish reading a book together, take some time to talk with your child about the pictures she/he may have imagined. If you wish, invite your child to imagine that there is a television set inside her or his head. Encourage your child to talk about the pictures that were on that TV set while you were reading.

Spending time with your child is important. Your contributions are vital to your child's future reading success.

Sincerely,

Learning to Listen

Date: _____

Dear Parents:

One of the most valuable skills your child can learn is that of listening. In fact, more than 50 percent of what your child will learn in school will depend on how well she or he is able to listen and follow directions. Young children need to be able to understand, remember, and act on what they hear—both at home and when they are in school.

You can help your child develop good listening skills through some of the following activities. Try to use some of them every day as you and your child learn and play together.

1. Read to your child on a regular basis. You may wish to point to words as you read them aloud. This helps your child understand the relationship between spoken and written language. As you read, leave out a word and let your child suggest one that makes sense.

2. Take time to listen to your child patiently and without interruption. Share the events in your day (at home or at work), using the terms *first*, *next*, *last*, *before*, and *after*. Ask your child about her or his day by using these sequence words. For example, you might ask, "What did you do first today?" or "What came right after lunch?"

3. As you make requests of your child, note the number of directions your child can recall and respond to correctly. Make a game of gradually increasing the number of directions she or he can follow. Let your child make up directions for you to follow as well.

4. From time to time, take a walk with your child around the neighborhood or block. Talk with your child about the things you see together. What new things do you see? What are some of the familiar things that you see together? Plan time after your walk to discuss your "neighborhood adventure."

I hope you and your child enjoy the time you spend together. I look forward to your continued involvement.

Sincerely,

Learning from Experiences

Date: _____

Dear Parents:

Childhood is filled with many new and exciting experiences. Helping your child discover and appreciate these experiences will be an important part of her/his growth in reading—both now and for the future. Readers tend to use the experiences they have encountered in their lives as a foundation for understanding and enjoying the ideas in books and magazines. Helping your child succeed in reading can be stimulated by offering a variety of experiences outside the home—in the community, the neighborhood, and beyond. Try these ideas:

1. Plan a simple family project such as planting a small garden, building a simple bookcase, or preparing for a party. Involve your child in some of the stages (as appropriate for her/his physical development) and talk about the steps involved.

2. Take time to visit some community buildings. The post office, fire or police station, or various stores offer wonderful opportunities for your child to expand his or her world of experiences.

3. Many industries conduct tours of their plants or factories. Call them and ask if you can arrange a tour for the family. Bring a camera and encourage your child to ask lots of questions.

4. Visit the airport, shopping mall, or downtown section of a nearby town where many people come and go. Discuss with your child the different people you see. Ask your child to guess what they may be doing or what their jobs may be.

Providing your child with many personal experiences outside the home is a critical factor in future reading success. I hope you and your youngster discover a new world of exploration near where you live.

Sincerely,

In the Public Library

Date: _____

Dear Parents:

The public library is an important part of your child's education. Not only does it contain thousands of books, but it can also offer your child a variety of reading-related activities, both during the school year as well as during vacation times. Every family should make the library a regular part of their weekly or monthly activities together. Doing so helps stimulate a lifelong reading habit. The following are some activities and programs that your public library may offer you and your child:

1. Get a family library card. Some libraries will permit even the youngest members of the family to sign up for their own cards.

2. Some libraries have special story hours for youngsters of all ages. Check with your local library for the time and day in your library.

3. Often the library will schedule special workshops for children. These sessions may include opportunities for children to create a wide variety of book-related projects or participate in active storytelling sessions with other youngsters.

4. Don't forget the library during vacation times. Many libraries offer special programs during the summer or during holiday times. Call and check on what's happening at your library.

5. Check with your local library to see if it offers a special series of children's films. These films, often keyed to popular children's books, can be a powerful stimulus in helping your child develop an interest in reading.

6. When you go shopping, make your local public library part of the trip. Stop by and pick up a new book for your child as a regular part of your "shopping list."

Working together, we can help your child become a successful reader. Thank you for your active role in this most important journey.

Sincerely,

Literature Letters

This section, like the previous one, offers you a collection of letters to duplicate and send home to parents. These letters provide parents with important information about children's books, especially those that can be successfully used with students in first and second grade.

Literature Letters — A

The letters in this section are divided into two parts. The first part contains book-related letters for duplication and distribution. These pages are designed to be duplicated on one sheet of paper to be sent home with children as an adjunct to your classroom activities. The activity page for each book contains the following:

- Bibliographic information (title, author, publisher).

- A brief summary of the book.

- Discussion questions that parents and children can share after the book has been read or during the reading of the story. The intent is not necessarily to have parents ask all the questions, but rather to stimulate parent-child discussion.

- Activities that parents and children can do together. These extensions of the book are appropriate to a wide range of abilities and interests of children.

- A list of related titles for students and parents to enjoy together. These include books on the same theme or books written by the same author.

Although the Literature Letters are listed alphabetically, there is no prescribed sequence for these letters. Feel free to distribute the pages in whatever order you wish. It is not necessary to "match" a book used in the classroom with a corresponding Literature Letter. Rather, these letters can be used as natural extensions of the literature activities you do with ALL books in your classroom.

Literature Letters — B

The second set of letters in this section includes letters related to recommended books for both first- and second-grade students. These letters are designed to alert parents to the wide range of recommended books appropriate for youngsters at this age. Included are books recommended by first- and second-grade teachers, books suggested by numerous professional organizations (e.g., American Library Association, International Reading Association), and award-winning literature in a variety of genres. These books are appropriate for read alouds (by parents) as well as independent reading (by youngsters). Equally important, these books are easily accessible by parents in any school or public library. There is no need for parents to purchase any of these recommended titles.

Introductory Literature Letter

Date: _____

Dear Parents:

One of the questions parents frequently ask is, "What are some appropriate books for my child to read?" To help you help your child experience good books, I will be sending you specially prepared activity pages. Each activity page identifies a specific children's book. Included will be a brief summary of the book, some discussion questions, and a selection of exciting activities for you and your child to work on together.

Each time you receive one of the activity pages, please obtain a copy of the recommended book. Read the book with your child over the course of several days. You may elect to read the book aloud to your child, your child may wish to read the book by himself or herself, or your child may want to read the book out loud to you. Set aside some time each day for you and your child to share some reading together.

Upon completion of the book, share some of the discussion questions with your child. These questions are designed to help your child think carefully about the book and what that book means to him or her; not to "test" your child on what he or she remembers about the book. Of course, you and your child are encouraged to think of other questions to talk about together.

Each activity page contains a variety of extending activities related to the book for you and your child to do together. Share the suggestions with your child and decide two or three you would enjoy working on together. Most of the activity materials can be easily found at home or inexpensively purchased at a nearby hardware, stationery, or variety store.

The time you spend with your child in reading these books and doing the suggested activities should be relaxed, comfortable, and supportive. By working together with your child in an encouraging way, you will be helping your child discover the wonder and excitement of good literature while also promoting his or her reading development.

I'm looking forward to working with you. Feel free to contact me at any time if I can provide you with any additional information or assistance.

Sincerely,

Alexander and the Terrible, Horrible, No Good, Very Bad Day
Judith Viorst
New York: MacMillan, 1972

Summary
One day Alexander wakes up with gum in his hair. From then on the whole day is filled with one misfortune after another. He wants to move to Australia, but he realizes terrible days happen everywhere, even in Australia.

Discussion Questions
1. If you were Alexander, what would you have done to change the day?

2. Could any of the other characters have helped Alexander so that he would have a good day?

3. Does everybody have bad days? Why?

4. Is Alexander's day similar to any day you have had? How did you deal with your "very bad day"?

Activities
1. Visit your local library and obtain some materials and resources on Australia (ask the reference librarian). Work with your child to put together a descriptive brochure (sheets of paper stapled together) on the climate, animals, lifestyles, and geography of Australia. What are some factors about Australia that make it unique?

2. Ask your child to write a brief essay about a recent horrible day. What happened? How did your child feel? Ask your child to share the essay with other family members. Did they see the "terrible day" in the same way your child did?

3. Ask your child to create an alternate version of the book entitled "Alexander and the Wonderful, Terrific, Super, Fantastic Day." Your child may wish to record the story on a tape recorder or write it for other family members to enjoy.

4. Ask your child to pretend to be an advice columnist. Have your child suggest some strategies or solutions for Alexander to consider in dealing with his terrible day.

5. Have your child interview an adult about the worst day that individual ever had. Your child may want to interview a parent, babysitter, neighbor, etc. Make sure your child takes notes during the interview. Have your child share his or her interviews with the rest of the family.

Related Children's Books
Today Was a Terrible Day by Patricia Reilly Giff
I Should Have Stayed in Bed by Joan M. Lexau
Sam's All Wrong Day by Gyo Fujikawa
The Quarreling Book by Charlotte Zototow
I Won't Go to Bed! by Harriet Ziefert
Alexander Who Used to be Rich Last Sunday by Judith Viorst
It Could Always Be Worse by Margot Zemach

Amazing Grace
Mary Hoffman
(New York: Dial, 1991)

Summary

Grace has a vivid imagination and loves to act out stories. However, when she wants to play the part of Peter Pan in a school play she is told that she cannot because she is a girl and black. Her mother and grandmother show her she can be anything she wants to be. Eventually, she wins the part of Peter Pan and a belief in her own abilities.

Discussion Questions

1. Are there any characters in this book who are similar to people in your family? Explain.

2. How was Grace able to overcome the "obstacles" in her life?

3. What did you enjoy most about Grace?

4. If you were to tell your friends about this book, what would you share?

Activities

1. Invite your child to obtain a copy of "Peter Pan" from the school or public library. Plan some time to share that book with your child. Discuss with your child the similarities between Peter Pan and Grace.

2. Invite your child to create a list entitled "Amazing Me." Encourage your child to write down personality characteristics or features that make him or her a distinctive individual. Take time periodically to discuss the items on that list.

3. Encourage your child to make a list of all the characters Grace liked to play (i.e., Joan of Arc, Anansa, Mowgli, etc.). Encourage your child to select one of those characters and to act out one or more scenes from that storybook character's life.

4. Take some time to talk with your child about a time in his or her life when he or she was told that he or she could not do something because of lacking a particular talent or skill. How did that event affect him or her? What did he or she do about it? What could be done in the future?

Related Children's Books

The Pain and the Great One by Judy Blume
I Like Me by Nancy Carlson
On the Day You Were Born by Debra Frasier
Much Bigger Than Martin by Steven Kellogg
Frederick by Leo Lionni
I'm the Best! by Marjorie Sharmot

Unit

13

Around One Cactus: Owls, Bats and Leaping Rats
Anthony D. Fredericks
(Nevada City, CA: Dawn Publications, 2003)

Summary
This dynamically illustrated book takes readers into the heart of the Sonoran Desert to watch the "happenings" that take place in and around a single Saguaro cactus. The young boy in the story doesn't think there is much going on at the cactus and so, near the end of the day, he leaves. But that's when all the activity begins.

Discussion Questions

1. Which of the creatures did you enjoy the most?

2. Which animal would you like to learn more about?

3. How did the illustrations help you enjoy the story?

4. If you could ask the author one question, what would it be?

Activities

1. Your child may enjoy creating a "Desert Dictionary." Invite him/her to gather words and definitions for several letters of the alphabet. For example:

   A—Arid, Arizona, Apache Indians; **B**—Beetles, Bats; **C**—Cactus, California Poppy; **D**—Diamondback rattlesnake, Dunes; **E**—Endangered environment; **F**—Fox, Flowers

2. Invite your child to read two other books by the author of *Around One Cactus: Owls, Bats and Leaping Rats*. They are *Under One Rock: Bugs, Slugs and Other Ughs* (Dawn Publications, 2001) and *In One Tidepool: Crabs, Snails and Salty Tails* (Dawn Publications, 2002). How are all three of these books similar?

3. Your child may be interested in obtaining travel and tourist information about Arizona. He/she can log on to http://www.arizonatourism.com/ and obtain a wide variety of resources.

4. Invite your child to create a "Wanted" poster for some of the more dangerous creatures (rattlesnake, scorpions) in the book. What information should be included on each poster?

5. Invite your child to tell part of the story from the perspective of one of the animals. For example, how would the rattlesnake view the actions of the other animals? How would the long-nose bat view the other creatures?

Related Children's Books
Desert Song by Tony Johnson
Cactus Hotel by Brenda Guiberson
Desert Giant: The World of the Saguaro Cactus by Barbara Bash
Cactus Poems by Frank Asch

Goodnight Moon
Margaret Wise Brown
New York: Harper & Row, 1947

Summary
This is the story of a little rabbit's bedtime ritual. He goes to sleep in the "Great Green Room" and bids goodnight to all his favorite things.

Discussion Questions
1. What kinds of things do you enjoy doing just before bedtime?

2. What would be different if you went to sleep in the daytime and were awake at night?

3. Why do you think the rabbit said "good night" to so many things?

4. What would you want to change in the story if you were the author? If you were the main character?

Activities
1. Discuss bedtime rituals with your child. As you talk, write down some of the things your child likes to do just before bed. Print each "activity" on a separate index card. Show each card to your child and have him or her put them into the correct order. For example, they might line up their shoes, hang up their clothes, put toys away, brush teeth, and read a favorite book. You may wish to read each card first and have your child arrange them in the correct sequence.

2. Talk with your child about various noises that can be heard at night. You and your child may wish to tape-record different sounds in and around the house that take place during the night. Talk with your child about reasons why some sounds are scary and others are not. What makes one sound scarier than another?

3. Talk with your child about occupations that require people to work at night. Try to make up a list (including illustrations, pictures, and brief descriptions) of some of the individuals who must work at night. What makes their jobs so much different from those of people who work during the day?

4. Visit your local public library and obtain recordings of several lullabies. Play them for your child and encourage your child to sing along. Talk with your child about the differences between several of the songs. You may wish to use The Lullaby Songbook by Jane Yolen (New York: Harcourt Brace, 1986) as a reference.

Related Children's Books
What the Moon Is Like by Franklyn M. Branley
Lullabies and Night Songs by William Engvick
Bedtime for Frances by Russell Hoban
Good Night, Richard Rabbit by Robert Kraus
Goodnight Max by Hanne Turk
Moonlight by Jan Ormerod

The Grouchy Ladybug
Eric Carle
New York: Thomas Y. Crowell, 1977

Summary
This is a story about a selfish and grouchy ladybug who wanted to prove he was better than everyone else. In the end he discovers that sharing and friendship are more important than power.

Discussion Questions
1. What do you think made the ladybug so grouchy?

2. What if the ladybug was not slapped by the whale's tail? What do you think the next animal would have been?

3. What did you enjoy most about this story? Why?

4. If you could write a letter to the author of this book, what would you want to say?

Activities
1. Work with your child to create his or her own clock out of paper plates. Use black construction paper for the hour and second hands and write numbers on the clock face with magic markers. Put holes on the clock hands and attach a paper fastener so the hands can move. Reread the story with your child and move the clock hands to the positions indicated in different sections of the story. Talk with your child about the different times indicated in the story.

2. Draw a large leaf on a piece of green construction paper. Attach the leaf to a wall of your child's room. Ask your child to draw an illustration of a ladybug and tape it to the leaf. Have your child draw a picture of one of the other animals in the story and tape that to the leaf, too. You may wish to work with your child to design and draw pictures of each of the animals in the story. Retell the story to your child and stop every so often to have your child place one of the illustrated animals on the leaf.

3. You and your child may wish to start an insect collection. Obtain a clean glass jar (a mayonnaise or pickle jar works best). Take a walk with your child and collect some soil to put in the bottom of the jar. Place a few twigs in the jar, too. Ask your child to collect several insects and put them in the jar. Upon returning home, have your child draw pictures of one or more of the insects. Take some time to talk about the similarities and/or differences between some of the collected insects. Later, you and your child may wish to visit the local public library to obtain one or more books about the collected insects. The Eyewitness Junior series from Knopf is an excellent reference. Most bookstores and libraries have it. After a few days, be sure to set the insects free in the same place they were found.

Related Children's Books
Tick-Tock, Let's Read the Clock by Bobbi Katz
Do You Know What Time It Is? by Roz Abisch
Lucy Ladybug by Gladys Conklin
Time by Jan Pienkowski
Ladybug, Ladybug! by Robert Kraus

In One Tidepool: Crabs, Snails and Salty Tails

Anthony D. Fredericks
(Nevada City, CA: Dawn Publications, 2002)

Summary

In this imaginatively illustrated book, a young girl takes readers into the magical and captivating world of a single tidepool. Together they discover an array of interesting and intriguing creatures including barnacles, anemones, a blood-red sponge, snail, crabs and a knobby sea star.

Discussion Questions

1. What was the most interesting creature in the book?

2. Which of the animals would you like to learn more about?

3. What are some other animals that might be found in a tidepool?

4. What did you like best about the book?

Activities

1. Provide your child with an assortment of magazines that contain pictures of small ocean animals—creatures that might be found in a tidepool. These may include (but not be limited to) Ranger Rick's Nature Magazine, National Geographic, Discover, etc. Encourage your child to make a collage by pasting pictures of different creatures on a sheet of plain paper.

2. Invite your child to select one of the animals mentioned in the book. Invite her/him to demonstrate the movement of that animal in a designated area. For example, a sea star moves very slowly over a surface; a crab scampers quickly from one hiding place to another. Provide opportunities for your child to describe her/his movements and why they may be unique for each animal.

3. You may enjoy obtaining some land hermit crabs for household pets. They make wonderful pets. They are easy to care for and fun to observe!

4. Cut the fingers from a pair of inexpensive work gloves. Invite your child to use a variety of art materials (crayons, yarn, felt-tip pens, sequins, etc.) to turn each "finger" into a puppet representing one of the creatures in the book. Your child can use these puppets as part of a finger play during a retelling of the story.

Related Children's Books

This Is the Sea That Feeds Us by Robert Baldwin
Along the Seashore by Ann Cooper
Seashells by the Seashore by Marianne Berkes
Seashore Babies by Kathy Darling
Beach Day by Karen Roosa

Miss Nelson Is Missing!
Harry Allard
Boston: Houghton Mifflin, 1977

Summary

The students of Room 207 were the most misbehaved students of the school. Miss Nelson, their teacher, suddenly disappears, and Miss Viola Swamp arrives with hours of homework. The class tries to figure out what has happened to Miss Nelson.

Discussion Questions

1. When you had a substitute, how was she similar to Miss Swamp? How was your substitute different?

2. Would you want to have Miss Nelson as a teacher?

3. How do you feel about having a substitute teacher like Viola Swamp?

4. If you were Detective McSmogg, where would you have started looking for Miss Nelson? Why?

5. How would you have felt if you were one of the students when Miss Nelson returned? Why?

Activities

1. Have your child make a "wanted" poster for Miss Nelson. What kind of information should be included on the poster? Post the finished poster on the door of the refrigerator.

2. Talk with your child about some of the qualities of a good teacher. What should good teachers do? How should they act towards their students? How should they teach?

3. Ask your child to dictate or write a sequel to the story. Have Detective McSmogg look for Miss Viola Swamp. Where would he look for her? Would he ever find her?

4. Your child will enjoy the two sequels to this story, including Miss Nelson Is Back and Miss Nelson Has a Field Day.

5. Ask your child to look through several old magazines and cut out pictures of children they would like to have in their classroom. Have your child paste these pictures on a large sheet of paper. Talk about the reasons why the selected children would make up an ideal class.

6. Have your child write a letter to Miss Nelson asking her to come back to the classroom. What would your child want to say to convince Miss Nelson that she should return?

Related Children's Books

Encyclopedia Brown by Donald Sobol (series)
The Case of the Cat's Meow by Crosby Bonsall
The Homework Caper by Joan Lexaw
Something Queer Is Going On by Elizabeth Levy
Sideways Stories from Wayside School by Louis Sachar

13

Parent
Involvement
Activities

The Napping House
Audrey Wood
San Diego: Harcourt, Brace, Jovanovich, 1984

Summary

In this book the author uses cumulative rhyme to tell of the sleeping granny and a host of others who join her for a nap. One individual after another joins the pile until the disastrous, yet humorous, ending.

Discussion Questions

1. How would you like to nap with so many other individuals? Do you think it would be fun? Why?

2. Do you have a favorite stuffed animal or pet you like to sleep with?

3. What else do you like to do on a dreary, rainy day? Who do you like to be with?

Activities

1. Before reading the book, ask your child what he or she thinks it will be about (according to the title). Write down any predictions your child has and discuss them after you have shared the story.

2. Discuss with your child the funniest, the scariest, the darkest, or the noisiest place he or she has ever slept. What is the most comfortable place your child has slept?

3. You and your child may wish to make some puppets using old socks, pieces of cloth, yarn, glue, and buttons or sequins (for eyes, mouth, buttons on shirt, etc.). Retell the story, providing opportunities for your child to "pile" the puppets on top of each other as in the book.

4. Talk with your child about babies' and toddlers' need for naps and what happens when they don't nap. Why is it important for growing babies to get lots of sleep?

Related Children's Books

Moonflute by Audrey Wood
Naptime by Gylbert Coker
The Nap Master by William Kotzwinkle
*I Know an Old Lady Who
    Swallowed a Fly* by Rose Bonne

The Snowy Day
Ezra Jack Keats
New York: Viking Press, 1962

Summary
Peter looks out his bedroom window one morning and sees snow all around. He spends a fun-filled day in the snow and comes home tired and wet. He is eager to play in the snow again the next day.

Discussion Questions
1. How did Peter feel when he saw all the snow outside his window? Would you have felt the same way?

2. Why do you think Peter decided not to join the big boys in a snowball fight?

3. How would your life be different if it snowed year-round?

4. How do you think Peter felt when he discovered that his snowball had melted?

5. Do you like snow? Why or why not?

6. How might Peter's day have been different if it had rained instead of snowed?

Activities
1. Talk with your child about ways in which we keep warm during the winter. Check out books from your local public library on winter fashions for various parts of the country or around the world. You may wish to use the book How to Keep Warm in Winter by David A. Ross (New York: Crowell, 1980) as a reference.

2. Talk with your child about the role of Peter's mother in the story. How did she feel when Peter was playing in the snow? What was she doing while he was outside? How did she feel when he came back in with wet clothes? How did she feel about the snow? Invite your child to dictate or rewrite the story from the mother's point of view.

3. Ask your child to create a story from the snowball's point of view, telling what it is like to fall from the sky, be packed into snow, stuffed into a pocket, and melt in the house. Your child can make a construction paper "pocket" by folding a 9x12 piece of construction paper in half and stapling two sides. Different stories can be written on large paper "snowballs" and inserted into the pocket for display.

4. Have your child write a sequel to The Snowy Day, describing Peter's adventures with his friend on the second day of snow. Have your child create pictures to illustrate the text by using paper cut-outs, similar to the style of Ezra Jack Keats.

Related Children's Books
Katy and the Big Snow by Virginia Lee Burton
A Walk on a Snowy Night by Judy Delton
Snow Company by Marc Harshman
The First Snowfall by Anne F. Rockwell
Snow Bunny by Bubbi Katz
The Snow Parade by Barbara Brenner
It's Snowing! It's Snowing! by Jack Prelutsky

The Teacher from the Black Lagoon
Mike Thaler
(New York: Scholastic, 1989)

Summary

It's the first day of school and a young boy wonders who his teacher will be. Imagine his surprise (and that of his classmates) when the teacher turns out to be a fearsome green creature—with claws! Horrible things happen to several kids, yet the principal seems unconcerned. A surprise ending adds to the hilarity in this delightful and humorous book.

Discussion Questions

1. How would you feel if you learned that your teacher was "from the Black Lagoon"?

2. Did you have any idea how the story was going to turn out? If you were writing this story, would you use the same ending?

3. What was the most terrible thing a teacher ever did to you?

4. What was the young boy's greatest worry?

Activities

1. Encourage your child (just for fun) to write a brief paragraph or story with the title "The Father/Mother from the Black Lagoon." What events in your child's life could be turned into a story similar to this one?

2. Invite your child to talk about the qualifications and/or qualities that good teachers must have. What makes a teacher outstanding? What kind of training do teachers need to have? What do teachers need to know about kids and how they learn?

3. Before your child reads the entire book, share the title with him or her. Invite your child to prepare an illustration of his or her "Teacher from the Black Lagoon." How does your child's illustration compare with those in the book? Is your child's illustration similar to anyone he or she knows?

4. Invite your child to prepare an advertisement or commercial promoting the book to his or her friends. What type of information should be included in order to "sell" the book to others? Should the advertisement/commercial be humorous or serious?

Related Children's Books

The Principal from the Black Lagoon by Mike Thaler
The Gym Teacher from the Black Lagoon by Mike Thaler
Miss Nelson Is Missing by Harry Allard
Miss Nelson Is Back by Harry Allard
"Could Be Worse!" by James Stevenson
Prince Cinders by Babette Cole
Princess Smartypants by Babette Cole

Unit

13

Literature
Letters

Thunder Cake
Patricia Polacco
(New York: Philomel, 1990)

Summary

A little girl is afraid of an approaching storm. With the help of her grandmother, she learns how to determine the distance of the storm and how to bake a "Thunder Cake"—which must be in the oven before the storm arrives. A marvelous story about overcoming fears and the special bond that exists between the generations.

Discussion Question

1. What are some things that scare you? What makes those things so scary?

2. What are some ways in which you overcome your fears?

3. Do either of the two characters in this book remind you of anyone else you know?

4. Do you think the girl knew she was being fooled by her grandmother?

5. What do you think the girl will do the next time a storm arrives?

Activities

1. After you have shared this story with your child, invite your child to create special sound effects for thunder or rain which could be used in an audiorecording. Your child may wish to beat on a cookie sheet to simulate the sound of thunder or tap on the plastic lid of a coffee can to simulate the sound of rain. Read the story again and record it with your child contributing the necessary sound effects.

2. The book contains the recipe for thunder cake. Work with your child in preparing that recipe together. When finished, serve the cake to family members and invite your child to tell everyone about the story that goes along with it.

3. You and your child may enjoy sharing other books by this author. These include Just Plain Fancy, Mrs. Katz and Tush, Babushka's Doll, Pink and Say, and Rechenka's Eggs. Plan some time to discuss the distinctive illustrative style of these books.

4. The next time a storm roars through your area, invite your child to count the time between a flash of lightning and the clap of thunder. Invite them to use that time to calculate the distance of an approaching storm just like in the book.

Related Children's Books

The Ghost-Eye Tree by Bill Martin and John Archambault
Brave Irene by William Steig
Storm in the Night by Mary Stolz
The Storm Book by Charlotte Zolotow
Grandma Gets Grumpy by Anna Hines

Where The Wild Things Are
Maurice Sendak
New York: Harper Row, 1963

Summary

A small boy, sent to his bed without his supper, imagines himself to be the master of the wild things. The smell of his dinner being brought to his room brings him back from monster land.

Discussion Questions

1. Why do you think Max was sent to bed without supper?

2. Would you like to visit the land of the wild things? Why or why not?

3. Why do you think Max became king of all the wild things?

4. Do you think Max will ever go back to visit the wild things?

5. Would your friends enjoy this book? Why?

Activities

1. Have your child pretend to be a reporter who has just spotted the wild things for the very first time. Direct your child to write a newspaper-style article that includes who, what, and where. An example might be: "A mysterious, 10-foot-tall creature called Wild Thing was spotted yesterday by a group of vacationing reporters in the jungle of Forty Winks."

2. Together create a scary costume catalog. Ask your child to draw several examples of scary costumes. Look through some old magazines for pictures of outfits that could be used as part of a scary costume. Put together a catalog that offers a variety of costumes that could be used in the Land of the Wild Things.

3. Have your child brainstorm all of the places that a monster or nightmare could hide in his or her room. Ask your child to draw up a plan for "monster proofing" his or her bedroom. Compile all ideas into a how-to manual for other kids who worry about monsters at night.

4. Your child may enjoy reading other books by Maurice Sendak, including In the Night Kitchen, Chicken Soup with Rice, and Rosie and Michael.

Related Children's Books

The Dream Child by David McPhail
The Night Flight by Joanne Ryder
Daddy Is a Monster...Sometimes by John Steptoe
Spence and the Sleeptime Monster by Christa Chevalier
A Monster in the Mailbox by Sheila Gordon
*My Mama Says There Aren't Any Zombies, Ghosts,
    Vampires, Creatures, Demons, Monsters, Fiends,
    Goblins, or Things* by Judith Viorst

Recommended Books—List #1

Date: _____

Dear Parents:

Following is a list of books highly recommended for children in first and second grade. These books have been selected on the basis of their appropriateness to children's interests and represent a wide range of award-winning and frequently cited books for this age level. Plan to visit the public library or your child's school library regularly and make these suggestions part of your child's reading adventures and explorations.

Aardema, Verna. *Bringing the Rain to Kapiti Plain*. New York: Puffin, 1993.

Ackerman, Karen. *Song and Dance Man*. New York: Knopf, 1988.

Allard, Harry. *Miss Nelson Is Missing*. Boston: Houghton Mifflin, 1993.

Allsburg, Chris. *The Polar Express*. Boston: Houghton Mifflin, 1985.

Auch, Mary Jane. *Eggs Mark the Spot*. New York: Holiday House, 1996.

Barracca, Debra. *Adventures of Taxi Dog*. New York: Dial, 1990.

Berger, Barbara. *Grandfather Twilight*. New York: Putnam, 1996.

Bogart, Jo Ellen. *Daniel's Dog*. New York: Scholastic, 1990.

Briggs, Raymond. *Jim and the Beanstalk*. New York: Putnam, 1997.

Brillhart, Julie. *Story Hour: Starring Megan!* New York: Dial, 1992.

Brown, Jeff. *Stanley in Space*. New York: HarperCollins, 2003.

Bunting, Eve. *Sunflower House*. New York: Harcourt, 1996.

Byars, Betsy. *Tornado*. New York: HarperCollins, 1996.

Carle, Eric. *The Very Hungry Caterpillar*. New York: Philomel, 1969.

Cauley, Lorinda Bryan. *The Ugly Duckling*. San Diego, CA: Harcourt Brace Jovanovich, 1979.

Coerr, Eleanor. *The Big Balloon Race*. New York: HarperCollins, 1992.

Cowley, Joy. *Agapanthus Hum and the Eyeglasses*. New York: Philomel, 1999.

Cushman, Doug. *Aunt Eater's Mystery Vacation*. New York: HarperCollins, 1992.

dePaola, Tomie. *Strega Nona*. New York: Aladdin, 1979.

Ernst, Laura. *Walter's Tail*. New York: Bradbury, 1992.

Fox, Mem. *Night Noises*. San Diego: Gulliver, 1989.

Fredericks, Anthony D. *Under One Rock: Bugs, Slugs and Other Ughs*. Nevada City, CA: Dawn, 2001.

Gackenbach, Dick. *King Wacky*. New York: Knopf, 1984.

Greene, Constance. *Odds on Oliver*. New York: Penguin, 1995.

Havill, Juanita. *Jamaica's Find*. Boston: Houghton Mifflin, 1986.

Hines, Anna Grossnickle. *Daddy Makes the Best Spaghetti*. New York: Clarion, 1986.

Horowitz, Ruth. *Breakout at the Bug Lab*. New York: Dial, 2001.

Hutchins, Pat. *The Very Worst Monster*. New York: HarperCollins, 1988.

Hyman, Trina Schart. *Sleeping Beauty*. Boston, MA: Little, Brown, 1977.

Sincerely,

Recommended Books—List #2

Date: _____

Dear Parents:

Following is a list of books highly recommended for children in first and second grade. These books have been selected on the basis of their appropriateness to children's interests and represent a wide range of award-winning and frequently cited books for this age level. Plan to visit the public library or your child's school library regularly and make these suggestions part of your child's reading adventures and explorations.

Ahlberg, Janet and Allan. *Each Peach Pear Plum*. New York: Penguin, 1978.

Borden, Louise. *Caps, Hats, Socks, and Mittens*. New York: Scholastic, 1989.

Burningham, John. *Granpa*. New York: Crown, 1985.

Christelow, Eileen. *Five Little Monkeys Jumping on the Bed*. New York: Clarion, 1989.

Henkes, Kevin. *Jessica*. New York: Greenwillow, 1989.

Hughes, Shirley. *An Evening at Alfie's*. New York: Lothrop, 1985.

Kellogg, Steven. *A Rose for Pinkerton*. New York: Dial, 1981.

Lawston, Lisa. *A Pair of Red Sneakers*. New York: Viking, 1998.

Leack, Laura. *My Monster Mama Loves Me So*. New York: Harper, 2002.

Levinson, Nancy. *Snowshoe Thompson*. New York: HarperCollins, 1992.

Lexau, Joan. *Striped Ice Cream*. New York: Scholastic, 1997.

Lindgren, Astrid. *Lotta on Troublemaker Street*. New York: Aladdin, 2001.

Little, Jean. *Emma's Magic Winter*. New York: HarperCollins, 1998.

Miller, Sara. *Three Stories You Can Read to Your Dog*. Boston: Houghton Mifflin, 2001.

Nolen, Jerdine. *Raising Dragons*. New York: Voyager, 2002.

Numeroff, Laura Joffe. *If You Give a Mouse a Cookie*. New York: Harper and Row, 1985.

Oxenbury, Helen. *Family*. New York: Wanderer, 1981.

Paterson, Katherine. *Smallest Cow in the World*. New York: HarperCollins, 1993.

Polacco, Patricia. *Chicken Sunday*. New York: Paper Star, 1998.

Rockwell, Ann. *First Comes Spring*. New York: Crowell, 1985.

Sharmot, Marjorie. *Gila Monsters Meet You at the Airport*. New York: Simon & Schuster, 1980.

Smallcomb, Pam. *Camp Buccaneer*. New York: Simon & Schuster, 2002.

Thaler, Mike. *The Teacher from the Black Lagoon*. New York: Scholastic, 1999.

Turner, Ann. *Dust for Dinner*. New York: HarperCollins, 1995.

Waddell, Martin. *My Great Grandpa*. New York: Putnam's, 1990.

Willey, Margaret. *Clever Beatrice*. New York: Aladdin, 2004.

Wood, Audrey. *Jubal's Wish*. New York: Blue Sky, 2000.

Sincerely,

Recommended Books—List #3

Date: _____

Dear Parents:

Following is a list of books highly recommended for children in first and second grade. These books have been selected on the basis of their appropriateness to children's interests and represent a wide range of award-winning and frequently cited books for this age level. Plan to visit the public library or your child's school library regularly and make these suggestions part of your child's reading adventures and explorations.

Ada, Alma Flor. *Yours Truly, Goldilocks*. New York: Atheneum, 1998.

Addy, Sharon. *When Wishes Were Horses*. Boston: Houghton Mifflin, 2002.

Alexander, Martha. *When the New Baby Comes I'm Moving Out*. New York: Dial, 1981.

Bauley, Lorinda Bryan. *Jack and the Beanstalk*. New York: Putnam, 1983.

Beith, Laura. *The Book of Bad Ideas*. New York: Megan Tingly, 2000.

Brown, Marc. *Arthur's Baby*. New York: Joy Street Books, 1987.

Bunting, Eve. *The Butterfly House*. New York: Scholastic, 1999.

Carlson, Nancy. *I Like Me!* New York: Viking, 1988.

Cazet, Denys. *Never Spit on Your Shoes*. New York: Orchard, 1990.

Clements, Andrew. *Dolores and the Big Fire*. New York: Simon & Schuster, 2002.

Cronin, Doreen. *Click, Clack, Moo*. New York: Simon & Schuster, 2000.

Fox, Mem. *Shoes from Grandpa*. New York: Orchard, 1992.

Freeman, Don. *Corduroy*. New York: Puffin, 1976.

Gould, Deborah. *Aaron's Shirt*. New York: Bradbury, 1989.

Herold, Ann. *The Butterfly Birthday*. New York: Simon & Schuster, 1991.

Hessell, Jenny. *Staying at Sam's*. New York: Lippincott, 1989.

Hoffman, Mary. *Amazing Grace*. New York: Dial, 1991.

Kirk, David. *Miss Spider's Tea Party*. New York: Scholastic, 1994.

Krensky, Stephen. *My Teacher's Secret Life*. New York: Aladdin, 1999.

Lester, Helen. *Tacky the Penguin*. Boston: Houghton Mifflin, 1988.

Long, Melinda. *How I Became a Pirate*. New York: Harcourt, 2003.

McCully, Emily. *Mirette on the High Wire*. New York: Putnam, 1997.

Ormerod, Jan. *Moonlight*. New York: Puffin, 1983.

Pearson, Tracey. *Old MacDonald Had a Farm*. New York: Dial, 1984.

Pizer, Abigail. *It's a Perfect Day*. New York: Lippincott, 1990.

Rockwell, Ann. *My Spring Robin*. New York: Macmillan, 1989.

Wagner, Karen. *Silly Fred*. New York: Macmillan, 1989.

Sincerely,

Recommended Books—List #4

Date: _____

Dear Parents:

Following is a list of books highly recommended for children in first and second grade. These books have been selected on the basis of their appropriateness to children's interests and represent a wide range of award-winning and frequently cited books for this age level. Plan to visit the public library or your child's school library regularly and make these suggestions part of your child's reading adventures and explorations.

Bennett, David. *One Cow Moo Moo*. New York: Henry Holt, 1990.

Brown, Margaret Wise. *Baby Animals*. New York: Random House, 1989.

Carle, Eric. *The Very Busy Spider*. New York: Philomel, 1985.

Carlstrom, Nancy. *Jesse Bear, What Will You Wear?* New York: Macmillan, 1986.

Hyman, Trina Schart. *Little Red Riding Hood*. New York: Holiday, 1984.

Kraus, Robert. *Leo the Late Bloomer*. New York: Windmill, 1971.

Martin, Bill. *Brown Bear, Brown Bear, What Do You See?* New York: Holt, 1967.

McMullan, Kate. *I Stink!* New York: HarperCollins, 2002.

McPhail, David. *Something Special*. Boston: Little Brown, 1988.

Meddaugh, Susan. *Hog-Eye*. Boston, Houghton Mifflin, 1998.

Olson, Mary. *Nice Try, Tooth Fairy*. New York: Simon & Schuster, 2000.

Ormerod, Jan and David Lloyd. *The Frog Prince*. New York: Lothrop, 1990.

Peters, Lisa. *When the Fly Flew In*. New York: Dial, 1994.

Polacco, Patricia. *Thank You, Mr. Falker*. New York: Philomel, 2001.

Rathman, Peggy. *Officer Buckle and Gloria*. New York: Putnam, 1995.

Riddle, Toby. *A Most Unusual Dog*. New York: Aladdin, 1995.

Say, Allen. *Grandfather's Journey*. Boston: Houghton Mifflin, 1993.

Schwartz, Amy. *Bea and Mr. Jones*. New York: Bradbury Press, 1983.

Simms, Laura. *Rotten Teeth*. Boston: Houghton Mifflin, 2002.

Viorst, Judith. *The Good-Bye Book*. New York: Atheneum, 1988.

Watson, Richard. *Tom Thumb*. San Diego, CA: Harcourt Brace, 1989.

Williams, Vera. *A Chair for My Mother*. New York: Greenwillow, 1982.

Wood, Audrey. *King Bidgood's in the Bathtub*. New York: Harcourt, 1985.

Yolen, Jane. *Owl Moon*. New York: Philomel, 1987.

Sincerely,

Family Reading Time Letters

The two parts that follow provide you with additional opportunities to encourage parent participation in your classroom reading program.

A Family Reading Checkup

This form can be duplicated and sent to parents one or more times throughout the school year. You may elect one of the following strategies:

- Send it out once at either the beginning of the school year.

- Send it out once at the end of the school year.

- Send it out twice—once at the beginning and once at the end of the school year.

- Send it out three times—once at the beginning, once in the middle, and once again at the end of the school year.

This form alerts parents to the reading behaviors that family members can practice at home to stimulate and encourage the reading development of all youngsters.

Family Read Aloud Calendar

This blank calendar can be sent to all families. It provides parents and children with an easy-to-use form that helps record family reading times. You may wish to duplicate multiple copies of this calendar and send it home with students at the beginning of each month. Also, it is important to plan time for the discussion and sharing of home reading opportunities within the context of your normal reading instruction. Let students know that when they and their parents make read aloud time a regular family activity, then their growth and development as readers escalates accordingly.

A Family Reading Checkup

Date: _____

Dear Parents:

The following suggestions give you an opportunity to examine your current family reading practices with an eye toward adding more positive reading practices to your family's schedule. Begin by placing a check before each true statement. Then place a star by one unchecked item that you and your family would like to try to do. In a month or so, recheck all true statements. Hopefully, the starred item will then become one of the ones you can check.

Note: Check only those items that you do on a regular basis.

- [ ] I read aloud to my children.
- [ ] I buy books for birthday and holiday gifts.
- [ ] The family goes on brief trips beyond the neighborhood so that everyone is exposed to new experiences.
- [ ] Family members make regular use of the library.
- [ ] I praise my child(ren) for at least one improvement or accomplishment each day.
- [ ] My child(ren) sees/see me reading for both pleasure and information from a variety of books, magazines, and newspapers.
- [ ] My child(ren) knows/know that I take a positive interest in all of his/her/their school activities.
- [ ] I am an active and attentive listener and encourage my child(ren) to tell me about his/her/their daily experiences.
- [ ] I make sure my child(ren) is/are well rested and has/have a good breakfast each day before school.
- [ ] My child(ren) has/have a collection of books in his/her/their room(s) and can obtain them easily.
- [ ] I show my child(ren) that reading is fun and enjoyable.
- [ ] I talk about the things I learn from reading.

Sincerely,

Unit

13

Family Reading Time Letters

Family Read Aloud Calendar

You can help promote a lifetime of reading enjoyment and success for your child by making reading a habit early in her or his life. Sharing the joys of good books and children's literature should be a regular family activity—one practiced every day. You can help your child get into the reading habit by using the following calendar. Post it on the family bulletin board or refrigerator for all to see. Plan a special time each day when you and your child can share a book or story together. Put your child in charge of "recording" each day's reading time with a mark or sticker in the appropriate spaces on the calendar. If you and your child read together for at least 20 days during the month, celebrate the occasion with a special treat or trip. Make another calendar for the following month and keep the reading habit going.

Sunday	Monday	Tuesday	Wednesday	Thursday	Friday	Saturday

Parents:

1. Put a check mark, star, funny face, or sticker in a box for each day you and your child read together for at least 15 minutes.

2. You may wish to write in the dates for this month.

3. At the end of the month, invite your child to post the calendar on the

refrigerator or some other appropriate place. Later, these calendars can be gathered together in a special notebook.

4. Try to read with your child for a minimum of 20 days each month. This will help establish the reading habit—one that will last a lifetime.

Unit 14
Questions and Answers

Like many competent readers, you tap into your background knowledge as you read a book. You also accessed some background knowledge as you read this book. For example, you probably had a vision of your classroom when you read some of the opening chapters. You undoubtedly had mental images of two or three of your students as you read a classroom scenario or pondered a specific comprehension strategy described in these pages. And you certainly thought about how all these ideas would work in your busy and overcrowded day.

Like many teachers, you had some very specific questions about the concepts and practices described in these pages. In my own work with children, as well as numerous conversations with teachers around the country who are implementing these practices into their classroom routines, several questions seem to predominate. Here are some of the ones most frequently asked:

Do Comprehension Circles work?

Yes (a very emphatic "YES"). They work for several reasons, not the least of which is the fact that children are invited to practice and become proficient in dynamic interactions with text—in short, they get to do the same kinds of things that accomplished readers do. By engaging students in the types of practices accomplished readers do, teachers can validate reading as something that everyone can aspire to. Many teachers have discovered that these practices establish a solid foundation that helps youngsters be successful readers throughout the primary grades and beyond.

I have a very crowded schedule. How can I add one more thing to my day?

At first glance, it may seem as though Comprehension Circles is another layer, another element, or another curricular requisite to "shoehorn" into an already busy and crowded schedule. However, it really isn't. It is a natural extension of two practices you already share with your students—reading aloud and shared reading time. By just focusing and extending the typical procedures you use in those two daily practices, you can make a major and significant impact on children's reading development. At most, you are looking at 20 minutes of time—20 minutes of

focused study that emanate from a book or story you would normally share with youngsters during the course of the day. It may mean five minutes less of the math centers or five minutes subtracted from journal writing time, but the payoffs more than make up for those very slight schedule modifications.

How do I start?

Start slowly! Don't try to rush your students into Comprehension Circles on the first day of school. Rather, ease them into these strategies through some "connections" with their background knowledge about reading. Debbie Miller (2002) does something at the start of the year that I particularly enjoy. She first talks to her students about some of the things readers do when they read. Students might volunteer the following ideas:

"They sit in a big chair and read a book."

"They go to the book place, you know, the library place."

"They look at lots of magazines."

"They read in bed. My mom reads in bed all the time."

"They read cookbooks when they cook."

Comments like these provide you with important insights into children's concepts about the role of reading in people's lives. Such comments also celebrate the fact that reading is a social expectation—it's something everybody does regularly and daily. This is an important concept for kids to grasp—one that underscores the value of the literacy activities you will share with them throughout the year.

From there you can invite children to note some of the behaviors that take place when people read. Ask them to watch their parents, older siblings, and other adults and note what kinds of things they do as they read. Children should also note the various places and locations that people read. Like Miller, I used to have my students suggest those places, behaviors, and feelings each day as they arrived. We would then copy them onto large sheets of newsprint and post them along one wall of the classroom. By the end of the first week, the wall was literally covered with reading behaviors ("My sister was laughing at the book."), reading locations ("Dad sometimes reads in his shop."), places to find books ("My granma gets me books at the Salvation Army store."), reading activities ("My mother sometimes reads the movie star magazines in the grocery stores."), and miscellaneous ("When granddaddy came for Thanksgiving, he told me about when he was growing up on a farm and they had a catalog of tractors and farm stuff. He said they used it a lot in the outhouse.").

From these beginnings, children get a sense of the importance and significance of reading in everyone's life. From here you can begin discussing some of the reasons why people read (and why people need to know how to read). I usually like to keep this conversation active and energetic, inviting suggestions and observations from all participants. I then ask the ultimate question, "Would you like to learn how to read?" Typically, the response is enthusiastic and energetic. At this point you can say, "Well, I'm going to teach you some of the things that readers do when they read. One of the things all readers do when they read is think. So, this year we're all going to work together to become good thinkers. When we become good thinkers, then we can also become good readers."

From these humble beginnings, the reading program is "off and running." Kids are "energized" about reading and especially about their involvement in learning to read. These initial activities signal to kids that reading instruction is not something done to them; but more important, it is something that is done as a cooperative venture between teacher and students. Here are some additional benefits of these initial activities (modified from Miller, 2002):

- Children are engaged early in the reading program.
- Children can practice and exhibit reading behaviors used by accomplished readers.
- All children can achieve a measure of reading success.
- Oral language development is an important part of learning to read.
- Children can make informed choices about their reading.
- "We're all in this together."—These activities help to build a community of learners, a community of readers.
- Youngsters learn that while we may learn how to read in school, reading also has a place of importance outside of school, too.
- Reading is something we can celebrate every day.
- Reading and thinking go hand in hand.

But these kids are so easily distracted!

It's happened to all of us who have ever worked with a classroom of first or second graders. Let's say you are going to share the book *Brown Bear, Brown Bear, What Do You See?* by Bill Martin, Jr., with your students. You start off by asking the class if anyone has ever seen a bear (sounds like a completely innocent inquiry). But then, they're "off to the races." Alisha mentions that she saw a polar bear at the zoo. José talks about the bear that his grandfather shot on a hunting trip. Tanya talks about the time she and her family went camping and during the night she *thought* she heard a bear in the woods. Carrie talks about the picture of a bear she once saw in a magazine that her mother was reading. And, of course, Robert tells everyone about the bears he has printed on his underwear ("Would you like to see them?").

Yes, kids do get distracted and they do tend to get off-target. My friend Jane Piepmeier, a first-grade teacher with considerable experience in these matters, says that she often finds these discussions frustrating simply because kids "keep making up experiences to top the experiences (real or imaginary) of those individuals who talked before them." The trick, she says, is to keep youngsters focused. This can be accomplished in several ways, including:

- Limit the responses to two or three.

- List four or five responses at the beginning of a book and then return to the list to determine which one or two were most specific to the topic of the book (good predictive activity).

- For each story read, select beforehand one or two youngsters to provide a personal experience. This can be determined based on your personal knowledge about each child's experiences.

- Redirect students' tangential responses immediately before they are perceived by others to be the accepted types of responses.

- "Prime the pump" by helping youngsters draw connections to a prior book.

- Place a time limit on this initial activity (2 minutes, for example).

The trick is to keep youngsters focused on the underlying concept or main idea of a book or story. Often the success of any oral encounters with youngsters can be determined by three words: focus, focus, focus.

Do I need to get any special books or literature?

No. One of the distinct advantages of Comprehension Circles is the fact that you can use them to promote comprehension development using the books and literature that are already a part of your classroom library or reading program. They require no additional books other than the ones you currently have. Throughout this resource, I have listed selected books in various categories of reading strategies, as well as in the various sections in the second half of the book. These are only recommendations, not absolutes. You can use these practices and procedures with any and all types of reading materials (trade books, magazines, basal readers) or language arts activities (nursery rhymes, songs, poetry).

Hey, what about phonics?

You may be wondering about the role of phonics instruction. That is, should phonics instruction take precedence over comprehension instruction, or should comprehension instruction take precedence over phonics instruction? Actually, the answer to that question is "neither." Based on conversations with many teachers,

I believe that both phonics instruction and comprehension instruction should take place concurrently. In other words, don't give up your phonics activities for the sake of comprehension instruction and vice versa.

Both phonics instruction and comprehension instruction should be based on children's authentic experiences with reading. When children use real books and real literature in a wide variety of literacy activities, they will understand the relevance and immediacy of these activities to other forms of authentic reading. Learning about sound/symbol relationships has the highest degree of success when done within the context of authentic text—a book, for example. Children are continually fascinated by words: how they work, what they do, how they can be broken down or built up, how parts of them sound, and how those sounds can be assembled to form whole units (words). When those words (and their attendant phonetic elements) come from the books and literature that children experience, then students begin making meaningful connections between learning and utility.

To take it one step further, Miller (2002) points out that the same strategies used for teaching words are also useful for teaching comprehension. These include:

- Explicit instruction

- Modeling

- Reading high-quality literature

- Giving children time to practice real reading

Indeed, the cornerstone for quality reading instruction lies in children's access to and use of good books and literature. These authentic experiences and interactions help youngsters acquire reading strategies that can be enhanced and expanded throughout the entire reading curriculum.

Is this another "fad" in reading instruction?

Throughout this book I have provided references to several research materials, including peer-reviewed articles, textbooks, monographs, and the writings of other teachers in the field. You can be assured that all of the ideas, concepts, and practices in this resource book have been classroom-tested, kid-approved and research-based. Comprehension is never a fad—it is the *raison d'etre* of reading instruction. The ideas here have been tested and are proven ways to engage youngsters in the dynamics of reading. Teachers just like you have used them in their classrooms with a wide diversity of students in a wide variety of instructional situations. Over time, you too can begin to see the success your colleagues have experienced through just a few minor modifications in your overall literacy program.

How can I teach kids to comprehend when many don't know how to read yet?

This is a query that is often on the minds of many teachers (perhaps many administrators and parents, too). It's best to look at reading as a process of thinking about text. Reading is not simply the match between the sounds of language and the written symbols of language or the understanding of new vocabulary words. In many ways, reading is a "conversation" between an author and a reader. It implies some responsibility on the part of the writer (providing a text has a beginning, middle, and end) and a responsibility on the part of a reader (understanding the message the author wishes to convey). As such, reading is an interaction between author and reader. As mentioned earlier in the book, we sometimes call this the *transactional approach to reading*. We could also say that there is a "conversation" between author and reader.

In any kind of conversation there is thinking going on. When you talk with a friend, you think about what you are going to say, you think about what you are saying when you speak, you think about what your friend is discussing, and you think about some of the meanings or interpretations of the conversation. In short, you do a lot of thinking. So it is with reading. Thus, it stands to reason that if we can assist youngsters in developing their thinking abilities, we can also assist them in comprehending all kinds of reading materials.

As teachers, we have a responsibility to provide instruction for our students that will enhance, stimulate, foster, and promote thinking in a wide array of activities. In so doing, we are helping to create a very viable foundation upon which more formal reading instruction can stand. Another side benefit is that students are engaged in reading-related behaviors that invite them into the "reading club." They are invited to use the same thinking/reading practices that independent readers use even before they master the transition from oral language to written language. This is both a revelation and a celebration!

So, the short story is that beginning and developmental readers CAN be active participants in the processes used by practicing readers. By assisting children in thinking like readers, we can help them to develop an active relationship with the books and stories that constitute a natural and normal part of their day—both in and out of the classroom.

Unit 15

Reproducibles

Page 244: Bookmarks. Duplicate and distribute to students.

Page 245: Story Pyramid. This form can be used to assist students in focusing on the important details of a story or book. It can be duplicated on a transparency master for use as a whole-class activity after reading a book. Or, it can be photocopied on sheets of paper for students to complete individually or in small groups after reading a selected book.

Page 246: Informational Story Frame. A story frame can be used to help students organize significant information or important details in an expository text. When completed, story frames serve as discussion starters for the components of good stories as well as an outline for students who need a support structure for the creation of their own stories. Duplicate this form and invite students to use it for selected nonfiction books.

Page 247: Group Data Sheet. This form allows students to share and discuss their respective background knowledge, how they used that knowledge in "tackling" the subject matter of the book, what they discovered while reading the book, and some projections for the future. This form places an emphasis on the Before, During and After stages of the reading process and encourages students to comprehend their connections and relationships.

Page 248: Student Self-Report Form. This form can be duplicated and distributed to individual members of the class at the end of a week or upon completion of a book or story. After students have completed this form, provide sufficient opportunities for them, both individually and collectively, to discuss their responses to the items on this form. These discussions can help students appreciate the interactive role they can have with books and authors.

Page 249: Story Map. Duplicate and distribute to students to use after they have completed reading a book.

Page 250: Mental Image x Two. Duplicate this form and distribute to individual students. Before reading a book to students, invite each student to create an image of the story or an image of the main idea based solely on the title of the book. (Don't show the cover illustration.) After finishing the read aloud, ask students to draw a final image of the story. Plan time for students to talk about changes made between their initial mental images and their post-story mental images.

Page 251: Comparing Two Books. Duplicate and distribute to students to use after they have completed reading two books on similar topics.

Page 252: Retelling Form. Duplicate and distribute to students to use after they have completed reading a book.

Pages 253–255: Award Certificates. Duplicate and distribute to students as appropriate.

Page 256: Comprehension Circles Teacher Self-Assessment. Use to assess how you are doing with your Comprehension Circles.

Teaching Comprehension in Grades 1–2

Bookmarks

Identifying Important Details

When I read, I

- Know why I'm reading this book.
- Can identify some important details.
- Can tell the main idea of the story.
- Can identify the beginning, middle, and end of the story.
- Can describe the main character in my own words.
- Can tell about the setting of the story.

Questioning

When I read, I ask myself the following questions:

Before

- Is this similar to anything I have read before?
- Why am I reading this?
- Do I have any questions about this book before I read it?

During

- Am I understanding what I'm reading?
- Why is this easy or difficult for me to understand?
- Is this interesting or enjoyable? Why?

After

- Can I retell this story to someone else?
- What did I learn in this book?
- Do I have some unanswered questions about this book?

Predicting and Inferring

When I read, I

- Make a prediction about the story from the title.
- Compare what I know with what I am reading.
- Make inferences about characters.
- Predict the story ending.
- Think about my predictions and how they help me enjoy the story.

Mental Imagery

When I read, I

- Make a picture in my head about the title.
- Make a painting in my mind when I begin reading.
- Think about my "mind pictures" while reading.
- Add details to my mental images.
- Change my mental images as I continue reading.
- Remember that my "mind pictures" may be different from the illustrations.

Name: _____   Date: _____

Story Pyramid

Book: _____

Line 1: Name of the main character
Line 2: Two words describing the main character
Line 3: Three words describing the setting
Line 4: Four words stating the problem
Line 5: Five words describing the main event
Line 6: Six words describing a second main event
Line 7: Seven words describing a third main event
Line 8: Eight words stating the solution to the problem

1._____

2._____ _____

3.____ ____ ____

4.____ ____ ____ ____

5.____ ____ ____ ____ ____

6.____ ____ ____ ____ ____ ____

7.____ ____ ____ ____ ____ ____ ____

8.____ ____ ____ ____ ____ ____ ____ ____

Name:_____ Date:_____

Informational Story Frame

Book:_____

This book was written to teach us about_____

_____

_____.

One important fact I learned was_____

_____

_____.

Another fact I learned was_____

_____

_____.

A third important fact I learned was_____

_____

_____.

If I were to remember one important thing from this book, it would be

_____

because_____

_____.

Name: _____ Date: _____

Group Data Sheet

Group members: _____ _____

_____ _____

Title of book read:_____

_____

What we knew:_____

_____

_____

What we did:_____

_____

What we discovered:_____

_____

What we still need to learn_____

_____

The most interesting thing we learned:_____

_____

Signed (Group Recorder):_____

Unit

15

Reproducibles

Name:_____   Date:_____

Student Self-Report Form

Directions: Please complete this report about your reading activities this week. Your comments will form the basis for a discussion with me later.

Book:_____

These are some of the things I learned this week_____

_____

_____

These are some of the things that gave me trouble this week:_____

_____

_____

I believe I have improved this week. Here's why:_____

_____

Here are some things I'd like to learn more about: _____

_____

Here is how I would rate my performance this week:_____

_____

This is what I'd like to do next week:_____

_____

248   Teaching Comprehension in Grades 1–2   © Harcourt Achieve Inc. All rights reserved.

Story Map

Title: _____

Setting:

Characters: _____

_____

Problem:

Event 1: _____

Event 2: _____

Event 3: _____

Event 4: _____

Solution:

Name: _____   Date: _____

Mental Image x Two

Pre-Reading Image:

Post-Reading Image:

Here are some differences between my two images: _____

_____

_____

_____

_____

Name: _____ Date: _____

Comparing Two Books

Book #1: _____

Book #2: _____

Similarities:

Differences:

Book #1	Book #2

Unit

15

Name: _____   Date: _____

Retelling Form

Book: _____

Main Character: _____

Other Characters: _____

_____

Setting: (place) _____

(time) _____

Problem: _____

_____

_____

_____

_____

Solution: _____

_____

_____

_____

_____

Award Certificates

Super Reader Award

This certificate is hereby presented to:

_____

For active participation in our classroom reading program

_____   _____
Teacher   Date

Family Reader Award

This certificate is hereby presented to the family of:

_____

For participating in _____ or more weeks of fun reading activities.

_____   _____
Teacher   Date

Award Certificates

_____

uses

mental imagery

to comprehend books and stories.

Thanks for all your efforts in our classroom reading program.

_____   _____
Teacher   Date

_____

uses

predicting and inferring

to comprehend books and stories.

Thanks for all your efforts in our classroom reading program.

_____   _____
Teacher   Date

_____

uses

good questions

to comprehend books and stories.

Thanks for all your efforts in our classroom reading program.

_____   _____
Teacher   Date

_____

identifies important information

to comprehend books and stories.

Thanks for all your efforts in our classroom reading program.

_____   _____
Teacher   Date

Comprehension Circles
Teacher Self-Assessment

Date: _____

Component	Self-Rating 5=always; 1=never	Self-suggestions for Improvement
Activate background knowledge.	5 4 3 2 1	
Talk about any misperceptions or misconceptions.	5 4 3 2 1	
Invite students to share relevant experiences.	5 4 3 2 1	
Link book to a previous book or story.	5 4 3 2 1	
Help establish a purpose for reading.	5 4 3 2 1	
Demonstrate a talk-aloud or think-aloud on a specific comprehension strategy.	5 4 3 2 1	
Permit students to "see" inside my head.	5 4 3 2 1	
Read the book aloud to students with expression and intonation.	5 4 3 2 1	
Demonstrate enthusiasm for book.	5 4 3 2 1	
Clarify reading strategy in "kid terms."	5 4 3 2 1	
Demonstrate the strategy within the context of the book.	5 4 3 2 1	
Invite students to "try out" the strategy.	5 4 3 2 1	
Encourage active discussion among all students.	5 4 3 2 1	
Use focused retelling activities.	5 4 3 2 1	
Invite reflection on identified strategy.	5 4 3 2 1	

Appendices

A: Reading Aloud to Students

Stimulating imaginations, enhancing listening skills, and introducing children to a variety of literature can all be facilitated when you read aloud to students, particularly when this sharing activity is made a regular and featured part of every school day. Children of all ages enjoy listening to someone read aloud from a new or familiar book. Reading aloud makes language active—it stimulates creativity, it develops an appreciation for the wide variety of literature that children can begin reading on their own, it assists children in the development of vivid mental pictures, and it promotes an easy and natural enjoyment of stories.

As you might suspect, there are many benefits associated with the "read aloud" experience. These include the following (adapted from Fredericks et al., 1997):

- Reading aloud stimulates children's interest in books and literature. Old "classics" as well as new tales broaden students' exposure to a variety of literature.

- Students' reading interests are broadened and enlarged when teachers utilize read aloud literature from several areas.

- Students are introduced to the patterns of language, including sentence structure, sequence, and the development of story themes.

- Children are provided access to books which may be beyond their independent reading level.

- Reading aloud fosters positive attitudes about reading and about books.

- Reading aloud helps develop a community of learners within the classroom.

- Reading books from many different sources helps children expand their backgrounds of experience—an important element in comprehension development.

- When teachers read books to their students, they are serving as positive reading models. Students see the pleasure, enjoyment, and excitement of reading demonstrated by an accomplished reader.

- Reading aloud enhances the development of appreciative, comprehensive, and critical listening skills in a variety of informal contexts.

- Reading aloud stimulates children's imaginations.

- Reading aloud provides a host of pleasurable sharing experiences and facilitates teacher-student communication.

- Reading aloud helps promote reading as a lifelong activity.

Following are some guidelines you should consider to make the read aloud experience enjoyable and gratifying for both you and your students:

Making Read Aloud Successful

1. Before reading a book to your students, take time to read the story beforehand. This will give you a sense of the story necessary for an effective reading.

2. Select a book you enjoy as well as a book your students will enjoy.

3. Occasionally provide opportunities for students to select the literature to be read.

4. Make reading aloud a daily part of your classroom schedule. When possible, include more than one read aloud session each day. Consider the beginning of the school day, immediately after a recess or gym period, after lunch, or just before students are dismissed at the end of the day.

5. Sit so that you are positioned in front of the children. This allows for appropriate voice projection and permits all youngsters an opportunity to listen. Also, if you wish to show illustrations in the book, everyone will be able to see them.

6. Emphasize that read aloud time is solely for the purpose of listening to a book read aloud. It should not be an opportunity to talk, interrupt, or fidget. Establish a set of "Read Aloud Rules" and adhere to them.

7. Practice reading with expression. Give different voices to each of the characters, highlight dramatic points in the plot through voice inflection, speed up or slow down the reading depending on the action. Dramatic readings (when appropriate) draw listeners in to the "action" of a book.

8. Be cognizant of the pace of your reading. Provide opportunities for youngsters to create "pictures" in their minds (e.g., mental imagery). It may be necessary to "slow down" your reading to allow children to develop appropriate images.

9. Provide frequent opportunities for youngsters to engage in directed reading strategies through Comprehension Circles. It is not necessary to do this for every read aloud book, but reading aloud can easily and naturally segue into appropriate comprehension strategies.

10. Begin your read aloud sessions with short stories and books and gradually progress to longer readings. Be mindful of your students' attention spans and adjust the reading time accordingly.

11. Expose youngsters to a wide variety of books. Throughout the year, select books from all of the genres of children's literature.

B. Bookwebbing

Providing youngsters with frequent exposure to good children's literature continues to be the focal point of any successful reading program. Children who have many opportunities to examine and explore all types of literature, particularly in a supportive and interactive environment, are those who develop a lifelong appreciation for books and stories. An effective reading program offers students a multiplicity of options to interact with authors and share those experiences with peers and adults.

Bookwebbing is a concept that extends a single piece of literature across the curriculum. It offers students a multitude of opportunities to make connections between subjects, to extend and expand their learning into a variety of topics, and to promote reading as a universal "subject." In other words, reading is linked to (and makes connections with) all the other subjects in the elementary curriculum.

The focal point of bookwebbing is a single piece of literature. From that book a variety of activities and projects can emanate, each related to a particular area of the curriculum. It is important that students have opportunities to create and design activities in keeping with their interests and needs, too. Thus, it is important to lead students through some of the following steps—the same steps you can follow in designing bookwebbing activities for other pieces of literature.

1. Select a book most students have read.

2. List the title of the book in the center of the chalkboard.

3. Discuss with students some of the events, characters, or settings from the book.

4. List the names of other curricular subjects around the sides of the chalkboard (see below).

5. Have students brainstorm related activities within each curricular area, each of which could be used to extend and enhance the book. Students can work in small groups—each group "assigned" one of the subjects of the curriculum—and generate an extensive list of possible projects.

6. Initially, you will want students to generate a quantity of ideas; later you can emphasize quality ideas.

7. After the master list has been created, provide students with an opportunity to select one or more of the listed activities and use them.

B: Bookwebbing

Here's a diagram of a bookweb design:

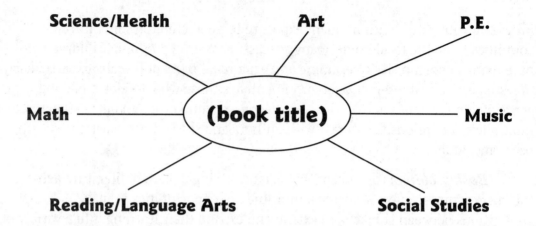

To complete the web, select relevant activities for each of the categories listed on the diagram above. The object is to generate a quantity of creative endeavors and dynamic activities that engage students in the dynamics of a single book. The first few bookwebs you use in your classroom can be developed and designed by you. However, as students become more engaged in this type of project, you will want to encourage them to create their own bookwebs as natural extensions of any piece of literature, particularly those you include in classroom Comprehension Circles.

For the most part the activities included within a bookweb are self-selected rather than teacher-assigned. As students engage in their self-selected activities, provide them with opportunities to refer to the book and draw relationships between the projects they are engaged in and the ideas, themes, or concepts presented in the literature selection. In this way, you will be ensuring that students understand the interrelationships that exist between literature and the rest of your primary curriculum. Students will begin to understand (and appreciate) how a single book can facilitate learning in a wide variety of learning opportunities.

Following are some examples of how some popular books were developed into multidisciplinary units for first- and second-grade classrooms using the bookwebbing strategy.

In my experience, students in the primary grades enthusiastically embrace bookwebbing as a positive adjunct to their Comprehension Circle activities. They discover an increasingly expanding range of learning extensions for any single book as well as an expanding array of academic pursuits tailored to their individual interests. In fact, I have discovered that there is no end to the possibilities that can be designed for any single book.

The Day Jimmy's Boa Ate the Wash

Trina Hakes Noble
New York: Dial Books, 1980

Summary

A boring class trip to the farm turns into an uproariously funny series of events involving cows, pigs, an egg fight, a busload of kids, and, of course, a boa constrictor.

Critical Thinking Questions

- Why wasn't the girl very excited about the class trip?
- What do you think the farmer and his wife will do with the boa constrictor?
- What was the funniest part of the story? Why?
- What do you think Jimmy will do with his new pet pig?
- Why would your friends enjoy this book?

Reading/Language Arts

- Encourage students to dictate or write a story about "The Day the Boa Came to Our School."

- Students will enjoy reading other books by this author including *Apple Tree Christmas*, *Hansy's Mermaid*, *The King's Tea*, and *Meanwhile Back at the Ranch*.

- Invite students to write a sequel to this story using a family pet or another familiar animal.

- Invite each student to choose an animal to study. Students can pretend that they are writing a newspaper birth announcement for the birth of their animal. They will need to do some research to collect necessary information. Provide the birth announcement section of daily newspapers for students to use as a reference for writing their article. Decorate a bulletin board to look like a section of a newspaper, and hang the animal birth announcements there. Students can include an illustration of the new "baby."

- Invite youngsters to each take on the role of a single animal. Encourage students to do the necessary library research on the habits and behaviors of their selected animals. Then have each student write a diary entry as their selected animal might record it on a day in the life of that species.

Science/Health

- If possible, call the biology department of a local college or university and ask if they have any snakes on display. Find out if it would be possible for someone to visit your classroom with one or more snakes for viewing. Encourage students to create a series of questions about snakes and how they live.

- Invite students to divide animals into several different categories. Invite them to think of some possible rules for categorizing animals. Next have the children compare several animals and write a list on the board stating the animals' similarities and differences. Compile a list of the general characteristics of each animal classification. Next, divide the class into several groups and assign an animal classification to each group. Encourage groups to record the qualifications of their animal classification on a piece of poster board using markers. The groups can also provide five sample animals for their animal group. Invite the groups to present their findings to the class. Allow the students time to debate whether the information provided by the groups is complete and accurate. Invite student groups to develop charts explaining general information about the development of their animal classification and how that information might be shared with students in other classes.

B: Bookwebbing

• Focus on a different group of animals each day, e.g., Monday—insects, Tuesday—fish, Wednesday—carnivores, etc. Each day include stories, songs, student-created plays, trivia, games, and environmental concerns related to the animal group. Invite a speaker from the community or local college to discuss current issues relating to the animals.

Art

• Obtain some discarded panty hose or nylon stockings. Work with students to stuff one of them with cloth scraps or crumpled newspaper. Paint a face on one end and turn the stocking into a replica of a boa constrictor. Retell the story and encourage students to manipulate the boa constrictor.

• Draw the outlines of several different items of clothing (shirts, pants, shoes, etc.) on pieces of construction paper and cut them out. Tie a piece of string between two places in the classroom. Invite students to write down one important word from the story on each piece of "clothing." Use clothespins to clip the words to the string. Occasionally encourage students to use one of the words in an original sentence.

Math

• Encourage students to keep an "Animal Journal." This can be a record of all the animals they see during the week. This should include pets, wild animals, insects, and animals seen on television or outside. Hang posters for mammals, fish, birds, reptiles and amphibians, etc. Students can add to the charts daily. Which group of animals has the largest number?

Music

• Provide students with an inexpensive tape recorder that has a corded microphone. Invite students to tape the microphone handle to the end of a broom handle or a long pole (be sure no tape covers the microphone itself). Encourage students to go outside on a clear and calm day (no wind blowing, for example) and place the microphone near one or more wildlife homes (i.e., a bird's nest, a beehive, a wasp's nest, etc.). The students should check first to be sure the animal(s) are at home. Invite them to record and catalog various animal sounds.

Social Studies

• Have a class pet show. Invite each student to sign up for a time slot to show his/her pet. If some students do not own pets, invite them to make a presentation on a pet they would like to own, or "adopt" a pet from a friend or neighbor for the day. Plan time to talk with students about the role or value of pets in the life of a family.

• Arrange for the local SPCA to give a presentation on pet care, adopting pets, and birth control for pets. How does pet ownership affect the local community? What is the role of other animals in the life of the community?

Physical Education

• Invite children to make a large chart (on an oversized piece of poster board, for example) that lists the speeds at which animals in the book travel. The students can rank order animals from the fastest to the slowest or vice versa. How much faster is their pet than the slowest animal on the chart? How much slower is the family dog than the fastest animal on the chart? Where would students place themselves on the chart? What physical activities would they need to practice to maintain their speed?

Ira Sleeps Over
Bernard Waber
Boston: Houghton Mifflin, 1972

Summary
Ira is invited to sleep over at his friend's house. However, he has one small problem—should he bring his teddy bear along? But Ira discovers that he isn't the only one with a teddy bear.

Critical Thinking Questions
- How would the story have been different if Reggie did not have a teddy bear?
- Where do you think Reggie and Ira got the names for their teddy bears?
- Why do you think Ira's sister made so much fun of him?
- If you spent the night at a friend's house, what would you want to do for fun?

Reading/Language Arts
- Invite students to create a written or oral story from the perspective of Tah-Tah. Do they think that Tah-Tah might have felt neglected?

- Invite students to pretend that they are a newsreporter for a local television station. Encourage students to make up a series of questions they would like to ask Ira. You can take on the role of Ira and respond to the questions students ask.

- Talk with students about some of their bedtime routines (watch TV, take a bath, put pajamas on, say goodnight to parents, etc.). Invite students to make up a list of bedtime routines shared by members of the class.

- Encourage students to write an invitation to Ira to sleep at their homes. Encourage students to tell about all of the activities planned.

- Discuss with students the funniest, the scariest, the darkest, or the noisiest place they have ever slept. What is the most comfortable place they have slept in? Invite students to construct a class book that records their thoughts and ideas.

Science/Health
- Talk with students about babies' and toddlers' need for naps and what happens when they don't nap. Why is it important for growing babies to get lots of sleep? If possible, invite a doctor or the school nurse to visit your classroom to discuss the importance of sleep in a growing person's life.

- The three major health needs for growing children are a nutritious diet, regular exercise, and sufficient sleep. Invite students to make a personal notebook divided into three sections. In the first section invite each student to record the foods he/she eats (even snacks) during the course of a week. Students may want to divide a sheet of paper into the four major food groups (vegetable-fruit group; bread-cereal group; meat-poultry-fish-bean group; and milk-cheese group) and record the types and amounts of each eaten during the week. In the next section invite each youngster to record the type and duration of various physical activities he/she participates in during the week. In the third section encourage each student to record the number of hours of sleep he/she gets during each night of the selected week. Invite students to share their notebooks with a family doctor for comments and suggestions.

B: Bookwebbing

Art

• Invite students to create bear collages by cutting pictures of various bears from old magazines and pasting them onto large pieces of paper.

• Encourage students to make some puppets using old socks, pieces of cloth, yarn, glue, and buttons or sequins (for eyes, mouth, buttons on shirt, etc.). Retell the story, providing opportunities for students to use the puppets during selected scenes in the story.

Math

• The average adult needs approximately eight hours of sleep a night. The average child needs approximately ten hours of sleep a night. The average baby sleeps for about 14–16 hours a day. At that rate, how many hours (approximately) has a ten-year-old slept since birth? A 21-year-old adult? A 65-year-old grandfather?

• Invite students to make charts and graphs of the sleep habits of members of their families. They may wish to record information such as: Who sleeps the longest? Who sleeps the least? What is the longest anyone has slept undisturbed?

Music

• Invite students to work with the school's music teacher to assemble a collection of bedtime music or lullabies. What are some traditional songs or tunes that can be included in the collection? Plan time for students to talk about the reasons these songs were created for young children.

Social Studies

• Students may be interested in conducting library research on the sleeping customs or habits of different peoples from around the world. How do children in other countries prepare for bed? What are some routines or habits in which they participate on a regular basis? Students may wish to put together an informational book illustrating some of those customs.

Physical Education

• Invite students to set up and carry out a bicycle rally. What kinds of events would be appropriate (obstacle courses, straight races, closed course for time, etc.)? Encourage students to plan as many different events as possible.

• • • • • • • • • • • • • •

Leo the Late Bloomer

Robert Kraus

New York: Simon & Schuster, 1971

Summary

Leo the tiger takes his time growing up. His parents are patient and eventually he does begin to bloom.

Critical Thinking Questions

• What makes Leo such an interesting character?

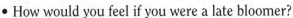

- How would you feel if you were a late bloomer?
- What does the term "late bloomer" mean to you?
- If you were Leo's friend, how would you treat him?
- What part of the book would you change if you could? Why?

Reading/Language Arts

- Obtain a large sheet of newsprint (available at most art or hobby stores). Invite students to lie down on the paper and trace their respective outlines. Invite children to cut out their outlines. Invite students to write (or dictate for you to write) words that best describe each one. Place these words randomly within the outline. Hang the outline in the classroom. Encourage students to think of other words to be added to the outline periodically. Encourage students to note that the descriptive words vary from individual to individual, indicating that everyone is unique and different from everyone else.

Science/Health

- Invite students to plant a bean or radish seed in a paper cup filled with potting soil. Talk about how even though students cannot see the seed growing inside the soil, eventually it will germinate and grow. Students can observe the cup every other day and keep a journal on the growth of the seed. Invite students to compare the hidden growth of the seed to the hidden growth of Leo.

Art

- Students may enjoy making casts of their feet or hands. This can be done with the following recipe for flour dough:

2 cups self-rising flour   2 tbsp. cooking oil
2 tbsp. alum   1 cup + 2 tbsp. boiling water
2 tbsp. salt

Carefully mix all ingredients and then knead until a doughy consistency. Roll out some of the mixture and have each child press a hand or foot into the mixture. Put the cast outside in the sun or bake in a slow oven (250 degrees) for several hours. The casts can be painted and kept for several months at which time students may wish to make additional ones to compare the amount of growth made during that time period.

Math

- Invite students to create personal time lines of important learning events in their own lives. When did they learn to walk, talk, read, or draw? Long strips of adding machine paper can be affixed to a bulletin board with each student recording his/her significant life events. The emphasis is not on comparing students, but rather on the fact that certain events occur at different times in everyone's life.

- Invite students to weigh and measure themselves. This data can be plotted on a large classroom chart. A separate chart can also be prepared on the various heights and weights of family pets.

Music

- Invite students to think of a theme song for this book. What popular tune would be most appropriate as background music when reading the book aloud to others? Invite students to defend their choices.

B: Bookwebbing

Social Studies
- Invite students to talk with various family members about when they learned to walk, talk, write, read, and/or draw. What differences do youngsters note? Are there any patterns, or does it seem as though everyone grows and learns at completely different times during their lives?

Physical Education
- Invite the school nurse or a local doctor to visit your classroom to discuss some of the developmental stages of youngsters. What are some physical activities that students at your grade level should be able to do? Make sure the emphasis is on the fact that not everyone develops at the same rate, but rather that there are averages to help gauge proper development.

- Students may wish to have short running races that can be timed. These can be repeated at selected intervals throughout the school year. Plan time to discuss with students the fact that their times may show improvement simply because they are developing important skills. The emphasis should not be on the competitive aspects of the races, but rather on the fact that each youngster will improve, grow, and develop at a rate different from everyone else throughout the year.

Under One Rock: Bugs, Slugs and Other Ughs
Anthony D. Fredericks
Nevada City, CA: Dawn Publications, 2001

Summary
In this creatively illustrated book, readers make some amazing discoveries about an ecosystem right in their own back yard. They'll journey with a youngster as he lifts up a single rock to find an amazing collection of creatures that take up residence on and in the ground. Using a rhythmic verse, this book introduces youngsters to some delightful inhabitants of this community of creatures. ("This is the spider with her eight-eyed face/Who builds a home in this cool dark place.")

Critical Thinking Questions
- Which of the creatures was most amazing?
- How did the illustrations help you learn about the animals in this book?
- Which of the animals would you like to learn more about?
- How are so many different animals able to live together in one place?
- What other animals do you think could be found under a single rock?
- If you could tell the author one thing, what would you like to say?

Reading/Language Arts
- Invite each student to choose an animal from the book to study. Students can pretend that they are writing a newspaper birth announcement for the birth of their animal. They will need to do some research to collect necessary information. Provide the birth announcement section of daily newspapers for students to use as a reference for writing their article. Decorate a bulletin board to look like a section of a newspaper, and hang the animal birth announcements there. Students can include an illustration of the new "baby."

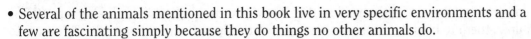

- Several of the animals mentioned in this book live in very specific environments and a few are fascinating simply because they do things no other animals do.

- As a class, brainstorm what the planet earth would be like if there were no insects. For example, imagine no more mosquito bites or bee stings, no more honey, no more flowers, no more butterflies, and so on. Invite students to list the positive and negative effects of insects. They can also write and illustrate stories about the planet with no insects.

- Encourage students to write a sequel to this book. What others creatures would the boy discover under other rocks?

- Invite each student in the class to select one of the animals illustrated in the book. Encourage each child to conduct necessary library research on his or her identified species. Then, invite each student to write a series of diary entries told from the perspective of the creature, for example, "A Day in the Life of a Slug" or "My Life as an Ant."

- Encourage students to create an original "rock" dictionary. Invite them to collect "rock-related" words and terms from various books and resources. These can be compiled into a dictionary (cut into the shape of a rock).

- Invite students to write and perform a "rock" skit. The skit could involve a meeting between two or more creatures who live under a rock. Or it could involve an imaginative scene in which a visitor to the rock shows up unexpectedly.

- Divide the class in half. One half can be predators and the other half can be prey. A predator is matched up with a prey. Invite each pair to construct a book on the life of a predator trying to catch its prey and the prey's attempt at escape. Illustrations should also be included.

Science/Health

- Encourage students to keep an "Animal Journal." This can be a record of all the animals they see during the week. This should include pets, wild animals, insects, and animals seen on television. Hang posters for mammals, fish, birds, reptiles, and amphibians, etc. Students can add to the charts daily.

- Invite youngsters to keep a journal of the activities, habits, travels, and motions of a single animal. Kids may want to select a house pet or some other animal that can be observed quite regularly throughout the day. Provide youngsters with a "Field Journal," a simple notebook wildlife biologists frequently use to track the activities of one or more wild animals over the course of an extended period of time.

- Invite children to go outside and select a section of grassy area (part of a yard, lawn, or playground). Encourage them to push four sharpened pencils into the soil in a one-foot square pattern. Have them tie string around the pencils, making a miniature "boxing ring" on the ground. Invite them to get on their hands and knees and look closely inside the square. Encourage them to make notes of all the different types of animals they see inside the ring. They should note the movements, habits, or behaviors of any animals (ants, grasshoppers, caterpillars, worms) as they travel (jump, crawl, slither) through the ring. Encourage youngsters to visit their "rings" frequently over a period of several weeks.

- Students may wish to "capture" their own spider webs. Materials needed: transparent self-adhesive plastic, dark-colored construction paper, masking tape, aerosol hair spray. Invite students to go outside with the hair spray, masking tape, and construction paper and locate several spider webs. Selected students can each make five rings of masking tape and slip them over the fingers of one hand. Instruct each student to press the

Teaching Comprehension in Grades 1–2

B: Bookwebbing

construction paper to their hand so that it sticks to the rings of the masking tape (this allows them to hold the construction paper vertically so that it doesn't fall). Tell them to carefully hold the construction paper just behind a spider web. With their other hand (or a friend can assist) gently spray the web from the other side. This will cause the web to stick to the construction paper. Invite students to carefully remove the web, and it will stick to the face of the construction paper. When they return to the classroom, they can place a sheet of the transparent self-adhesive plastic over the web (or laminate it) and seal it. This will preserve the spider web. (NOTE: This process takes some practice, so tell students not to get discouraged if they can't do it the first time.) Students may wish to collect several different examples of spider webs from around the school or neighborhood. A scrapbook of different webs can be put together.

- Invite students to create a variety of birdfeeders. These can be hung in various locations around the school. Bird populations, as well as the various varieties of birds in your area, can be recorded over an extended period of time. Following are several possible birdfeeders:

- Tie a string to a pinecone. Fill the crevices in the cone with peanut butter and roll the cone in birdseed. Hang the cone from a tree branch.

- Cut a large section from the side of a waxed or plastic milk carton. Fill with birdseed and hang from a branch.

- Tie several pieces of orange peel onto lengths of string. Hang these in various places in a nearby tree.

- Tie some unsalted peanuts onto various lengths of string. Hang these in a tree.

Art
- Invite youngsters to create "Wanted" posters for some of the animals in the book. What information should be included on each poster? What are some of the "vital statistics" that students would want to share with others on their posters? If possible, obtain one or more "Wanted" posters from your local post office and use them as models for your students' posters.

- Provide inked stamp pads and invite students to use their thumbprints to make insect/spider bodies and then draw legs and antennae. Encourage students to also illustrate the environment in which they would find their selected creatures.

- Cut the fingers from two pairs of inexpensive work gloves. Invite students to use a variety of inexpensive art materials (crayons, yarn, felt-tip pens, sequins, etc.) to turn each "finger" into a puppet representing one of the animals in the book. Students can use these puppets as part of a finger play they create or they can display them in an appropriate "museum" in the classroom.

- Provide students with some modeling clay (available at any hobby store). Work with them to make small models of each of the animals mentioned in the book. These can be displayed in a special "museum" in the classroom.

Math
- Invite students to develop charts and graphs that record the number of species of each of the animals described in the book. Which species has the greatest number of

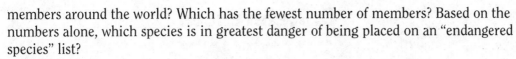

members around the world? Which has the fewest number of members? Based on the numbers alone, which species is in greatest danger of being placed on an "endangered species" list?

- Invite students to list all the animals in the book and categorize those animals from smallest to largest.

Music

- Invite students as a class to generate a list of creature characteristics (squiggly, wiggly, etc.) and use this list to create a class song set to the tune of a popular children's song. For example (to the tune of "Old MacDonald"):

> Old MacDonald had a rock,
> E-I-E-I-O.
> And 'neath this rock he had an earthworm,
> E-I-E-I-O.
> With a squiggle, squiggle here,
> And a wriggle, wriggle there,
> Here a squiggle,
> There a wriggle,
> Everywhere a squiggle, wriggle.
> Old MacDonald had a rock,
> E-I-E-I-O.

Social Studies

- People live in a wide variety of houses or dwellings and so do animals. Invite youngsters to create a chart and investigate the wide variety of homes and dwellings used by animals. They may wish to use some of the following examples and add to the list through their library readings:

nest	burrow
cave	tunnel
branch	ledge

- Invite students to discuss the similarities between human dwellings and animal homes. What are some of the things that determine where an animal lives? Are those conditions or features similar to the considerations of humans in selecting a living site? Invite youngsters to create a chart of animal homes and examples of the animals that might live in or on those spaces. Do animals have more options for living spaces than humans do?

Physical Education

- The human character in the book asks the question, "What could be hiding in the red-rich ground?" Invite students to create their own version of "Hide and Seek" in which selected students take on the roles of certain designated animals and hide from other members of the class.

C: References

Anderson, R.C., and Pearson, P.D. (1984). A schema-theoretic view of basic processes in reading. In P.D. Pearson (Ed.), *Handbook of reading research*. White Plains, NY: Longman.

Bandura, A. (1986). *Psychological modeling: Conflicting theories*. Chicago: Aldine-Atherton.

Baumann, J., Hoffman, J., Duffy-Hester, A., & Ro, J. (2000). The first R yesterday and today: US elementary reading instruction practices reported by teachers and administrators. *Reading Research Quarterly*, 35, 338-377.

Brown, A.L., Day, J.D., and Jones, E.S. (1983). The development of plans for summarizing texts. *Child Development*, 54, 968–979.

Carin, A.A. and Bass, J.E. (2001). *Teaching science as inquiry*. Upper Saddle River, NJ: Merrill.

Cooper, D.J., and Kiger, N.D. (2003). *Literacy: Helping children construct meaning*. Boston: Houghton Mifflin.

Early Childhood and Literacy Development Committee of the International Reading Association. (no date). *Literacy development and early childhood (preschool through grade 3)*. Newark, DE: International Reading Association.

Ford, M.P., and Opitz, M.F. (2002). Using centers to engage children during guided reading time: Intensifying learning experiences away from the teacher. *The Reading Teacher*, 55(2), 710-717.

Fredericks, A.D. (1986). Mental imagery activities to improve comprehension. *The Reading Teacher*, 40, 78–81.

Fredericks, A.D. and Cheesebrough, D. (1993). *Science for all children*. New York: HarperCollins.

Fredericks, A.D., Blake-Kline, B., and Kristo, J.V. (1997). *Teaching the integrated language arts: Process and practice*. New York: Longman.

Fredericks, A.D. (2001). *The complete phonemic awareness handbook: More than 300 playful activities for early reading success*. Barrington, IL: Rigby.

Fredericks, A.D. (2003). *Guided reading in grades K-2: Guided reading strategies, activities, and lesson plans for reading success*. Austin, TX: Harcourt.

Grigorenko, E.L. (1998). Mastering tools of the mind in school (Trying out Vygotsky's ideas in classrooms). In R.J. Strenberg and W.M. Williams (Eds.), *Intelligence, instruction, and assessment*. Mahwah, NJ: Erlbaum.

Hansen, J. (1981). The effects of inference training and practice on young children's reading comprehension. *Reading Research Quarterly*, 16, 391–417.

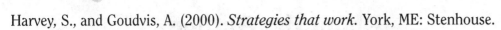
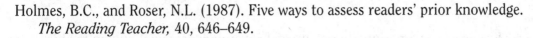
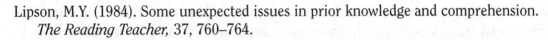

Harvey, S., and Goudvis, A. (2000). *Strategies that work*. York, ME: Stenhouse.

Holmes, B.C., and Roser, N.L. (1987). Five ways to assess readers' prior knowledge. *The Reading Teacher,* 40, 646–649.

Lipson, M.Y. (1984). Some unexpected issues in prior knowledge and comprehension. *The Reading Teacher,* 37, 760–764.

Miller, D. (2002). *Reading with meaning: Teaching comprehension in the primary grades*. Portland, ME: Stenhouse.

Mooney, M. (1990). *Reading to, with, and by children*. Kanotah, NY: Richard C. Owen.

Palinscar, A.M., and Brown, A.L. (1984). Reciprocal teaching of comprehension fostering and monitoring activities. *Cognition and Instruction* I, 117–175.

Pearson, P.D., Roehler, L.R., Dole, J.A., and Duffy, G.G. (1990). *Developing expertise in reading comprehension: What should be taught? How should it be taught?* (Tech. Rep. No. 512). Urbana: University of Illinois Press, Center for the Study of Reading.

Pearson, P.D., Dole, J.A., Duffy, G.G., and Roehler, L.R. (1992). Developing expertise in reading comprehension: What should be taught and how should it be taught? In J. Farstup and S.J. Samuels (Eds.), *What research has to say to the teacher of reading, 2nd ed.* Newark, DE: International Reading Association.

Pressley, G.M. (1976). Mental imagery helps eight-year-olds remember what they read. *Journal of Educational Psychology,* 68, 355–359.

Pressley, M. (2000). What should comprehension instruction be the instruction of? In M.L. Kamil, P.B. Mosenthal, P.D. Pearson, and R. Barr (Eds.), *Handbook of reading research,* (Vol. 3, pp. 545-562). Mahweh, NJ: Lawrence Erlbaum Associates.

Raphael, T.E. (1984). Teaching learners about sources of information for answering questions. *Journal of Reading,* 27, 303–311.

Roehler, L.R., and Cantlon, D.J. (1997). Scaffolding: A powerful tool in social constructivist classrooms. In K. Hogan and M. Pressley (Eds.), *Scaffolding student learning: Instructional approaches and issues.* Cambridge, MA: Brookline Books.

Roehler, L.R. and Duffy, G.G. (1991). Teacher's instructional actions. In R. Barr, M.L. Kamil, P. Mosentahl, and P.D. Pearson (Eds.), *Handbook of reading research* (Vol. 2, pp. 861–883). New York: Longman.

Rosenblatt, L. (1978). *The reader, the text, the poem*. Carbondale, IL: Southern Illinois University Press.

Strickland, D. (1995). Reinventing our literacy programs. *The Reading Teacher*, 48, 294–302.

Wiggens, G., and McTighe, J. (1998). *Understanding by design*. Alexandria, VA: Association for Supervision and Curriculum Development.

Wiske, M.S. (Ed.) (1998). *Teaching for understanding*. San Francisco, CA: Jossey-Bass.

About the Author

Tony Fredericks is a nationally recognized reading expert well known for his practical, down-to-earth, and stimulating resources. His teacher books in language arts, social studies, and science have captivated thousands of educators from coast to coast and border to border—all with rave reviews! His background includes extensive experience as a classroom teacher, reading specialist, curriculum coordinator, staff developer, children's author, professional storyteller, and university specialist in children's literature.

Tony has written more than 60 teacher resource books in a variety of areas, including several best-selling books for Harcourt. These include the hugely praised *Guided Reading in Grades 3-6: 300+ Guided Reading Strategies, Activities, and Lesson Plans for Reading Success* (ISBN: 0-7635-7750-2); the incredibly successful *The Complete Phonemic Awareness Handbook: More Than 300 Playful Activities for Early Reading Success* (ISBN: 0-7635-7347-7), the very down-to-earth *Guided Reading in Grades K-2: Guided Reading Strategies, Activities, and Lesson Plans for Reading Success* (ISBN: 0-7398-8060-8), and the wildly applauded *Redefining the Three R's: Relax, Refocus, Recharge* (ISBN: 0-7398-7598-1) which has quickly become a valued resource on teachers' desks in thousands of schools.

Tony is also an award-winning children's author of more than 30 highly acclaimed nonfiction books. These include the 2003 Teacher's Choice (Learning Magazine) Award-winning *Under One Rock: Bugs, Slugs and Other Ughs* (Dawn Publications), the 2001 Children's Book Council Outstanding Science Trade Book, *Slugs* (Lerner), *In One Tidepool: Crabs, Snails and Salty Tails* (Dawn Publications), and the 2004 Teacher's Choice (International Reading Association) Award-winning *Around One Cactus: Owls, Bats and Leaping Rats* (Dawn Publications), among many others.

Tony is currently a professor of education at York College in York, Pennsylvania. There, he teaches elementary methods courses in children's literature, reading, and science. Additionally, each year he is a visiting children's author at numerous elementary schools around the country where he conducts humor-packed assemblies and shares the writing life with the next generation of young authors. He maintains a children's author web site (**www.afredericks.com**) designed specifically for elementary educators.